D0116863

Grim Death
and Bill the Electrocuted Criminal

Also by Mike Mignola

Father Gaetano's Puppet Catechism: A Novella
(with Christopher Golden)

"Joe Golem and the Copper Girl:
A Short Story"
(with Christopher Golden)

Joe Golem and the Drowning City:
An Illustrated Novel (with Christopher Golden)

The Hellboy Series

The Amazing Screw-On Head
and Other Curious Objects
(with Dave Stewart)

B.P.R.D.: Plagues of Frogs Series
(with Guy Davis)

Baltimore: Or the Steadfast
Tin Soldier and the Vampire
(with Christopher Golden)

The Abe Sapien Series
(with various other authors)

Lobster Johnson Series
(with various other authors)

Witchfinder Series
(with various other authors)

ZombieWorld: Champion of the Worms
(with Pat McEown)

Also by Thomas E. Sniegoski

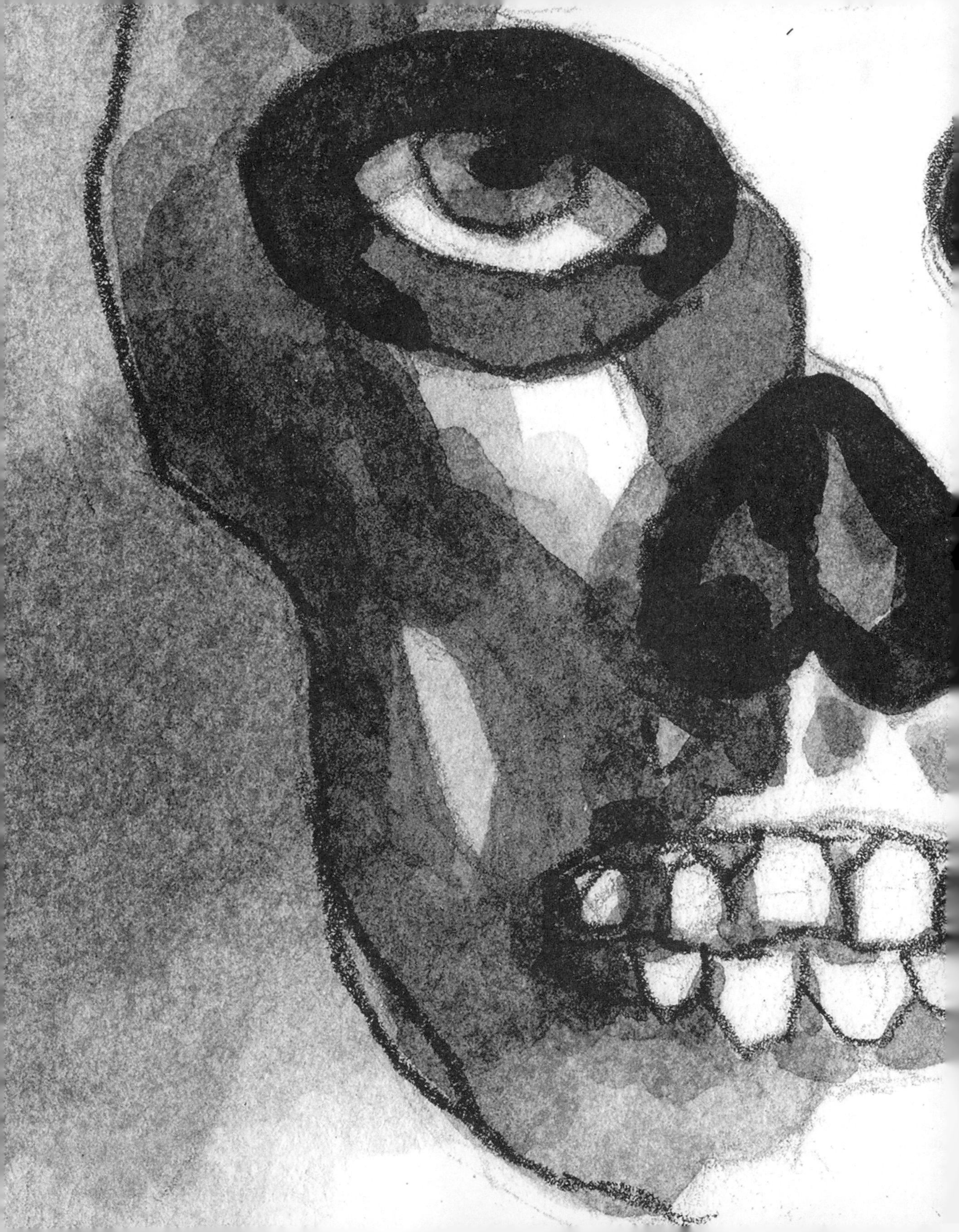

Grim Death

and Bill the Electrocuted Criminal

An Illustrated Novel

**Mike Mignola
& Thomas E. Sniegoski**

ST. MARTIN'S PRESS
NEW YORK

GRIM DEATH AND BILL THE ELECTROCUTED CRIMINAL. Copyright © 2017 by Mike Mignola and Thomas E. Sniegoski. All rights reserved. Printed in the United States of America. For information, address St. Martin's Press, 175 Fifth Avenue, New York, N.Y. 10010.

www.stmartins.com

The Library of Congress Cataloging-in-Publication Data is available upon request.

ISBN 978-1-250-07768-4 (hardcover)
ISBN 978-1-4668-8987-3 (e-book)

Our books may be purchased in bulk for promotional, educational, or business use. Please contact your local bookseller or the Macmillan Corporate and Premium Sales Department at 1-800-221-7945, extension 5442, or by e-mail at MacmillanSpecialMarkets@macmillan.com.

First Edition: February 2017

10 9 8 7 6 5 4 3 2 1

This book is dedicated to Mike Mignola.
It's amazing what a crazy idea and a phone call can end up
turning into. To think it all started with a guy with no pants
talking to himself in the mirror.

Acknowledgments

As always, a zillion and one thanks to my wife, LeeAnne, and evil incarnate, Kirby.

Special thinks to Christopher Golden, the amazing Michael Homler, Howard Morhaim, Frank Cho, Thomas Fitzgerald, Tom McWeeney, Dale Queenan, Larry Johnson, Nicole Scopa, Mom Sniegoski, Mom & Dad Fogg, and the wretched hive of scum and villainy down at Cole's Comics in Lynn.

And a very special thanks to Dave Kraus: knowing how much you would have loved this one just made it all the more special to write.

Chapter One

I must look a sight, Bentley Hawthorne thought as he stood in the doorway of his family home, adorned in a ragged black suit, slouch hat atop his head, face hidden by a grinning skull mask.

He could just imagine the thoughts racing through his manservant's mind at the moment.

"I seem to have misplaced my key," Bentley said as he reached up with a gloved hand and removed the gruesome mask.

"Dear God, sir!" Pym exclaimed, clutching the heavy bathrobe about his throat. "You gave me a fright. I had no idea . . ."

A sudden wave of overwhelming fatigue caused Bentley to slump against the doorframe, interrupting the butler's rant.

"You're hurt," Pym observed, and quickly reached out to take the young man's arm. "Come inside, you'll catch your death."

"Too late for that," Bentley muttered, and then chuckled as he was drawn into the warmth of the foyer.

The servant closed the door on the frigid morning rain and turned his full attention on Bentley. "Here, let me look at you," he said. "You're bleeding."

"Yes, but not all of the blood is mine. Some of it's monkey."

"Monkey?"

Bentley nodded. "Trained to commit the act of murder. Wouldn't have believed it myself if I hadn't seen it with my own eyes; furry devils wielding straight razors and . . ."

"Monkeys—with straight razors?" Pym asked incredulously.

There was that look in the manservant's eyes. Bentley knew it well; he'd seen it so many times over the many years the two men had been together— first when he'd been horribly sick as a child, and most recently as Pym worried about what strangeness had come over his charge of late.

"Where on earth have you been?" the butler asked, a touch of petulance in his tone. "I thought we retired hours ago."

The skull mask dropped from where Bentley had held it clutched beneath the arm of his jacket, the visage of death grinning up at them from the marble floor where it landed.

"The ghost of a murdered innocent roused me from the comfort of my bed," he explained as he reached down for the mask. His black-gloved fingers hooked the eyeholes, but the effort nearly cost him his balance.

Pym rushed closer, placing a supporting grip upon his master's elbow. "Perhaps we should call the doctor."

"No need," Bentley said quickly. "All I require is a warm bath, and then to slip beneath the covers of my bed and into Morpheus's soothing embrace. I'll soon be right as rain." He forced a smile to lighten the mood, but Pym was having none of it.

"Bentley . . . sir, I don't understand what—"

"It is my burden alone to bear," the young man interrupted, placing a comforting hand on his servant's shoulder. "Yours is the preparation of that bath I've been yearning for since I encountered those filthy monkeys. Have I told you how much I despise monkeys, Pym?"

The butler looked as though he might burst, a multitude of questions desperate to come forth, but he held his tongue.

"I'll draw that bath," was all he said as he turned away.

A wise decision, the young man thought as he watched Pym head for the stairs.

For to know the world within which Bentley existed was to tempt the touch of madness.

———

By the time Bentley had climbed the winding staircase to his suite of rooms on the second floor and sloughed off his wet clothing, Pym had finished filling the tub with steaming-hot water.

It took all that Bentley could muster to scrub his body clean of the grime

of conflict. Drying off quickly, he slipped into his robe and padded bare-foot from the bath, sidestepping the pile of wet clothes still lying where he'd shed them. He fell upon the bed and barely managed to squirm beneath the heavy blanket before the blackness of sleep engulfed him.

In seconds, he was firmly in the clutches of unconsciousness and began to dream, reliving the evening's dark endeavors. Once again he faced the bitter scientist driven to madness with the belief that his life's work had been stolen. With the injection of an experimental hormone believed to increase the intelligence of lesser life, the scientist had orchestrated the murder of the one he believed had wronged him. His engineered instruments of revenge: capuchin monkeys.

Capuchin monkeys taught to murder for a mad scientist's twisted cause.

Bentley saw them again as he'd seen them earlier that evening, freed from their cages and scampering across the floor of the secret laboratory, knives and straight razors clutched in tiny, long-fingered hands, dark beady eyes filled with intelligence and wild with the promise of bloodshed.

He'd felt a twinge of pity for the things as he had pulled the twin automatics from within the pockets of his coat. But Death had no patience for such emotions, and he'd opened fire upon the murderous simians.

The pistols had made short work of the monkeys, leaving Bentley with only one remaining task: dispensing justice upon the scientist responsible for the gruesome murder of his colleague. The guilty one had tried to escape by fleeing across the rooftops as the storm had raged overhead.

But Death gave chase.

Bentley smiled in his sleep. The villain had believed he could actually escape the inevitable—right up until he was pierced by a lightning rod, thrown like a javelin just as a jagged bolt of lightning zigzagged down from the heavens to strike the alluring shaft of iron—and in a blinding flash, another wrongful death was avenged.

Bentley's new purpose once again defined.

The young man's eyes flew open, the scientist's piercing scream receding into his subconscious. Bentley sat up suddenly, realizing he wasn't alone; Pym stood before the bed, holding a silver tray.

"I took the liberty of preparing some breakfast," the man said as he placed the tray on a nearby table.

"How long was I asleep?" Bentley asked, languidly stretching.

"Not long enough for an average person to function," Pym replied dryly.

"Ah, but Hawthornes are better than average," Bentley said as he left the comfort of his bed to see what his servant had brought him. He was suddenly famished. "At least that's what Father always told me."

He lifted the silver cover to reveal two pieces of lightly toasted white bread, exactly how he preferred it.

"I'm guessing these require laundering?" Pym asked as he reached down to pick up the pile of filthy clothes that were still on the floor.

"If you wouldn't mind," Bentley answered around a mouthful of toast. "Take the shoes as well; they got a bit scuffed with all the running about."

An image flashed in his mind of his quarry, jumping from rooftop to rooftop, glancing over his shoulder with eyes growing wider in terror at seeing how close Death was to him.

It had been very close indeed.

"And this?" Pym asked. He was holding the skull mask with two fingers, as if it were contaminated with some wretched disease. "Will this need to be laundered as well?"

Bentley experienced both a sickening wave of dread and a flash of excitement at the sight of the grinning visage dangling from the tips of the butler's fingers.

"No, that can stay here."

Was it his imagination, or had the grin upon the skull face grown wider as Pym set it down atop a nearby dresser?

The butler left without another word, and Bentley returned to his breakfast. He ate another slice of toast and poured himself a cup of steaming coffee. Pym had placed a single, freshly cut rose in a small crystal vase at the corner of the tray, and the young man found himself staring at its beauty, but imagining it slowly wilting and dying.

As with all things, death and decay would eventually have their way.

He picked up the folded newspaper on the opposite end of the tray. The headlines still decried the so-called Great Depression and what President Hoover was or wasn't doing about it. In between bites of toast and sips of coffee, Bentley perused the news of the day.

He had just started to read about the convicted murderer of a circus trapeze artist when he felt a terrible cold that made the short hairs at the nape of his neck bristle. He'd felt similar sensations since his transformation, and braced himself as he turned for what he knew would be looming behind him.

The ghost stood not two feet away.

"Hello," Bentley said, knowing full well that it would not answer.

The female specter hovered above the floor, this one's body in even worse condition than the others that had previously appeared to him. The ghosts often came to him adorned with the damage that had claimed their lives: bullet wounds, broken necks, flesh charred black; this one was naked and missing part of an arm and the opposite leg. Pieces of flesh had been removed from her side, exposing the bones of her rib cage.

"Who did such terrible things to you?" Bentley asked, knowing that was what the spirit was waiting for, what they were all waiting for: the invitation to share the horrible fate that had befallen them.

Bentley steeled himself. If there was one thing he had learned since coming to serve his master, it was that the poor souls taken before their time could be very creative. The last had turned his dreams to grisly visions of its murder.

"I'm ready," he said, taking a deep breath. "Show me how you—"

The ghost came at him in a rush of frigid air, the spectral woman's mouth open wide in a silent scream. Bentley instinctively recoiled, stumbling back against the table, enveloped in a choking miasma that froze him to the bone. He crumpled to the floor, fighting to breathe, his lungs aching. He could feel the spirit inside him, desperate to share—desperate for him to know.

And then the images came, visions of the fate that had befallen this poor soul who now sought his aid.

For retribution.

He saw the woman, vibrant, alive, until . . .

Until she wasn't.

He could not see the person responsible for the woman's murder, the perpetrator's features hidden in darkness as they crept up behind her. Bentley felt her terror as cold hands wrapped about her throat, closing off the flow of air, beginning a countdown to the end of her existence. She fought her assailant for as long as she was able, but time ran out, and she could fight no more.

Bentley could feel her life slipping away, writhing curtains of shadow falling down over her bulging eyes. It was the end of the line, but only the beginning of further indignities to be heaped upon her.

The next of the visions came in searing flashes, glimpses of events that followed after the woman's untimely demise: weeping family members, ineffective law enforcement too stupid or uninterested to find her killer, a roaring oven fire, the flash of a metal blade, and a grinning mouth of razor-sharp teeth stained red with blood.

"Is everything all right, sir?" A familiar voice brought him back from where the spirit had taken him.

Bentley opened his eyes to see Pym, who wore an expression of concern.

"I heard you cry out, and . . ."

"I'm fine, Pym, thank you," the young man said. His eyes searched the room for a sign of the ghost, but she had gone.

"Are you certain, sir?" the butler asked.

"I am," Bentley replied. He was sitting at the table, the newspaper open before him. "Another ghostly visitation has occurred, I'm afraid; another departed soul in need of vindication."

Under the sway of the specter, he had turned to the death notices. One particular listing had been circled repeatedly. It was only then that he noticed he was holding a pencil in a clawlike grip.

It was the obituary of Constance Dyer, due to be waked at the Hargrove and Sons Funeral Home.

"Was that you, Constance?" he asked the ether, reading further. It wasn't likely, for Mrs. Dyer was listed as being sixty-five years of age. The apparition couldn't have been much older than thirty.

But there was a reason the spirit had made him take note of this particular viewing, and Bentley knew he had no choice but to investigate further.

"Pym," Bentley said, sensing the butler still standing in the doorway, "I'm going to need clothes."

"Are we going out again this evening, sir?"

"I am." Bentley closed the newspaper and turned in his chair. "And I'll be needing a car."

"And a driver?"

"I am more than capable of driving myself, thank you."

"Then you haven't seen the Packard since your last foray into the city."

Bentley rose from the table, folded the newspaper and put it beneath his arm. He approached the skull mask still sitting atop the dresser.

"Perhaps it's time for me to become more involved with what you're doing," Pym said quietly, watching as Bentley picked up the mask.

An electric charge went through the young man's fingers. "A part of me would truly welcome the companionship," Bentley said as he stared into the yawning darkness of the mask's hollow eyes. "But there's also a part of me that fears what I might be exposing you to."

He managed to lift his gaze from the skull's face to his servant and loyal friend. There was most definitely a tinge of fear on Pym's stern features, but there was also something else. Resolve.

Bentley waited, praying for the butler's retraction, but it did not come.

"I'll go and find another suit," Pym said instead, turning and leaving Bentley alone.

Though it might have just been the old house settling, Bentley could have sworn he'd heard a chuckle.

And that it had come from the mask in his hand.

—

Pym, chauffeur's hat poised jauntily atop his head, brought the black Packard sedan to a stop in front of an old brownstone. Traffic into the city had been surprisingly light, and he and Bentley had made the drive with little trouble.

"I believe this is it," he said, putting the gear in park.

Bentley leaned toward the backseat window, gazing out at the brick building. He could read the gold-lettered sign of HARGROVE AND SONS FUNERAL HOME over the door.

"Doesn't look like much, does it?" he commented, still wondering what the connection to the dismembered ghost might be.

"A family-run business, obviously," Pym said. "Probably been here for decades."

"But what is it hiding beneath its inconspicuous facade?"

Pym turned in the driver's seat to look at Bentley. "Does it have to be hiding anything?"

"I wouldn't be here otherwise," the young man said, still gazing out the car window. "The dead do not send me to places that have nothing to do with their demise."

"I suppose," Pym commented, his skepticism evident.

"Do you doubt me, Pym?"

The butler didn't answer.

"How about an easier question, then," Bentley said. "Do you think me mad?"

"Sir, please," Pym began. "I know you've been through some difficult times over these last months, and I'm well aware that—"

"Answer without fear of repercussions," Bentley instructed him. "Do you think I am insane?"

"Perhaps . . ." the servant said with a hesitant shrug. "A little."

Bentley laughed, a short, barking sound of disbelief rather than humor. "Does this honestly look like the face of madness?" he asked the man who had looked out for him nearly since birth.

Again, Pym did not answer.

"Never mind that," Bentley said. "Let me assure you that I am of sound mind and that I speak nothing but the truth. I must ask you to trust me, as well as my judgment."

They sat in silence for several minutes.

"So what now?" Pym finally asked. "Have the spirits that communicate with you told you what to do next?"

"The spirits only share so much," Bentley said, "nudging me in the direction of their retribution."

"That's rather inconsiderate," Pym said. "If you're going to take the time to avenge them, they should have the common courtesy to tell you more."

Bentley appreciated the butler's feelings, but who were they to question the way in which his objectives were delivered? There was still much he himself was learning about being an avatar of Death.

"They give me what they are capable of giving," Bentley tried to explain. "Then it becomes my responsibility to unravel the mystery of their untimely expiration."

"And how exactly do you do that?" Pym asked. "Do you enter the building wearing your fright mask with your father's guns blazing?" He stared at Bentley, his gaze hard and accusatory.

"I've told you before," Bentley stated. "I use violence only when it is necessary." He looked out the backseat window of the Packard at the building again. "When the answers are found and the villains exposed." He paused, flashes of the insane bloodletting that he had perpetrated— that *Death* had perpetrated—over the last weeks parading before his mind's eye.

"And until then?"

"Until then?" Bentley repeated, opening the passenger door and stepping out onto the sidewalk. "Until then, there is an investigation to complete, and purveyors of evil to be routed."

He told his driver to wait for his return before slamming closed the car door and climbing the steps to the building's front doors.

Into the lion's den.

—

The thick, sickly smell of flowers was almost palpable as Bentley entered a wood-paneled foyer. A tall, dark-suited, middle-aged man stepped from an office on the right and greeted him with a serene smile.

"Good evening, sir," said the man with a slight bow. Bentley took note of his voice; he had a sibilance to his speech. "May I first say how sorry I am for your loss. Constance and her mourners are in the Serenity Room. This way, if you please."

The woman's name came out as *Conssssstanssse*.

Bentley followed the man down a short hall. They stopped at the doorway to a room on the left.

"Right in here," the man said, motioning with his hand into the room.

"Thank you," Bentley said.

The man bowed again, leaving Bentley standing in the entryway. There were chairs on either side of a short aisle, leading to the casket containing the departed in the center of the back of the room. A smattering of black-clad mourners were seated here and there, speaking in whispers so as not to disrespect the dead. Some turned to stare as Bentley entered, and he quickly found a seat in the last row.

He sat and watched as more mourners arrived and approached the casket, where they knelt for a moment, bowing their heads. Then, prayers completed, they would step away, politely offering their condolences to the grieving family before finding a chair and sitting only long enough to avoid seeming rude.

It went on like that for hours, people coming and going, and still Bentley saw nothing out of the ordinary. He was becoming antsy; usually by then the reason for his presence in a particular place would have become evident. Once again he carefully studied the room. His eyes finally settled upon the casket, and he made up his mind as to what he would do.

Bentley rose from his chair and walked toward the deceased.

Constance Dyer lay in her coffin, hands folded atop her ample chest. Her fingers had been wrapped in rosary beads, a silver crucifix dangling at one of her wrists. Bentley knelt upon the cushioned kneeler as if to pray, but instead studied the corpse. There appeared to be nothing wrong; the large woman's face was heavily adorned in makeup that made her flesh appear waxy in the room's lighting. She wore a string of pearls around her thick, powdered neck and a flowered dress that made him think of the jungle. He wondered how had she come to meet her end and what form Death had worn when it had taken her hand.

Bentley remembered a beautiful little girl with a beaming smile and curly blond hair the color of the sun, and how she had come for him, but his parents had had other plans—and things had not turned out so well.

Sensing that another mourner had arrived, Bentley stood, his eyes furtively searching one last time for any sign—any clue—as to why the ghost had brought him here.

As if he had somehow summoned her, the ghost appeared to his left, looking even more grotesque in the funeral-home lighting than she had in his bedroom. This time the top of her head had been removed, the inside of her skull fully visible and lacking its gray, cerebral contents. She tipped her head forward to be sure he saw the empty, bloody bowl. Even though she was a phantasm, Bentley reacted, stepping quickly back from the gruesome vision and losing his balance.

To prevent himself from falling, he reached out, grabbing hold of the coffin's edge. The world began to spin, a spell of vertigo and nausea causing him to sway in an attempt to regain his balance. His gaze fell to the inside of the coffin, and he was surprised to see that Constance was gone, replaced by another.

It is the female spirit's physical form, but intact from what he can see. The vision shifts. He sees the lid of the casket being slowly lowered, and then the container is wheeled from the viewing room down the hallway to what appears to be an open elevator.

The coffin begins its descent, the elevator door opening into some sort of stone basement. It is like something out of Dante: cold, wet stone, the ceiling lined with rows of iron hooks that sway in the dank, fetid air. He feels the sensation as the woman's body is roughly hauled from her resting place, her clothes torn away and discarded, exposing her pale, naked flesh. At the end of a stone chamber, in front of a blazing oven, a man works. He is wearing a heavy, crimson-stained apron, his fearsome cleaver coming down with great force upon a wooden cutting board.

A butcher doing as a butcher does.

The woman is being brought to him.

Bentley sees that the man hacks at a thick and bloody piece of flesh, a limb, but he can't tell whether arm or leg. The meat is expertly trimmed from the bone, then slid aside to be added to a larger pile later, while the clean-picked bone is tossed upon a heap of offal.

The butcher turns toward Bentley, his eyes a solid black in the firelight cast from the great oven. He motions for the woman's corpse to be brought closer and smiles, exposing jagged teeth like razors, as the body is unceremoniously laid before him upon the bloody, gouged wood. He looks her over, assessing his work before raising the cleaver and bringing it down with a sound like thunder.

The hand that dropped down upon Bentley's shoulder was firm, drawing him back from the nightmarish vision. He turned to focus upon a concerned face—the face of the butcher, but clean and unspattered with blood.

"Are you all right?" the older man asked. "You look quite pale."

His teeth were normal, and instead of a bloody apron, he was wearing a fine black suit, with a white shirt and black tie. The middle-aged man who had met him at the door was standing beside him, as was another younger man.

"I'm fine," Bentley managed to say as he tried to shake off the horrors of the vision. "I always look this way—pale, I mean. I'm just overwhelmed by grief, I suppose."

The butcher offered an understanding nod. "Constance was a fine woman, and she will most assuredly be missed."

Bentley was surprised to hear that the butcher had the same speech impediment as the middle-aged man.

"Would you care to sit down?" the butcher asked him kindly. "One of my sons can bring you a glass of water, if you'd like."

One of my sons? Bentley realized that he was in the presence of the funeral home's owner. The butcher in his vision was the senior Hargrove.

The eldest son began to walk away to fetch the glass of water.

"No, no that's quite all right," Bentley said quickly, stopping him. "I think I'll just take my leave now. Thank you anyway." He turned to face

the aisle and found other mourners staring from their seats, concern on
their faces.

"I'm sorry for your loss," he said to no one in particular as he marched
down the aisle and back into the hallway.

He pushed through the front door, but as he headed down the stairs, he
could suddenly feel eyes upon him, and turned to see Hargrove and his two

sons watching him go. There was something in their gazes, something that chilled him to the core and stirred him to action.

Now he knew why he'd been sent.

———

Bentley slipped into the backseat of his car, startling Pym, who had fallen asleep.

"So?" the butler asked, rubbing sleep from his eyes as he turned to address Bentley.

"It was as I feared," he said. "Behind the veneer of a family-run business something incredibly dark and evil thrives."

Pym sighed, his shoulders slumping in the driver's seat. "And that means what, exactly?"

"It means that I am now forced to act," Bentley explained. "It was why I was summoned here."

"What do you intend to do?"

Bentley stared out the side window at the building. "I wait until the innocent have departed."

He reached down below the seat and retrieved the two guns he had placed there earlier. Taking one in hand, he chambered a round.

"Then I make evil pay."

———

Bentley Hawthorne had no idea why he had been chosen. He knew that it had something to do with his parents, and the lengths they had gone to to keep him alive, even though they had been told by many a medical expert that his demise was inevitable.

They had attempted to ignore the laws of life, and death, and had paid a terrible price.

A price Bentley continued to pay.

———

"Do you have to wear that?" Pym asked with distaste.

Bentley glanced up through the eyeholes of the skull mask and saw the butler staring at him through the rearview mirror.

"I do," he said. "When I wear it, I'm somebody else—some*thing* else—with an important job to do."

"I mean no disrespect, sir, truly, but do you realize how insane this all sounds?" Pym turned in the driver's seat to face him. "Ghosts sending you out in the middle of the night to God knows where, dressed in black, wearing a skull mask and carrying two automatic pistols. If I were to inform the proper authorities, you would be locked away in an asylum for certain."

Bentley reached up with a gloved hand to remove the mask. He found it easier to talk to his friend this way.

"But you would never do that."

Pym's look softened, and he sighed. "You're right. A long time ago, I made a promise to your parents. I promised that I would always look after you."

"And you've done that quite well," Bentley told him.

"But it hasn't been easy," Pym retorted, "especially of late."

"Things have changed, my friend." Bentley slowly returned the yellowish-white mask to his face. "I have been given a job," he said, his voice taking on a more menacing tone.

A voice he barely recognized.

——

The lights inside the funeral home finally went dark. The last of the mourners had filed through the front door a little more than an hour before, leaving only the owners of the establishment inside.

"It's time that I get to it," Bentley said. "The Grim Death has work to do."

He slid across the backseat and opened the door, allowing a rush of chilling air to enter.

"Is that what you actually call yourself when you're like this?" Pym asked. "Grim Death?"

"It is the death I deliver to those deserving of it . . . It seemed appropriate," he said, half in and half out of the car. "Why?"

"Oh, nothing," Pym said.

"Why?" Bentley asked again, only more firmly, and came farther back into the car.

"It seems silly," Pym said bluntly.

"Silly. Well, let me tell you it's not that, I assure you. I'm the kind of death they deserve, you see."

"Yes," Pym said with a little nod.

"I'm not a happy death," Bentley continued to explain. "These people I'm visiting . . . they've done horrible things. I'm the one who will remind them of their terrible actions and make them pay the price."

"I see. Yes," Pym said.

"Do you?" Bentley asked him. "Not so silly now, correct?"

Pym just shook his head no, ever so slowly.

Not entirely sure he believed the butler, and no longer having the patience to argue, Bentley slunk from the car, pushing the door silently closed behind him.

He darted to the nearest shadows thrown by the buildings on the street, using the darkness to conceal his movements. There was an alley between buildings, and he went down it, pressing close to the wall until it opened onto a large lot and the service entrance to the funeral home.

Bentley tried the heavy door but was not surprised to find it locked. He looked around, searching for some other way to gain entrance. His eyes fell on a rectangular basement window that he might have been able to break, but he paused when he heard the sound of a truck engine drawing closer. A closed gate at the far end of the lot was suddenly illuminated by headlights, and he quickly ran for cover.

A truck stopped in front of the gate, and the driver got out to push it open. Then he climbed back into the truck and drove into the lot, parking near the back door to the funeral home.

From his hiding place, Bentley could see the sign on the side of the truck—SALVY'S FLORIST, obviously making a delivery for the next day's services. He watched as the driver again left the cab, this time walking to the door. The man fished inside one of the pockets of his baggy pants and produced a key, then unlocked the door and let it swing open into darkness.

Bentley saw his opportunity as the man turned from the open door and went around to the back of the truck, pulling open its double doors and climbing inside to retrieve his delivery. Stealthily, he raced from the shadows and plunged through the open door, just as he heard the delivery truck's doors slam closed. He managed to slip behind a large brick support before the man came through the door carrying two large floral arrangements, carefully stepping down the three steps into the basement. He walked past where the masked Bentley had secreted himself and placed the flowers just outside another door at the far end of the room. Finished, the driver quickly left the basement, whistling a Gilbert and Sullivan tune as he closed the door and locked it behind him.

Bentley listened as the truck engine started up and then faded off as the florist drove away. He waited a few moments in the silence of the funeral home basement to be sure there would be no further interruptions before he cautiously emerged from behind the pillar. The basement was dark, but his eyes quickly adjusted. He could see the shapes of multiple caskets across from him. Even in the semidarkness he could make out the high quality of some, with ornate carving and silver and gold detailing, in sharp contrast to others that appeared to be little more than pine boxes.

He was surprised by how large the basement seemed to be, and as he prowled about he noticed several other doors, some closed, some open. He peered through one open doorway to find some sort of workroom, the wall covered in shelving littered with bottles of chemicals. A long metal table, which could only have been used for the preparation of the deceased for burial, sat ominously in the room's center.

He also noticed that there were children's toys—a tricycle, a doll, and a striped ball—just outside the workroom's door, and thought how odd it was to see items such as these in a space where—

The silence was suddenly interrupted by the grinding of gears and the hum of machinery. Bentley scanned the shadows of the basement until his eyes fell upon a larger metal door with a heavy accordion gate across it. Ducking into a patch of concealing shadow, he watched as the door drew sideways, and a hand reached out from within to unlatch the gate and slide it aside. A casket resting atop a wheeled cart was pushed from the elevator, followed by the middle-aged undertaker who had greeted Bentley earlier that evening.

The undertaker left the coffin, disappearing for a moment somewhere in the basement, only to return with a wheeled stretcher. With growing fascination, Bentley watched as the man opened the lid of the coffin, roughly hauled the stiffened corpse of Constance Dyer from her resting place, and laid her body upon the stretcher.

Making certain the body was stable and would not tumble off, the undertaker left again, only to return with what appeared to Grim Death's eyes to be multiple sandbags, which he then proceeded to lay inside the now empty casket. Satisfied with his work, the man then closed the lid.

They don't intend to bury the body, Bentley realized. The sandbags were intended to give the impression of weight—the impression that Constance was inside.

But what of the body? he pondered. *What is to be done with it?* He recalled the horrific visions he'd experienced at the woman's wake and hoped his suspicions were wrong, but . . .

Death roiled within him, already sure that it knew what was happening here, eager to make those responsible pay.

Bentley watched as the door where the delivery man had left the flower arrangements came open, and the youngest of the Hargrove sons appeared.

"The casket is ready to be sealed," the older brother told his sibling. "When you're finished, take it back upstairs and load it into the hearse. Burial is tomorrow morning at eight sharp."

The older then got behind the cart that held Constance's remains and pushed it toward where the youngest had just exited. "And bring these flowers upstairs while you're at it."

The youngest grunted something in response, getting behind the sandbag-filled casket and pushing it back onto the elevator. The older Hargrove got the other door opened and maneuvered the stretcher carrying Constance through the passage and into the area beyond; the door slammed closed when he was through.

Bentley knew that was where he needed to go—*where Grim Death needed to be*—observing the young man as he did as he had been told and returned for the flowers. The youth bent to pick up both arrangements. As Grim Death leaned farther out to observe, he unknowingly stepped upon a child's toy and unleashed an ear-piercing squeak into the quiet of the room.

If the situation had not been so dire, he would almost have found it comical.

Almost.

His clumsiness had alerted the youngest Hargrove to his presence.

The youth charged across the basement with a feral growl. Bentley met his lunge, resisting the temptation to reach inside his coat pocket and draw one of his guns. That would have been the most efficient way of dealing with the situation, but he didn't want to risk alerting anybody else to his presence. This needed to be handled as quickly and quietly as possible.

The young man was strong. Hitting Bentley like a bull, the younger Hargrove drove him back against a brick column, knocking the wind from his lungs in an explosive rush. Bentley had never been the greatest physical specimen, weighing no more than 125 pounds soaking wet, but since being inducted into Death's service, he'd found that when needed he could tap into some reserve of preternatural strength.

A gift to him, perhaps, in case of dire situations such as this.

Bentley felt his limbs flush with power and he lashed out, kicking the youngest Hargrove away with great force. His attacker flew backward across the basement, landing just before the elevator. He was climbing to his feet as Bentley hurled himself at his prey, coat splayed out like bat wings as he collided with the youth. The impact carried them both back into the elevator, crashing up against the bodyless casket, their furious struggles tipping it onto its side.

Young Hargrove managed to crawl atop Bentley within the cramped space, raised fists preparing to fall. The casket's contents had spilled out onto the elevator floor, and Bentley grabbed one of the sandbags, using it first to absorb the young man's wild blows and then as a weapon, slapping the heavy sack across the young man's face. Something flew from the undertaker's mouth as he fell out of the elevator. Bentley quickly climbed to his feet, ready to continue the fight, but found that his opponent was unconscious. Catching his breath, he looked to the floor to see what appeared to be a row of teeth lying next to the young man's head—false teeth, by the looks of them. Kneeling beside the unconscious Hargrove, Bentley reached down, pulling open his bloody lips and gasping at what was revealed. There were still teeth within the youth's mouth, but they were unnatural. Jagged and sharp, filed to points, they called to mind the disturbing visions he'd experienced earlier in the evening. He retrieved the row of artificial teeth: they were hollow, designed to be worn over the man's real teeth. A disguise.

He recalled the speech impediment he'd heard in both Hargrove and his eldest, and wondered.

After some searching, Bentley found a length of old rope and bound the man's hands and feet. He shoved a rag into his mouth and dragged him into the elevator, closing the heavy door and accordion gate.

Turning toward the closed door where he'd seen the middle-aged

Hargrove wheel the woman's body, Bentley experienced an icy chill down the length of his spine. He reached into his pockets, feeling for the reassurance of his guns.

Death impatiently urged him on.

Carefully, he opened the door and found himself looking into a long corridor that descended at a precarious slant. He guessed there was an entire other sublevel below the cellar.

Abandon hope all ye who enter, he thought as he proceeded into the corridor. The first thing he noticed was the smell, a thick, coppery miasma of blood and decay. The Bentley he had been would have turned tail and run for the closest exit.

But now, as Grim Death, he plunged deeper, drawn to what awaited him like metal filings to a magnet.

Thunk.

He stopped at the sound, reaching into his coat for one of his guns.

Thunk.

Bentley listened, cocking his head to discern from where the sound originated.

Thunk.

It was close, and he began walking again, pistol clenched in his gloved hand.

Thunk.

There was no mistaking the sound of chopping. His mind flashed back to his childhood, and one of the many cooks they'd had—he believed her name was Ida—busily working in the kitchen, cutting up a whole chicken for his parents' supper.

Thunk.

He was close now, just about able to make out an opening at the left of the corridor.

Thunk.

Bentley slowly approached, eyes darting about, searching for any potential threats. He noticed that the temperature had become much warmer the closer he got to the room. His eyes fell upon an enormous metal stove that seemed to take up one side of a stone wall, its two doors hanging wide open, a roaring wood fire blazing within.

Thunk.

Now standing just inside the room, Bentley saw where he was, and for a moment believed he had somehow found his way into one of the lower levels of Hell.

It was a kitchen of a sort, but one that could have belonged to some kind of demonic chef. It was dark, the stone walls sweating with moisture. Huge hooks at the ends of chains hung from a large portion of the wood-planked ceiling.

And from the ends of the hooks dangled . . .

Thunk.

He found the source of the sound in the corner of the room. A lone figure, his back to Bentley, dressed in a heavy apron, stood before a huge butcher's table, his heavy cleaver coming down upon the pieces of meat that he was cutting.

Thunk.

Pieces of meat that had until very recently been parts of Constance Dyer.

The sound of scuffling feet from behind alerted him, and Bentley spun around, gun raised in defense. The eldest of the Hargrove sons swung a meat hook, knocking the pistol from Bentley's hand. Bentley jumped back, going for his other weapon, but he slipped on an overly saturated pile of sawdust and lost his balance. The eldest Hargrove son came at him hard, lashing out with the hook, its tip easily piercing Bentley's clothing and burying itself in the meat of his shoulder. The young man behind the mask cried out as he did all he could to dislodge the foreign object, but it was already too late—he was set upon by his foe and beaten to the floor, the son's powerful blows nearly sending him into unconsciousness.

"So, what do we have here?" asked a familiar voice, hissing speech impediment and all.

Bentley looked up blearily through the eyeholes of the mask into the blood-spattered face of the butcher—and owner of the funeral home.

"Caught him watching you prepare the meat," the eldest son said to his father. He squatted down, then reached out with filthy hands, taking hold of the mask and ripping it from Bentley's face. "Look familiar, Da?"

"In fact he does," Hargrove said. "It's the little fella that took a spell while viewing Mrs. Dyer. Thought we were going to need to fetch a doctor for him."

The older man dropped down on his haunches beside his son.

"So, what brings you down here dressed like that, my boy?" the undertaker asked. "And don't you wish now that you'd minded your business?"

Bentley said nothing as he glared up at the man, his silence inspiring the son to yank and twist the meat hook that was still embedded in his shoulder.

"My father asked you a question," the eldest said as Bentley hissed in pain.

Pushing past the burning agony, he answered.

"The act of murder has brought me here," Bentley said.

Hargrove shook his head. "Harsh words," the older man said. "But what else can we expect from one who does not understand. Ancestry has shaped us into something rare upon this world, but murderers we are not."

Hargrove rose, his knees cracking noisily as he stood erect.

Bentley glanced over at the cutting board, and the chains hanging down, and the remnants of those who had once been whole, reduced now to little more than butchered meat.

"I'm having a difficult time seeing anything but."

The eldest son reached for the hook again, to punish him for his flippancy, but the older man stopped him.

"We are hunters, sir," Hargrove said indignantly. "I want you to know that."

He then glanced off to where Bentley had been looking, toward the dangling body parts, toward the meat. By the serene expression upon Hargrove's face, Bentley could tell he was seeing something other than a monstrous act of savagery.

"My grandfather wanted what was best for his family when he emigrated from eastern Europe. He and others continued to chase that dream, embarking on a journey to California."

The older man grew misty-eyed, reverence obvious in the tone of his voice.

"The wagon train set out in the late spring of 1846, but a series of mishaps caused their progress to suffer, eventually stranding the pioneers in the Sierra Nevada, where the harsh winter took its toll and their food resources grew low."

Mr. Hargrove paused, looking down at the bloodstained meat cleaver that he still held in hand.

"They began to die, to grow sicker and sicker with the brutal cold. It was my grandfather who determined how they could survive, but it was a decision he knew would change them forever."

"They became cannibals," Bentley said with obvious disdain.

Hargrove's son lashed out, pulling savagely on the meat hook stuck in his shoulder. Bentley cried out, falling over onto his side. He could feel the blood flowing from the wound, soaking through his shirt and into the sleeve of his coat. It looked as though yet another suit would find its way to the rag pile.

Mr. Hargrove went on with his story as Bentley lay there bleeding.

"The others refused to partake, even though it meant their imminent demise. Some even attempted to prevent my grandfather from doing what had to be done to survive . . . but he wouldn't let them stop him."

Bentley listened, trying to keep the metal point of the hook from grinding against the bone in his shoulder. As Hargrove continued to speak, Bentley focused his eyes on the mask—the face that he wore in service to a higher power—its empty eyes telling him that he had wasted too much time, that it was time for him to act.

Now.

Bentley made a show of going for the hook, to pull it from his flesh. As he'd hoped would happen, the son reacted.

"There'll be none of that," the elder son said as he swatted Bentley's hand away, taking hold of the hook once more. Bentley used the distraction to dig down into his coat pocket with his other hand for the second gun.

As the undertaker's son gleefully tugged on the hook, Bentley rolled onto his back, revealing the pistol in his hand. The son's eyes went wide as he saw what was about to happen.

"Death has a message," Bentley said.

The gun roared within the subbasement enclosure, the .45-caliber bullet punching the man in the stomach and throwing him backward into his father.

"Elijah!" Mr. Hargrove cried out, as he caught his son and lowered him to the ground, cradling him on the blood- and sawdust-covered floor.

Gun clutched tightly in hand, Bentley climbed painfully to his feet. He switched his weapon to the other hand so he could remove the hook from his flesh, and tossed it to the floor with a resounding clatter.

The undertaker glared at Bentley as he held his dying boy.

"Grandfather could never understand their unwillingness to accept how he provided his family with a means to survive the harshest of winters, so he silenced those who opposed him."

"He murdered them," Bentley said as he looked for his mask. "He murdered them, and then he and his family ate them."

"He saw it as a form of sacrifice in order for them all to live."

Bentley slipped the mask over his face, covering his scowl as he once again assumed the guise of Grim Death.

"How long?" Bentley demanded, his voice changed with the mask. "How long has your bloodline fed upon the innocents of this city?"

He watched the old man's expression gradually change with the realization that he was now in the presence of something more than human.

Bentley could feel Death struggle at his core to be set loose, but he held it at bay, curious to know the rest of the story.

"We had no choice," the old man went on. "The act of consumption changed us . . . Normal sustenance could no longer sustain us. The forbidden meat was the only way. After all my grandfather and his children had been through, they had to find yet another way to survive . . ."

"A funeral home," Bentley said, impressed with yet disgusted by the concept.

"We would do no harm . . . We became carrion eaters," Mr. Hargrove explained as he continued to hold his son close. "It was an acceptable life, until . . ."

Bentley gripped the pistol tightly, and kept his hold upon an impatient Death even as the pain in his shoulder throbbed unmercifully. Hargrove looked at his son and saw that he was no longer moving, and his tear-filled eyes grew dark as he recognized that his boy was gone.

"Before he died, Grandfather always cautioned his sons and their wives and their own children about the temptation of the fresh kill."

Hargrove let his son's still body slide from his arms as he got to his feet, picking up his cleaver.

"'Feed upon the naturally dead,' he'd always say, 'keep our ways secret—or be damned for all eternity.'"

The old man sighed as he hefted the heavy metal tool. "I'd suspected that they might be partaking . . . hunting the living. I warned them that it wasn't smart to hunt so close to home." He shook his head sadly.

"But they didn't listen," Bentley said, aiming his gun.

"No," Hargrove said. "They didn't, and neither did I. It was just too damn tempting."

The old man looked at him, and then removed his false teeth, flashing a smile that showcased razor-sharp teeth. "I've always feared someone like you," he said, no longer emphasizing the *S*. "Someone who would come and take away everything we've worked so hard to achieve. Someone who would mete out punishment for what we have done."

Blossoms of color had started to expand in front of Bentley's eyes as the blood continued to flow down his arm. It was taking all that he had not to swoon.

"The innocents you and your family have murdered and defiled cannot truly rest until you are punished," he declared.

Hargrove stepped back, nodding slowly as if accepting his fate.

"Grandfather warned that the road of the fresh kill would lead to all sorts of trouble," the old man explained. "He never got too specific . . . but there was something in his eyes when he talked about it, like something really bad would happen."

Hargrove lifted the cleaver, and Bentley reacted, his finger tightening on the pistol's trigger. The gun spat fire as the undertaker cried out, falling back against the doorframe.

Bentley experienced a wave of vertigo that threatened to bring him to his knees; he swayed drunkenly, grabbing one of the dangling chains to keep himself upright.

The old man had not been brought down with the shot. Through unfocused eyes Bentley watched as Hargrove proceeded to whack the side of the metal cleaver repeatedly against the damp stone wall, the noise resounding throughout the subbasement.

"He should have told us what the fresh kill would do to our bloodline," Hargrove said. "He should have told us the price the mothers would pay . . . what it would do to the children."

Children?

And then Bentley remembered the toys in the basement.

He heard them before he saw them—skittering, scratching sounds from all around him.

They came out of hiding, crawling from shadows and squeezing out from behind spaces that appeared too small for anything with a skeleton to fit.

At first glance they seemed as though they might have some human ancestry, but the more he studied their pale, malformed bodies, the less he was sure. They watched him with eyes like black marbles. Twin vertical slits in their flat, pasty faces, which he guessed served the function of noses, twitched nervously as they leaked milky liquid into open mouths where mottled pink-and-black gums were lined with rows of saw-blade teeth.

The creatures kept their distance, looking nervously from him to Hargrove, chattering in some strange, guttural tongue.

Chattering to their grandfather.

"You're right," the old man said to the children in a soft, grandfatherly tone. "He doesn't belong here . . . He's a bad man."

The things immediately responded to the man's words, turning in Bentley's direction, their malformed faces twisting into guises of animalistic savagery.

"And what do we do to bad men?" Hargrove asked them.

The monstrous children reacted with bloodcurdling screams, giving Bentley their full attention.

Hargrove made a move for the doorway, and Bentley fired his pistol once more, but the shot went wild, missing the man as he escaped into the corridor.

"Damn it," Bentley hissed, wanting to give pursuit. But he had other matters to attend to now as the children, transformed by the sin of cannibalism, stalked toward him. Some had picked up implements, mostly knives of various sizes, from around the room. Some even brandished jagged pieces of dried bone. He backed up as they came closer. Noticing the pistol he had dropped earlier, Bentley snatched it from the ground. Now fully armed, he aimed with both weapons but found that he could not bring himself to fire.

Even though they were hideous, twisted things, created from murder and the consumption of human meat, they were still children, and he could not squeeze the triggers.

Sensing his hesitation, one of the misshapen youths charged forward ahead of his brethren, thrusting the tines of a filthy, gore-encrusted fork into Bentley's calf with an inhuman wail.

Bentley cried out, gazing down into the malicious grin of something seemingly void of humanity, and as the Death that resided within him took control, he suddenly found he no longer had any qualms about firing a bullet into the distorted face.

In fact, it was the proper thing to do.

The Colt.45 boomed its retort. Grim Death's diminutive foe flipped backward to the cellar floor with a pathetic squawk, to lie there perfectly still. The others stopped their advance, gathering around their newly deceased brother, staring in wide-eyed awe at his fate. Grim Death wondered if they were capable of understanding that he meant business, that they could share their brethren's fate or choose to live, returning to their hiding places in the shadows of the nightmarish slaughterhouse.

One by one they looked up from their fallen brother to stare at Bentley with eyes glistening black.

"Children of nightmare, choose your fate," Grim Death warned, his thumbs pulling back the guns' hammers with an audible *click*.

One after the other they began to whoop their war cries, coming at him all at once in a tidal wave of enraged deformity, and Grim Death, twin pistols at the ready and with no further compunction, began to fire. He had given them a choice, and they had chosen death.

The abominations screamed. Some managed to avoid being struck, while others were savaged by the .45-caliber bullets that tore unmercifully through their twisted bodies.

Death temporarily satisfied, Bentley saw his opportunity and dashed toward the exit, turning as he ran to see a few survivors emerge from hiding places to resume their pursuit. Running low on bullets and feeling the heat upon his back, he turned his gaze to the large oven, still burning with a blistering intensity, and formulated an idea.

Bentley found a wrought-iron shovel and leaned into the oppressive heat. He drove the shovel into the burning matter inside the great stove

and was horrified to see a blackened skull staring back at him from a pile of ash and bones.

He scooped a white-hot mound onto the shovel and spun toward his attackers, throwing the burning remains into their path.

The advancing monster children were driven back by the blazing vestiges, some of the rolling bones igniting drying puddles of grease and oily rags into hungry pyres.

From the doorway he watched as the twisted products of cannibalism reacted to the flames, their futile attempts at extinguishing the fire causing the voracious conflagration to spread.

That particular threat temporarily contained, Bentley rushed down the corridor to the funeral home's basement, the smoke from the fire growing thicker as it followed him into the main building. From out of the writhing smoke the youngest Hargrove leapt, colliding with him and sending them both sprawling to the floor. The youngest, having escaped his bonds and internment in the casket elevator, was savage in his attack. Bentley worked his forearm beneath the young man's throat as they struggled, driving him back and preventing the youth from biting him with snapping, knife-sharp teeth. Having no further patience for fisticuffs, Bentley brought one of his pistols up and jammed the barrel against the youth's chest, firing a single shot through his black heart. The youngest Hargrove went down, but still showed signs of life. At Death's urging, Bentley fired another slug into the young man's skull to make certain he would not be getting up.

The Death inside him grew anxious, urging him to find the patriarch of the cannibal clan. The cellar was now filled with smoke, and Bentley carefully made his way through the choking fog in search of the undertaker. From somewhere in the haze there came a terrible screaming, like the tormented cries of suffering animals.

"What have you done to them?" asked a voice much closer to him than expected. "What have you done to the children?"

Bentley threw himself back, barely evading the looming shape that came at him from out of the roiling vapor. The blade of Hargrove's ax came down upon the concrete floor in an explosion of sparks. Reacting before Hargrove could raise the weapon again, Bentley lashed out with one of his pistols, slapping the cold steel across the man's jaw. Hargrove lurched back with a pained grunt as Bentley took aim with the other gun, but the smoke was now too thick, and the undertaker was gone.

Again came the disturbing, pain-racked cries, only this time they were closer. Bentley prowled the hidden landscape of the funeral home basement, through the shifting smoke, every sense attuned to possible danger. The ghost of the woman who had brought him here suddenly appeared, her damaged body taking form in the smoke. Her mouth was open in a pleading wail, her one untouched arm raised to point behind him. Trusting that the spirit had his best interests in mind, Bentley spun and fired into the curtain of obscuring gray.

There came a grunt, and the clatter of something heavy falling to the floor. Bentley advanced toward the sound and found the discarded ax and a serpentine trail of blood leading off farther into the labyrinthine basement.

He followed the crimson trail to the workroom he'd seen earlier, filled with the chemicals and tools of the undertaking trade. Hargrove lay upon the floor, blood leaking from two bullet wounds in his chest into a circular drain in the floor.

"I see you now," Hargrove began, eyes fixed upon the specter of Death standing in the doorway, "see you for what you truly are."

The older man attempted to stand, grabbing the wooden shelving for support—shelves that held dusty bottles of formaldehyde. The shelves creaked in protest, then tipped forward onto the injured man, the bottles of chemicals exploding at they hit the concrete. Hargrove lay there covered in glass and embalming fluid, the heavy wooden shelving pinning him to the floor. The drifting smoke and fumes from the spilled chemicals were nearly overwhelming, and Bentley found himself bringing a hand to his mask to filter out some of the choking vapors.

"Please," Hargrove begged weakly, bloody hands reaching out to Death's emissary. "Haven't I served you well?"

The Death inside him stirred excitedly, sensing an end to the moment, and Bentley found himself beginning to raise one of his guns.

And then there came the screams again, and through the thickening smoke he saw a glow—a glow that was coming closer and closer.

"Please!" Hargrove begged again as Bentley moved from the doorway into a shadowed corner of the supply room.

The surviving Hargrove grandchildren swarmed into the room, their bodies aflame, screaming in agony, driven to madness by their pain. They were looking for somebody to help them—somebody to take away their torment.

They fell upon their trapped grandfather, all their emotions pouring out as they hugged, bit, and clawed at him with spindly arms burnt practically to blackened sticks.

And Hargrove, too, began to burn, the formaldehyde on his clothing and collected upon the floor beneath him igniting in a rush. The flames spread voraciously about the room as the Hargrove clan screamed for far longer than Bentley would have thought imaginable.

It was only a matter of time before the entire building would be engulfed. Bentley found his way back to the door from which he'd originally gained entrance and pushed it open; a rush of cool early morning air fed the fire behind him.

Bentley collapsed to his knees just outside the entrance, choking on purifying gulps of oxygen.

"Bentley?" he heard a familiar voice call out, and looked up through watering eyes to see Pym coming toward him. He continued to cough and gasp as the butler helped him stand, supporting him as they went down the alley between buildings to where the sedan was still parked.

"Perhaps if you removed the damned mask," the man growled, reaching up to rip away his other face.

"Ah," Bentley wheezed. "That's better."

It was still early enough that the streets were free of life as Bentley and Pym emerged from the alley and made their way to the car.

"I think it wise that we leave here at once," Pym said, opening the rear passenger door before quickly going around to the driver's side.

Bentley chanced a look at the funeral home before climbing in. The windows were illuminated with a ghostly orange light, and smoke was beginning to seep from beneath the sills and doors.

And then he saw them. There had to be at least a hundred, maybe more: the ghosts of all those who had been fed upon by the Hargrove cannibals. They were standing before the building, watching as it burned.

"Are we done here?" Pym called out from inside the car, revving the engine.

"Yes," Bentley said as he practically fell onto the seat. His shoulder, his whole body, throbbed painfully, and he barely managed to reach out to grab hold of the door handle and pull it closed. "Yes, I think we are."

Bentley slumped down in the backseat, helplessly weak, as the car screeched away from the curb. The Death that resided within him sighed contentedly, satisfied—

For now.

—

Bentley slipped in and out of consciousness through the long drive home, the sun having climbed higher in the morning sky each time he opened his eyes. By the time they returned to Hawthorne House, it would be a particularly lovely fall day—not that he would see any of it.

As soon as Pym parked the sedan, he helped Bentley out and into the mansion, where the butler assumed another of his seemingly endless responsibilities: cleaning and dressing Bentley's wounds.

Painfully sore, and stinking of formaldehyde and cooked meat, Bentley slowly climbed the stairs to his room, while Pym did what he did to keep the great house in order. There was a part of him that would have loved another bath, but at the moment his body needed sleep far more than cleanliness.

Bentley entered his bedchambers, shucking off his stinking clothes. As he kicked off his trousers, he saw that his breakfast tray from the previous day was still sitting upon the table, reminding him that it had been close to twenty-four hours since he'd last eaten. Some of his breakfast still remained, a single piece of cold toast lying upon a plate. Bentley picked up the bread and brought it to his mouth, too tired to do anything but nibble on the crust. When he felt that he'd had enough to temporarily sustain him, he dropped the toast's remains to the table and turned languidly toward the bed.

Another ghost had appeared, blocking his way.

Bentley didn't want to see it, closing his eyes hard before opening them again. The little boy still stood there, large eyes piercing and beckoning to him. And that was when he noticed the ornate dagger protruding from the center of the child's chest, phantasmal blood leaking out from the wound to form a halo of crimson around his small head. Bentley looked away, trying to get to his bed, but the small spirit continued to drift to block his way, his pale hands reaching out—beckoning.

"I have to sleep, little boy," he told the child. "I'm so very tired. When I awaken I will . . ."

Bentley felt the odd stirring at his core telling him that the power he served had again awakened. It wanted him to act.

At once.

The ghost mouthed the word *please,* and Bentley felt his resolve collapse.

"Pym," he called out in his loudest voice, "I have need of you."

The door to his suite came open.

"What is it, sir?" the butler asked.

"I'm going to need another suit," he told the man, his fatigue forgotten as he watched the expression on the ghost's face turn from sadness to joy.

"But I thought you were exhausted?" Pym asked.

"I'm fine," he told his friend, his heart beginning to race. "We have work to do."

Death had no time for weariness.

Chapter Two

BEFORE:

Six-year-old Bentley Hawthorne raised his toy pistol and fired repeatedly at the large man, who dove behind the sofa to avoid being hit by the imaginary bullets.

Abraham Hawthorne exploded up from the other side of the elegant piece of furniture and lunged at his son, who continued to snap away with his pistol as his father snatched him up into his arms.

"You're dead!" Bentley shrieked as he wriggled in his father's grasp. "I shot you!"

"That pistol of yours only holds six shots," Abraham told his son knowingly, and began to tickle him unmercifully. "Anything after that was like firing blanks."

"No!" Bentley squealed as his father continued the onslaught of tickling. "The bad guy can't win . . . The bad guy can never win!"

"And that is why you must always be prepared," Abraham instructed. "You should always be aware of your rounds, and carry appropriate amounts of ammunition, or perhaps even another weapon if—"

"Abraham!" a woman's soft but stern voice interrupted.

The large man holding his child upside down stopped his antics and stared.

Edwina Hawthorne continued with her cross stitch.

"That's quite enough of the gun talk," she said, pulling up on a stitch. "This is supposed to be family time, not talking-shop time."

"Of course, my dear," her husband said, letting the still squirming child down to the floor. "I just thought it might benefit the lad to bestow some important tidbits of information and . . ."

"Certainly, my dear," she said. "I quite understand."

Bentley stumbled back from his father. "I'm putting more bullets in my gun," he said, going through the motions of loading invisible ammunition into the gun's chambers. "And then the good guy will shoot the bad guy . . . and the good guy will win."

The child was breathless, and soon coughing and gasping for air.

"Bentley?" his mother called from the sofa, setting her cross stitch aside to go to her son.

His father was already there, holding his son as he choked and gasped.

"It's okay, boy," his father said, attempting to calm him. "Just try to breathe in and out. Slowly, that's it."

"The good guy . . . The good guy has to win," Bentley wheezed.

"Yes," Abraham told him, stroking his sweat-damped hair and rocking him. "You're right. The good guy always wins."

"Give him to me," his mother commanded, and Abraham did as he was told, lifting the gasping child and placing him in his mother's arms.

"You shouldn't have let him get so excited," Edwina reprimanded.

"We were just playing, my dear," Abraham explained.

"But he can't play as others do," she scolded. "His condition . . ."

The father stroked his son's hair, gazing down at the little boy nestled in his mother's arms, now breathing shallowly.

A tall, imposing figure dressed in butler's attire appeared in the doorway.

"Is there anything that I may do?" Pym asked.

"I think he's all right," Edwina said, bending down to kiss the boy's sweat-dappled brow. "He just needs some rest."

"You can take him to his room, Pym," Abraham said, stepping back to allow the butler access.

"Very good, sir," Pym said, taking the child from his mother and into his arms. "Right this way, Master Bentley," he continued, as he carried the child from the study.

His parents watched them as they left.

"I'll just take a little nap," the boy called out weakly, his voice sounding hoarse. "And then I'll come back and we can play some more."

The butler carried him to the staircase that led up to his bedroom and began to climb, and when the little boy was out of sight, his mother began to cry.

The pain his parents felt was palpable.

"He just needs some rest," Abraham said. "He overdid it, is all. He'll be fine in a few hours or so."

Edwina's back was to her husband as she stared out the window at the late-summer blooms.

"If only that were true," she said, turning from the view to gaze at her husband. "He'll never be better."

"Don't say that," Abraham commanded, anger and frustration in his tone.

"Someone has to say it," she said, tears streaming down her full cheeks. "Our boy is unwell, and has been since he came into this world. There's no amount of love we can give him that will change that."

"But the doctor said . . ."

"You hear what you want to hear. The doctor said that he will grow weaker over time, but then . . ."

"I refuse to accept that outcome," Abraham barked, puffing out his chest powerfully. He had been in control of the Hawthorne family munitions business since he was eighteen years old, and was not in the least bit used to being denied his every want.

His wife came to him, her face damp with sadness.

"But it's an inevitable truth that we need to confront," she said as she put her arms around him, laying her wet cheek against his broad chest. "Our sweet boy will never grow to be an adult."

"Don't say that," Abraham growled.

"But I must," the boy's mother cried. "I can't help but hope that the more I say it, the less excruciatingly painful the inescapable will be."

Abraham irritably shrugged his wife off and turned his back on her, heading to the windows. "I will not accept that Bentley will die," he said forcefully, gazing out at the deep woods beyond the backyard. "The answer is out there," he muttered, brain churning with the intensity of thought, "the solution to keeping my son alive."

He turned from the window to look at his wife, still standing where he had left her, looking so brittle and forlorn.

"I swear to you, we will find the answer," he said, reassuring her. "If I have to wrestle Death itself, our son will live."

Chapter Three

Lying in the darkness, halfway between waking and sleep, Bentley could sense that he was no longer alone.

He listened to the sounds of the presence from the protection of the darkness behind his eyes, and at once recognized the familiar footfalls. He attempted to dive deeper, back into unconsciousness, praying for the intruder to go away and leave him to his sweet oblivion.

He heard a sudden hissing sound, which could only have been the curtains covering his windows being drawn apart, and then felt the warmth of the midday sun searing the pale skin of his face.

"No!" Bentley cried out, certain that he would explode into flames if exposed much longer to the blistering rays. He grabbed his sheets and blanket and yanked them up over his head for protection.

"I can't stand it anymore," Pym said, from somewhere near his bed. "You've been entombed in this room for days. I refuse to let you rot away in the darkness like some sort of bizarre fungus."

"I'm not listening to you," Bentley said from beneath his protective covering. "Go away or you're fired."

"Don't do me any favors," he heard his manservant mutter beneath his breath as he strode from the room.

Bentley chanced a look, pulling down the covers and squinting across the room to the open door, hoping that Pym had left, but doubting that was the case. He heard the clattering of silverware and ducked down beneath the protection of his sheets and blankets again as Pym entered the room carrying a silver serving tray holding plates of food and a pot of coffee.

Bentley's stomach gurgled as the smells on the tray wafted about the room, invading the air beneath the sheets. "You're fired," he said from under his shroud.

"So be it," Pym replied, setting the tray down atop a small desk across from Bentley's bed. "But before I begin my life of unemployment and seek out the nearest soup line, I've taken it upon myself to cook you some breakfast, although it is closer to dinnertime."

The gurgling of Bentley's stomach was followed by a gnawing pain, as if something asleep in his belly had come awake and was attempting to eat its way out.

How long, exactly, have I been asleep? he wondered as he drew the bedclothes down to watch Pym setting the place where he would eat.

"Is there toast?" Bentley asked Pym's back.

"I'm truly not obliged to answer, seeing as I am no longer in your employ," the butler responded sarcastically.

"You're hired again," Bentley said, emerging from his cocoon of sheets and blankets. "But you're on probation." He swung his legs over the edge of the bed with a grunt and placed his feet on the floor.

"Then I will strive to be on my best behavior, sir," Pym said, turning from the makeshift place setting upon the desk.

"You need to let me rest, Pym," Bentley said, sitting slumped over on the side of the bed. "I need to heal."

Bentley lifted the sleeve of his silk pajamas to examine his most recent wounds, and found the cuts and gashes already puckered and healed over. "Amazing," he said aloud, lifting up his pajama top to find that the extraordinary healing process had occurred with even the more severe of his wounds. "It appears that my prolonged slumber has actually done me well," Bentley said, experiencing a sudden jolt of reinvigorating energy as he stood up from his bed.

"What's to eat?" he asked, rubbing his hands together eagerly. "I'm famished."

Pym stepped aside, allowing Bentley access. "I imagine you would be, sir. It's been three days since you've had anything to eat."

Bentley's hand froze with a slice of toast midway to his mouth. "Three days?"

"Three days, yes," Pym reaffirmed, continuing to stare straight ahead. "I was beginning to think you might have died."

The image of a little girl, arms wide, appeared inside Bentley's head, the vision of innocence transforming into a ghastly, shrieking visage.

"No," he said, raising the toast to his mouth and taking a bite. "Not yet." He suddenly felt overwhelmingly tired again, the weight of the future and the things expected of him as an agent of Death draining him of his new-found strength.

"I think I'd like to rest some more, Pym," he told his friend and man-servant, finishing the last bite of his single piece of toast. He wiped the crumbs from his hands and started toward the windows to pull the curtains closed.

The apparition of a woman appeared before him, and he gasped aloud.

"Sir?" Pym questioned. "Are you all right?"

Bentley sighed, knowing that there would be no more rest for him, at least not in the immediate future.

"I'm fine, Pym," he said, staring into the haunted eyes of the ghostly beauty. "I guess I won't be going back to bed after all . . .

"There's something I need to do."

Chapter Four

BEFORE:

Professor Romulus had the most fascinating theory on death.

He was giving a standing-room-only lecture in the meeting hall rented once a month by the spiritualist group the Blessed Brothers and Sisters of the Afterlife, and held the crowd in rapt attention with the details of his thrilling research.

Using an invention of his own design, Romulus projected photographs he had taken over the last ten years, depicting individuals as they neared the end of their lives. Some had been taken in hospitals around the country, others in homes where sickness had taken root. Besides the individuals close to death, all the pictures depicted something else. Something that the professor said could only be seen using a special camera—also of his own creation—that was able to record a specific kind of energy present at the time of a person's demise.

An energy given off only by beings he referred to as Death Avatars.

Professor Romulus was convinced that every living person had a Death Avatar, and that this representation of death was responsible for escorting the life-force from the body when it ceased to live.

Each series of pictures showed a strangely shaped shadow near the dying individual, its shape growing more and more defined as the person drew closer to the end of life—then gone as soon as the individual expired.

The spiritualists who had gathered for his presentation appeared riveted by his words, but none more so than Abraham and Edwina Hawthorne. They sat side by side, holding hands, their grip upon each other becoming more and more intense the longer the professor spoke of his theory.

This concept . . . this theory . . . if true, gave a kind of identity to the force that threatened to take their child.

A face to their foe.

The tall and powerfully built professor finished his talk, then took a bow as the crowd rose to its feet in a standing ovation.

Abraham and Edwina waited, silently and patiently, at the back of the auditorium, watching as individual members of the audience took turns shaking the professor's hand and thanking him for his time—thanks that he graciously accepted. They continued to stand there, even after all the others had gone and the professor had begun to disassemble the screen and strange whirring machine that continued to project the last image he had shown.

"Is this true?" Abraham finally asked, releasing his grip upon his wife's hand and striding toward Professor Romulus.

The professor turned, startled by the power behind the question.

"So sorry," he apologized. "I thought everyone had left."

"That." Abraham Hawthorne pointed to the dark shape hovering over the bed of what appeared to be a young woman ravaged by some horrible illness. "That shape . . . that avatar, as you called it . . ."

"Yes," Professor Romulus answered, his tone urging Abraham to continue.

"Is it real?" he asked. "I've seen much in my many years as a student in the ways of spirit. Some things were fascinating, while others were clearly devised to create false hope, meant only to separate the desperate from their money."

He strode closer to the professor, his mere presence usually quite intimidating, but Romulus stood his ground. "Do you believe these death entities to be a reality?"

"I do," the professor stated unequivocally.

Abraham's eyes drifted back to the screen, to the frozen moment of a stranger's death projected there. He stared at the grayish-black shape looming above the dying woman, waiting like a vulture to take her.

Familiarizing himself with the image of his enemy.

Before a declaration of war.

———

Professor Romulus daintily sipped his coffee from the fine china cup, then gently set it down upon its saucer.

"I must say I was a bit surprised to receive your invitation," he said, smiling at his hosts, "and then to find out who you are."

Abraham and his wife sat across from the man, sipping from their own cups of coffee.

"I had no idea that the man who appeared so passionate about my life's work was, in fact, the illustrious Abraham Hawthorne," Romulus continued. "Needless to say, I'm thrilled to have made your acquaintance, as well as to have been invited to your beautiful home." He gazed around the room.

Pym entered carrying a platter of cookies, which he immediately held out to the professor. "Cookie?" he asked.

Romulus considered the variety before selecting one. "Thank you."

Pym bowed slightly and approached his employers.

"No, thank you, Pym," Edwina said.

The butler nodded and set the platter down atop the coffee serving cart before leaving the room.

"We were quite excited that you accepted our invitation to coffee," Edwina began, as she raised her cup and delicately sipped.

"Quite," Abraham agreed, leaning forward to place his cup and saucer down upon the table in front of the sofa. "We were hoping to be able to further discuss your research."

Professor Romulus beamed, cookie crumbs falling into his gunmetal-gray beard. "Excellent," he said, grabbing for his cloth napkin and brushing crumbs from his chest and lap. "What would you like to know?"

Edwina glanced quickly at her husband before setting her own cup and saucer down. He met her eyes, a silent message passing between them before Abraham returned his attention to their guest.

"The Death Avatars," Abraham stated.

Professor Romulus sat back in the chair, anticipating the question to follow.

"You're saying that these beings are present at the time of death . . . that these creatures are there to transport the soul of the departed to the next adventure in the afterlife."

Professor Romulus smiled, slowly nodding. "This is what my research has shown, yes."

"These avatars," Abraham continued, growing even more intense, "have you ever had any interaction with them . . . or they with you?"

Romulus stood and approached the coffee cart, then lifted the silver decanter to pour himself another cup.

"I can say I have been tempted," the professor said, "but I fear the repercussions of interfering with the cosmic scheme of things, of interfering with the very forces of life and death."

"But could you?" Abraham asked, sitting at the very edge of the sofa, waiting with great anticipation for the professor's response.

Romulus reached for another cookie as he considered the question.

"Perhaps," he finally replied, returning to his chair with his cookie and fresh cup of coffee. "But why would . . . ?"

A pale young man stepped into the study.

"Pym said that we had company," the boy said, walking over to stand beside the couch where the Hawthornes were seated. "Hello," he acknowledged the professor.

"Bentley," Edwina said, getting up to wrap her arms lovingly around the boy. "You're supposed to be resting."

"This is our son, Bentley," Abraham said. "Bentley, this is Professor Romulus."

"Hello there, Professor Romulus," the boy said, going over to shake the professor's hand. "It's very nice to meet you."

"It's a pleasure to meet you as well, Bentley," the professor said.

The young man looked as if he were going to continue the pleasantries, but suddenly began to cough, as if choking on his words.

"Are you all right?" Romulus asked.

"He's fine," Abraham answered sternly.

Edwina went to her child, putting her arms around him again and rubbing his back.

"Take him back to his room," Abraham commanded. "He needs his rest."

Edwina hesitated for a moment, but saw the look in her husband's eyes. Hugging her child close, she escorted the choking youth away.

"Nice meeting you, Bentley," Professor Romulus called after them.

"He isn't well," Abraham stated flatly.

"Is it something that he can be treated for or—"

"We've taken him to every specialist," the boy's father interrupted, "the best that money can buy, but his prognosis remains the same." He paused, as if needing to adjust to the painful knowledge.

"My son will die in the not too distant future," Abraham finished.

"I'm terribly sorry," Professor Romulus said.

"Unless," Abraham said quietly, turning his dark, intense gaze fully on the professor.

"Yes?" Romulus asked, his curiosity whetted.

"Unless his death spirit . . . my son's avatar," Abraham began.

The professor's stare widened as the man spoke.

"Unless it was captured at the instant before my son's death . . ."

Romulus raised a hand to his beard and stroked it thoughtfully. "In theory," he said, "he would not die."

Abraham Hawthorne nodded slowly in agreement. "Help us, Professor . . .

"Help us save our son."

Chapter Five

Bentley returned to his breakfast tray, and the spectral woman followed.

"Should I look at this as a minor victory?" Pym asked proudly, standing by the desk.

"What is that?" Bentley pulled his gaze from the woman who hovered above the floor mere feet from them.

"You're returning to eating," Pym explained. "May I categorize this as a win?"

"Of course," Bentley replied distractedly, looking away from his manservant and back to the woman floating in the air. "Think of it however you like."

"Is there anything else that I might—"

"No," Bentley interrupted, sensing the woman's need. "You can leave me now."

"Very good, sir." Pym crossed the room and opened the door to the hallway.

Bentley heard it close as he reached for another piece of dry toast, continuing to stare at the woman as she watched him with dark, haunted eyes.

Beckoning eyes.

He chewed the toast, studying her details, taking in all that defined her appearance. He could see that she had been a pretty woman, with long, dark hair and a small frame. She was wearing a costume, sequined and glittering in a strange light that he assumed was found in the afterlife. At first he believed her to be a dancer of some kind, but then corrected himself.

No, I'll bet she was an aerialist. A trapeze artist.

The ghost floated closer, moving her dark, flowing hair aside to show him the wounds upon her throat.

Dear God, he thought, leaning forward in his desk chair for a closer look. The marks upon her delicate, ghostly throat were dark, bruised, as if her neck had been squeezed by a pair of powerful hands.

"I see," he said aloud, and watched as tears of ghostly ectoplasm leaked from her eyes to float about the room.

Bentley knew it was time.

Time for her to show him more.

Sitting up straighter, he brushed the toast crumbs from his fingers and pajama legs, and readied himself.

"Show me," he said, tightly gripping the arms of the chair. "Show me how you died."

The ghost responded to his invitation, flowing toward him . . . onto him . . . inside him . . .

Showing him what he needed to know.

Showing him what she had been, and how sad it all was that it had been so quickly and cruelly taken from her.

Her name was Tianna Hoops, and Bentley had been right in his observations: the woman had been aerialist—an acrobat—for a small traveling circus and sideshow called Doctor Nocturne's Circus of Unearthly Wonderment.

In the blink of an eye, he experienced everything that had made her who she was. She had come from a small village in Germany, moving from tiny circus to tiny circus before ending up in the United States, with the Circus of Unearthly Wonderment. Tianna loved what she did; loved the cheers and gasps of the audience as she performed her death-defying feats high above the circus floor. She imagined herself a kind of angel as she soared through the sky, from one trapeze to the next, the circus life her Heaven.

Bentley shuddered with her excitement, feeling the rushing air upon his—*her*—face.

But she had another love besides the trapeze, of the earthbound variety.

He—*she*—watched the handsome man as he worked, shirtless and brawny, swinging a sledgehammer, pounding into place the spikes that

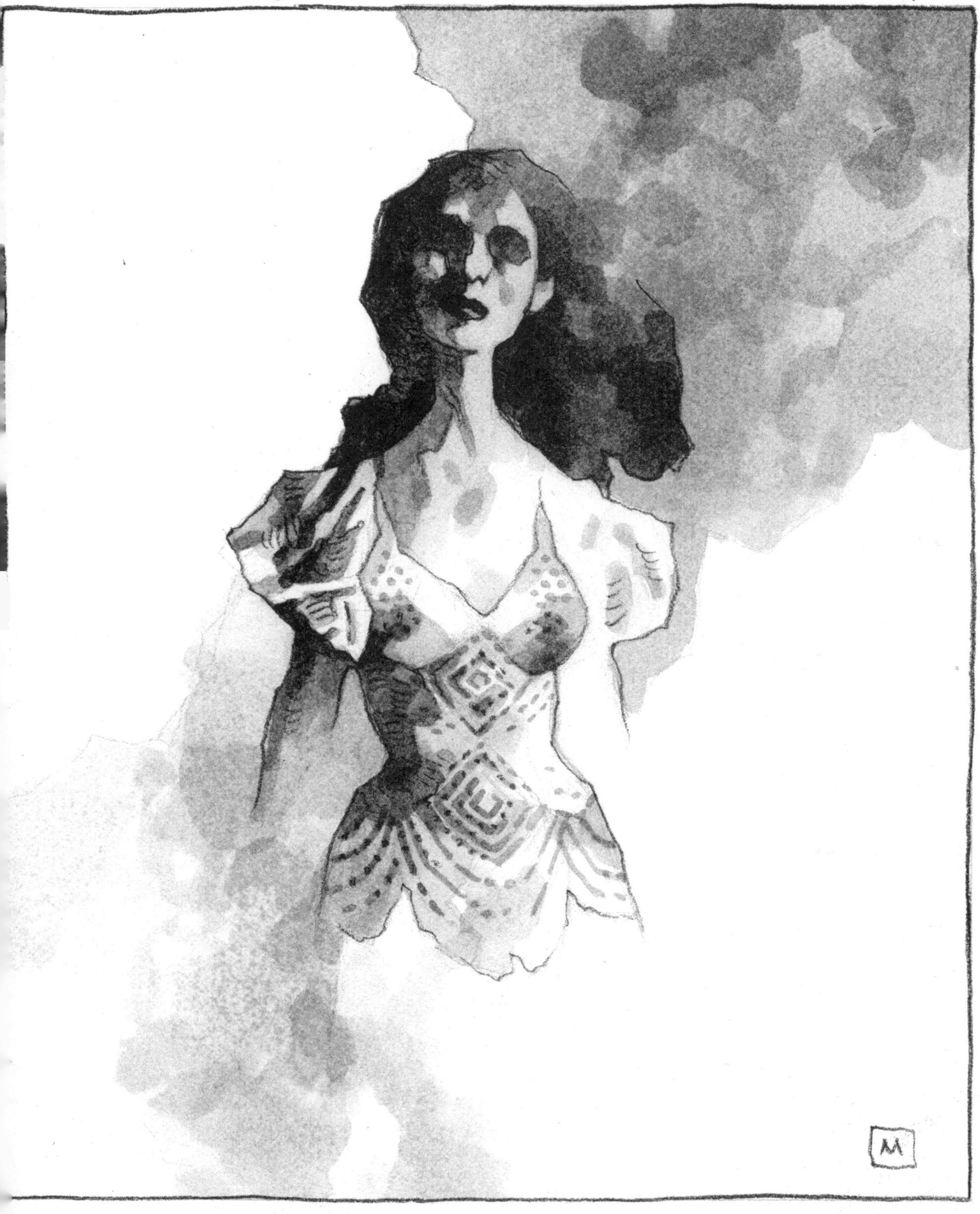

would hold up the circus tent. His name was Bill Tuttle, and she loved him almost as much as she loved soaring through the air. And he loved her as well.

But then, why had he killed her?

The moments traveled quickly from romance to death. First they are kissing, then the roustabout's large hands are wrapped around her throat.

Squeezing the life from her.

She tried to fight him but he was too strong, and suddenly she was weightless, flying again above the circus, but without the need of trapeze and wires.

He—*she*—could see the results of her murder, an emotional Bill being dragged away in handcuffs by the police, found guilty in a court of law and sentenced to death in the electric chair.

Bentley saw the murderer, as he was then, the large man sitting alone in his cell, tears of sadness streaming down his face.

Waiting for the inevitable.

Waiting to be punished—waiting to die.

———

The ghost of Tianna Hoops flowed out of Bentley's body like smoke from a waning fire, leaving him cold and trembling.

He sat for a few minutes, collecting his thoughts and remembering who he was, instead of the spirit that had just shared her life and death with him. Then he slowly stood and poured himself a steaming cup of the revitalizing coffee Pym had left on the desk with the toast. His hand shook as he raised the cup to his mouth and slurped loudly.

Bentley turned and found that the ghost of the murdered trapeze artist was still there, floating above the floor behind him.

He drank more of the coffee, his thoughts returning more to his own. There was something about this visitation that was different than the others he'd experienced, and it confused him.

"I don't understand," he said to the drifting apparition. "Sadly, I witnessed your untimely demise." He slowly approached the ghostly female who continued to watch him intently. "But my purpose, as defined by Death, is to avenge those who are taken before their time, to make their murderers pay the most horrible of prices for cutting a life span short," Bentley explained to the specter. "Your killer has been caught, tried, and put in prison, where he awaits his final punishment. What is left for me to do?"

The ghost's tears stretched and flowed freely from her eyes once more, drifting through the air toward him. Bentley attempted to move, to step from their path, but they followed, moving like serpents toward his face.

Believing that he knew what her intent was, Bentley allowed the ecto-plasmic representation of her sorrow to move toward his eyes, coating the bulging orbs inside his skull with her sadness.

And then he saw why she had not gone to her rest.

What was still left for him to do.

"The man," he said nearly breathless. "Bill . . . your lover . . ."

Tianna continued to cry, her tears filling the room like smoke.

"Even though I saw . . . that he took your life . . ."

The ghost of Tianna Hoops covered her face, and cried and cried.

"Somehow you believe he's innocent."

The spectral aerialist lowered her hands from her face, and her look was desperate—beckoning.

Catch my killer, her stare said.

And despite the fact that the man whose hands had squeezed the life from her throat already sat upstate in a maximum security prison, await-ing punishment for the crime of killing Tianna, Bentley had no choice but to investigate, to satisfy the desires of the departed aerialist.

As well as the demands of Death itself.

Chapter Six

BEFORE:

Because I could not stop for Death—
He kindly stopped for me—
The Carriage held but just Ourselves—
And Immortality.

Bentley looked up from the Emily Dickinson book he had received on his eleventh birthday, and smiled.

He imagined the carriage that would come for him, a black '32 Packard driven by a skull-faced chauffeur who held the door to the backseat open for him, bowing as Bentley approached.

He wondered where the black car would go . . . where Death would take him.

"Bentley!" called the familiar voice of Pym. "Bentley, where are you?"

The boy made himself smaller in a secret section of the attic that he considered his special hiding place. It was time for his medicine, and he had no desire to ingest that foul-tasting liquid this day, thank you very much.

He remained very quiet, moving the book ever so slightly to capture the light shining into the crowded, darkened space of the attic, so that he could continue to read Miss Dickinson's captivating words.

We slowly drove—He knew no haste
And I had put away
My labor and my leisure too,
For His Civility—

Pym continued to call for him. The butler was close by, checking some of the empty rooms where Bentley used to hide when he was much younger, and not as smart as he was now. The attic was practically forgotten these days, which was perfect for Bentley, and his desire to escape the trials of his health.

The butler's calls receded into the distance, and Bentley relaxed. He imagined that he had at least another half hour or so before his parents joined the search for him, but then again . . .

His parents had become quite entranced with their new houseguest, Professor Romulus. A shiver that Bentley couldn't quite understand coursed up and down his spine with the recollection of the strange machinery he had seen being built in the mansion's solarium, and the look upon his mother's face when he'd asked what it was for.

His father had then called for Pym to escort Bentley away—to get him out from underfoot—but he still could see his mother's eyes and couldn't quite decide whether it was sadness or fear that he saw there.

Or was it a strange intermingling of them both? Bentley wondered as he closed his special book and stood, going to the attic window to gaze at the wooded property. He enjoyed looking out over the forest, at the examples of life and death on display there. As if not wanting to disappoint, a hawk swooped down out of the sky toward the body of a felled tree. A tiny rabbit attempted to escape the hawk's keen eye, but soon found itself clutched in the bird of prey's talons, and was carried off.

Nature is sometimes cruel, the boy thought, watching the flapping hawk disappear in the distance with its prize, but he doubted that it was anything personal.

There was more movement below, and he craned his neck to see out of the far lower corner of the window.

Is that somebody outside?

Yes! he realized excitedly, as he spotted a blond-haired little girl stealthily creeping around the trees.

He wondered who she could be, and then realized that he was smiling. He certainly didn't know the girl, but for some reason she seemed to make him happy. Bentley was about to rap on the window as loudly as he could to attract her attention when she looked up at the house.

He could have sworn she was looking directly at him, but that was impossible, he was too far away to . . .

Bentley could just about make out that she was smiling, when she began to wave.

She *did* see him. He waved back, thinking that she must have had eyes like a . . . like a hawk, he thought, and began to laugh.

Suddenly, he had a nearly irresistible urge to go outside and meet the pretty little stranger. He bolted for the trapdoor to the attic, lifting it carefully so as not to alert anyone who might still be looking for him. Then he cautiously skulked down the stairs to the first floor and into the warmth of the kitchen, where something boiled noisily upon the stove. He grabbed an old jacket hanging on a hook beside the back door and pulled it on. For some strange reason he was desperate—anxious that the mysterious little girl would be gone by the time he managed to get outside.

He opened the door, no longer worried about attracting the attention of Pym or his parents, and raced out into the backyard, only to feel his hopes dashed to the rocks as he reached the edge of the wooded area and found it barren of life. With shoulders slumped, he was about to return to his home when he sensed her presence.

Turning around, he found her peering out from behind a mighty oak, smiling slyly.

"I thought you'd left," Bentley said, ecstatic to see her there.

"Why would I leave?" she asked, stepping out from her hiding place so that he could see her. For a moment he wondered why she wasn't wearing a coat, only a pretty, red velvet dress, but that thought was quickly forgotten as she continued to speak. "I was waiting for you, Bentley."

"How do you know my name?" Bentley asked, with a curious tilt of his head.

"I know lots of things," she said, moving closer to take his hand in hers. Her touch was very cold, but it was cold outside, and he thought nothing more about it as they went off into the woods to play.

It was as if they had been friends since the day he was born.

Chapter Seven

Pym worried about Bentley.

He smiled slightly as he flicked the feather duster over the top of the heavy piece of furniture in the foyer, remembering the sickly child that he'd cared for in his early days at Hawthorne House.

Bentley may no longer have been a child, but as far as Pym was concerned, his services were still required.

Someone needed to look after the boy, especially since he'd taken up his rather bizarre, and potentially quite dangerous, hobby.

Pym recalled the first time he'd come to the realization that something about the boy was changing dramatically, and that he might need to keep a watchful eye on him.

The voice had been unrecognizable—ragged and raw sounding. Pym had actually believed that intruders had found their way into Hawthorne House and were talking as they prepared to plunder the home. He remembered how he'd taken hold of a silver candlestick, ready to bludgeon the first stranger that he came across.

The horrible-sounding voice had been coming from one of the empty guest rooms on the building's third floor, an odd place for burglars to be searching for valuables, he'd thought. Those rooms had been empty for quite a long time, ever since most of the staff had been let go. They were primarily used for storage now.

Pym remembered his terror as he'd taken hold of the doorknob, turning it quickly and throwing open the door, candlestick raised. At that moment he had believed he was ready to face just about anything.

And he had been wrong.

Inside the room he'd found Bentley, wearing the hideous skeleton mask that he'd recently found in the attic, standing in front of a dresser mirror, speaking to his gruesome reflection. He was wearing the top coat of one of his deceased father's suits, but not any pants, just his underwear.

"Look upon this visage of death and tremble," Pym remembered Bentley growling at his skeletal reflection, not even realizing that he was no longer alone in the room.

"Bentley?" Pym had called softly, lowering his candlestick weapon.

It had taken a moment for the youth to respond, to pull his eyes from his reflection in the old mirror.

"Yes, Pym?"

"What are you doing?"

"Practicing," he'd said, turning back to his masked reflection.

Pym had been ready to question his charge, but decided that perhaps it might be wise to let it go, yet another phase that the boy was going through.

And he'd left him there. Practicing. But truly having no idea as to what Bentley was making reference to.

Now Pym was more than aware. That initial belief—hope, actually— that Bentley's odd behavior was simply another youthful fancy had gone by the wayside.

It was so much more than that.

"Pym!" Bentley called out, startling the butler.

He looked up to see Bentley, fully clothed, trotting down the staircase, and felt his heart flutter with worry once more. *There must be something terribly wrong,* he thought. It was far too early for the young man to be out of his bedroom, never mind fully dressed.

"What is it?" he asked, rushing to meet Bentley at the foot of the stairs.

"Newspapers."

"Newspapers, sir?"

"Yes. Do we still have the old copies about?"

Pym had to pause and think for a moment. "Yes, I believe we do," he answered slowly. "They're down in the basement, ready to be burned in the furnace."

"Are there any from a few weeks back?"

"Yes, and some more recent than that. Why?"

"Excellent." Bentley rubbed his hands together. "I need you to bring them up to my room at once!"

"Up to your . . . all of them?" Pym asked incredulously.

"Yes, and the quicker you get them, the better," Bentley said, turning around on the last step and heading back up the stairs.

"May I inquire as to why?"

"Research, Pym," Bentley called over his shoulder as he continued to climb. "I must do my research."

The question of what kind of research danced on the tip of the butler's tongue, but once again, he decided not to ask it, fearful of the response. Instead, he retreated to the kitchen, and the cellar door.

There were newspapers to retrieve.

———

Bentley had never stopped to really think about how much was going on in the city, and the world as well. It was a perpetual machine of constant happenings, but only the events that managed to be noticed were written up in the papers.

Fascinating, he thought as he flipped through the pages, his eyes scanning them from top to bottom, in search of any information about the murder of Tianna Hoops and her supposed killer, William Tuttle. He vaguely remembered having read something about the trial and the conviction of the trapeze artist's murderer.

The ghost of Tianna stood resolutely nearby as he perused the news. He could feel her presence, a cold sensation radiating upon his back.

"I'm trying," he told her. "Without specific dates it's difficult for me to . . ."

The door to his bedroom flew open, and Pym stumbled in, his arms loaded with yet another stack of newsprint.

"This is the last of them," the butler wheezed, dropping the pile on the floor beside the last he'd hauled up from the basement.

"Thank you, Pym."

"How goes your research?" the butler asked, catching his breath as he carefully stretched his spine.

"Slowly, I'm afraid," Bentley said, scanning and turning the page. "There is so much . . . news here."

"That's to be expected in a daily periodical," Pym said. "Is there anything that I might do to . . . ?"

"Here," Bentley said, his eyes finally falling on a story about William Tuttle's sentencing. He leaned forward to read. "It says here that he was convicted unanimously and sentenced to death by the electric chair," he said.

"And who would that be?"

"William Tuttle," Bentley said.

"And he's important to us why?"

"Supposedly he murdered his girlfriend," Bentley said, setting the paper back down upon the table. He glanced over to see that Tianna's ghost was silently crying again.

"Supposedly?" Pym questioned.

"He confessed to the act," Bentley said, again looking to the ghost for answers. "And all the evidence was right there."

"Yet you said 'supposedly,'" Pym reiterated. "You don't believe he did it?"

"It doesn't matter what I believe." Bentley watched as the ghost of the woman with the horribly bruised neck continued to cry, her tears of absolute sorrow flowing about the room like smoke.

"If there's even a suspicion of innocence, then the true perpetrator must be found."

Chapter Eight

BEFORE:

braham did everything he could not to notice: distracting himself with the magnitude of running one of the country's largest munitions manufacturers, as well as little things, like immersing himself in the news of the world with his morning paper while having his coffee.

They were all shields. And as long as they were up, he didn't have to see. He didn't have to pay attention.

He didn't have to feel.

"Good morning, Poppa," a young voice said, suddenly chipping away at his wall.

Abraham lowered his paper to see that his son had risen early and had joined him at the dining room table.

"Hmmm," the boy's father replied, hoping the conversation would go no further than that. The wall had to be maintained.

But he could feel the child's eyes upon him—upon his wall—burning through the surface of the newspaper to get to him on the other side.

Abraham lowered his paper again. "Can I help you with something?" he asked. "Where's your mother? Perhaps you should go find her and . . ."

"What are you reading about?" young Bentley asked.

"The world," Abraham replied, raising the paper again. "Things about which a young man like yourself should not yet concern himself. There will be plenty of time for that in your coming years."

He lowered his paper again to look upon the child—*Why did I do that? Why did I let my shield go down?* he scolded himself.

And he saw the sadness of it all, and what he had been trying to hide from himself in the smiling face of a little boy.

Abraham saw the vitality in the smile, but he also saw the manifestations of illness around it: the paleness of his son's skin, the cracking of the flesh at the corners of Bentley's exuberant expression. He appeared even more ill than he had the last time Abraham had looked at him.

The last time he'd let the wall come down.

"What is it, Poppa?" Bentley asked, real concern evident in the child's tone. "Is something wrong?"

Is something wrong, the child asked. Of course there was something wrong. How could something like this be happening to the likes of Abraham Hawthorne? How dare the gods in the sky torture him in this way? Didn't they know who he was? How powerful the Hawthorne family was?

But the gods don't care, Abraham thought, swearing that he could actually see his son dwindling away before his eyes. The gods were cruel, of that he had no doubt.

"There's nothing wrong," he lied. "Go find Pym and have him make you a healthy breakfast," he commanded the boy.

Without another word, Bentley slid off the high wooden chair and ran off toward the kitchen.

Abraham was angry—angry and desperate. He quickly folded up his newspaper, the barrier between his feelings and cold, harsh reality, and threw it down upon the tabletop.

His wife came into the room carrying a vase of freshly cut flowers. There was the hint of a smile on her face as she set them down, but then she saw the look on his own.

"What is it?" she asked, her fear growing.

"Time is running out," he said, and he could tell by the way she stared that she understood what he was talking about. "I'm going to talk to him."

"He—he said that the—the process would take time," she stammered. "That he'd never attempted anything like this before and—"

"We don't have the time," Abraham interrupted rather frantically. "I have to know if he's going to be ready . . . if *it's* going to be ready."

———

Abraham Hawthorne barreled through the halls of his sprawling home, feeling his anxiety turn to anger as he made his way toward the renovated solarium.

The twin doors to the room given to the professor for his work were closed, which usually meant the man didn't want to be disturbed, but Abraham was beyond such polite considerations.

"Romulus!" Abraham bellowed as he threw open the doors to the room, now filled with banks of strange machines that hummed like hives of aroused bees.

The professor was handling a long glass tube very carefully.

"The filaments in this bulb are incredibly delicate," he said, his eyes not leaving the trembling strands of extremely thin wire inside the glass container. "One sudden move could cause them to disconnect and set us back weeks."

Abraham watched, and found himself actually holding his breath as the professor carried the bulb over to one of the humming machines. Romulus bent forward toward an open hatch that exposed the complex internal workings of the machine, carefully inserted the tube into the hatch, then slowly withdrew his hands from the device.

"There," he said, a smile of accomplishment gradually appearing on his bearded face as he gently closed the metal hatch and turned toward Abraham. "What can I do for you this fine morning, sir?"

Abraham's eyes darted about the room, at the machines of all sizes and shapes that had been built to Professor Romulus's detailed specifications—at considerable cost to the Hawthorne fortune, no less.

"This," Abraham said, hearing the edge to his voice, "all this"—he moved his hand around, indicating the room, as the Professor listened and waited—"will it be ready when the time comes?"

Professor Romulus looked about the room as well. "I guess it all depends," he said. "It depends on when it might be needed."

Abraham moved toward the man, fixing him with a powerful gaze.

"Soon," he said, attempting to keep his emotions in check. He did not know how he knew this, but he sensed that time was indeed running out.

"Oh," Professor Romulus responded, walking toward his special mechanisms. "Well, there are still some things to be done . . . I'm not sure we'll be ready before—"

Abraham surged forward, taking hold of the professor's arm in a powerful grip and spinning him around. "It needs to be ready," he said, the intensity in his voice saying it all. "And you will do all that you must to make it so."

The dying boy's father paused for effect.

"Do we understand each other, Professor?" Abraham asked.

"Completely," Romulus replied.

Abraham released the man's arm, fully aware of how tightly he'd been gripping it.

"Then I'll let you return to your work," he said, turning toward the door.

And just as he was about to leave the solarium, he looked back to see Professor Romulus standing as he'd left him, rubbing his arm where Abraham had gripped it.

—

Bentley didn't recall what had happened exactly, only that his head had felt incredibly light before the entire world had somehow been plunged into total darkness.

He'd come around eventually and found himself back in his room, stuffed beneath the covers of his bed.

Things like that were beginning to happen more and more often, and he pondered briefly the quality of the life that was ahead of him. This might be something that he would need to discuss with his mother and father in the not too distant future.

He was about to attempt to climb from his bed when the door to his room swung open to reveal the imposing figure of Pym.

"Pym," the boy said. "I was just getting up."

"You'll do no such thing," the butler corrected, coming into his room, making sure that the covers were down on both sides and he was nicely tucked beneath them.

"I feel fine," Bentley said as Pym swiped wrinkles from the heavy duvet.

"I found you unconscious in the kitchen," the manservant informed him. "You are not fine."

The boy considered the argument presented.

"I wasn't then, but now . . ."

Pym made a sound Bentley had learned to associate with displeasure.

"You need to rest."

"For how long?"

"Until you are rested."

"I feel rested now."

"But you're really not."

"Am I going to die?"

Bentley watched for Pym's reaction, searching for any tic or twitch that might let on that things were perhaps worse than he suspected. He saw something going on around the man's eyes that was concerning.

"What kind of question is that?" Pym scolded, proceeding to straighten the sheets and blankets again. "You just need your rest."

"We all die, Pym," Bentley told him. "Some just sooner than others."

Pym stared at him for what felt like quite some time, the activity around his eyes becoming even more intense.

"And your time is a long ways off," he finally said briskly. "I'm going to go down to the kitchen and fix you a bowl of soup."

"I really don't want soup," Bentley told him.

Pym stood taller, clasping his hands behind his back.

"I will fix you soup, and I will bring it to your bed, and you will eat it, even if I'm forced to feed it to you myself."

Bentley considered that.

"I'll eat the soup," he said. "But only if you let me get out of bed after."

Pym was silent for a moment.

"After the soup, we will discuss the matter further."

"Deal," Bentley said, and brought his hand up and out from beneath the covers, extending it for Pym to shake.

Pym considered the boy's hand for a moment, and then, slowly, brought his own to it. They shook. Pym's grip was strong, powerful even, and Bentley wasn't sure if he'd ever realized the strength Pym had inside.

"Rest," the butler then ordered, tucking Bentley's hand and arm back beneath the covers.

He left the room, closing the door behind him and leaving Bentley alone with the silence of the room and his own thoughts.

He pulled his hand out from underneath the bedclothes and looked at it, still feeling Pym's warmth and the pressure of his grip.

He also noticed a tremble, and could not make it stop no matter how hard he thought about it. Pushing his hand back down beneath the warming layers, he tried to forget his shaking limb, and to do what Pym had asked of him.

To rest.

Bentley was just on the verge of falling asleep when he heard a very faint tapping upon his window. At first he thought it to be rain, but there was something more—something solid about it.

Unable to lie there any longer, the boy squirmed out from beneath his protective coverings into the cold of his room, and looked toward the window.

He smiled at what he saw there. He had been right—it wasn't rain at all. It was snow.

He ran to the window, looking out at the gray world now made a little more special—a little more magical—by the frozen flakes drifting down from the sky.

And to make it even more special, even more magical, he saw *her* out there.

His special friend. He hadn't seen her in a few days, and he felt his heart begin to pound as he saw her moving out from behind the cover of the forest trees.

Bentley was about to rap upon the glass when she darted out from behind an oak and ran toward the back of the house, stopping abruptly beneath his window to look up at him. She smiled and beckoned to him.

Come out, Bentley, her dainty hand said as she started back toward the wood.

Come out, and we will play in the snow.

Bentley ran excitedly for the door to do as she requested of him.

How could he not?

Chapter Nine

Lost in thought, Bentley didn't realize where his wanderings had brought him. He looked up, surprised to see that he was standing in front of the high double doors to the solarium.

Even though the room still bore the blackened scars from the fire that had nearly burned down the southern side of the mansion, as well as the painful memories of what had transpired within, Bentley often found himself drawn to this burnt-out shell.

It had become a kind of church to him, a place where he was able to gather his thoughts.

He pushed open the doors and stepped inside, remembering how it had looked before the incident; recalling when it had been just a sun-room, before Professor Romulus had come to stay with his strange machines.

Bentley made a mental note—as he had many times in the past—to talk to Pym about hiring a crew to clean out the space and haul away the blackened remains of the professor's devices. *Maybe the room can be used again*, he thought as he looked around at the charred wood and walls.

Or maybe it should just be left alone.

A memorial to remind him, and anyone else who should enter, of the dangers in playing with the forces of nature.

The powers of the universe.

He closed his eyes and breathed in the thick, damp, smoky smell, attempting to gather his thoughts on the murder of Tianna Hoops and what he still had to do to satisfy the needs of the ghostly trapeze artist.

"What more is there to do?" Bentley found himself muttering as he moved piles of ash around with the tips of his shoes.

"*You're not very good at this, are you?*" The voice came out of nowhere, so very close to Bentley's ear, that it seemed to come from inside his skull.

"Where are you?" he asked, startled, eyes darting about darkness.

"*Right here,*" the raven named Roderick said.

It was if a piece of shadow had come alive, emerging from a wall of black in the corner of the room to perch atop the wreckage of one of Professor Romulus's machines.

"Oh, I thought I was alone."

"*Alone and talking to yourself,*" the bird muttered, fluttering his shiny wings. "*They say that's one of the first signs that you're cracking up.*"

"Not cracking up," Bentley said. "It's just like you said . . . I'm not very good at this whole 'agent of Death' rigmarole."

Roderick spread his wings and flew to a machine closer to Bentley.

"*You had better get better,*" the bird warned. "*Wouldn't want to disappoint the boss.*"

"Why wouldn't I?" Bentley asked, seeing a glimmer of hope in the situation. "If I perform the job badly enough, maybe he'll fire me."

"*Believe me, you don't want to be fired.*" Roderick pretended to shiver, the shiny black feathers around his neck puffing out. "*It's nothing pleasant, getting let go by the boss.*"

Bentley wasn't quite sure exactly what job the raven filled in the afterlife, but the bird would appear from time to time in the living world to offer the young man some guidance.

"All right, do you have any suggestions, then?" Bentley asked, more than confident that Roderick already knew every detail of the case as well as he did himself.

The raven tilted his black head from side to side, fixing Bentley with his dark brown eyes. *"Hey, you're the avatar."*

Bentley started to pace about the remains of the sunroom. "I know that, but I'm not sure where to go with this one. My job is all about finding the guilty—to punish those who have interfered in the natural order of things by taking a life early."

"Well, at least you have that part down," Roderick said with sarcasm.

"But this one," Bentley said, feeling his frustration surge. "This case . . ."

"Go on," the bird urged.

"This one isn't like the others," the young man said.

"How so?"

"We know who killed the girl," Bentley told the raven. "We know that Tianna Hoops was killed by her boyfriend, William Tuttle."

"You don't say."

"Yeah," Bentley went on. "He confessed to the crime, was tried, and now is awaiting execution upstate."

"Fascinating," Roderick said, lifting his taloned foot and scratching at the side of his feathered neck.

"Not really," Bentley said. "It's terrible . . . She really loved him . . . Still loves him, actually. I felt it when she showed me what happened."

"Why'd he do it?" the bird croaked.

Bentley shrugged his shoulders. "I really don't know."

"And you don't find that strange?"

"People kill each other all the time," Bentley said. "The reasons are all over the place . . . jealousy, anger, fear."

"Did you feel any of those when she showed you her murder?" Roderick asked.

Bentley remembered the feelings that had washed over him when the ghost flowed into his body. He remembered all of her emotions until the moment of her death. But he felt nothing from *him*. Nothing from William Tuttle that would bring him to murder.

"No."

"*Strange,*" Roderick said with a tilt of his head.

"Yes," Bentley agreed thoughtfully.

"*I think there are still some questions to be asked,*" Roderick said.

"I should speak with him," Bentley said. "I should ask William Tuttle the questions." He looked to the bird for confirmation, but as it usually was with Death's messenger, Roderick was gone.

Never mind. He knew what he had to do. Turning around, he strode through the room with renewed purpose and direction. But as he reached the doors, swinging them open into the hallway, he questioned how he might achieve that.

How would he get into a maximum-security prison and how would he convince a convicted murderer to speak to him?

Bentley smiled, the answer to his question suddenly materializing before him like a certain raven.

He had to pay a visit to the attic.

Chapter Ten

BEFORE:

Reginald Pym had never married, nor had he ever experienced the true bond of fatherhood, but he imagined that what he'd been experiencing throughout the years in his service to the Hawthornes, and more specifically to the boy, Bentley, was somehow akin to it. He worried about the child, about his worsening maladies, as well as his strange disconnection to the living world about him. Pym had lost count of the times he'd found the child sitting alone, nose planted in the rather gloomy works of Edgar Allan Poe, Emily Dickinson, or William Blake.

He'd done as much as he felt he could to encourage the child to mingle with children of his own age, partaking of the outdoors and the many seasonal activities that were offered, but the boy would only feign the effects of illness and return to his books. To his comforting solitude.

Pym often wondered if he shouldn't have done more to encourage the boy, but would then pull back, reminding himself that he was not the child's father.

No matter how it sometimes felt.

As he climbed the winding staircase up to the boy's room, carrying a tray with the promised soup before him, he attempted to imagine what it would be like if Bentley should succumb to his ailments. How he would feel. A sudden and sickly feeling passed through his body, and he found himself thinking of the mister and missus, and the strange guest they'd allowed into their home.

The man and his machines.

He hadn't bothered to ask them about the man . . . this so-called professor, but he couldn't help but overhear some of the conversations they'd had over coffee.

Somehow the professor was there for the boy; somehow he and his machines were going to save him. Pym had no idea what that meant, or how it was to be, but if it were true . . . if this man could somehow save young Bentley . . .

He stopped in front of the child's door and, balancing the tray upon one hand, knocked before entering.

"Now, I expect you to eat every bite of this or—"

Pym's eyes fell upon the empty bed, staring at the slight indentation where a body once lay.

"Bentley?" he called out, looking around the room, paying extra-close attention to the patches of shadow where the boy sometimes liked to hide. The room was empty. He set the tray down on the boy's desk and looked around again, just to be sure.

"Bentley? Where are you?" he called out a little louder, just in case the boy was out of the room nearby.

He was about to begin a search of the house's upper levels when he heard it—something just below the sound of the snow ticking off the room's windowpanes. Pym moved closer the window and was surprised to see how hard it was coming down, the snow piling up much more quickly than he would have thought.

And then he saw.

At first he thought it might be his imagination, but stepping closer he saw the back of Bentley trudging through the collecting snow, heading deeper into the woods.

"Dear God," Pym muttered, as the boy was quickly swallowed up by the storm.

⬧

Bentley shivered as the snow piled up around him.

"I don't feel so well," he told his friend, as he looked back in the direction from which he had come. His footprints were already nearly filled in by the storm.

She came out from behind a tree, took his hand, and smiled at him, the warmth of her loving look making him feel not quite so cold or sick.

"Maybe you just need to play some more," she suggested.

The little girl turned her gaze up to the falling snow, letting the large, downy flakes land upon her face. He noticed again that she wasn't dressed for this kind of weather; a pretty party dress was not sufficient, as far as he was aware, for keeping one warm.

"Aren't you cold?" he asked her.

She looked down from the sky to him, and he noticed that the snow that had fallen upon her face had formed a crusty mask; the heavy flakes had not melted.

Bentley started to laugh, and she did as well.

"No, silly," she said as she bent down to scoop up a handful of the powdery white stuff and threw it at him.

"Hey!" Bentley shrieked, jumping backward as snow struck his front.

The little girl was laughing hysterically as she ran deeper into the woods.

"C'mon!" she called to him.

"Where are we going?" he asked, running after her.

He noticed that she moved incredibly fast, leaving no visible trace of her passing in the snow as she ran.

How odd.

"Over here!" she cried out as she stopped in the center of a clearing surrounded by swaying birch trees and waited for him to reach her.

"What are we doing?" he asked, feeling the cold as it flowed beneath his coat to his skin, and down into his bones.

"We're going to make angels," she said, again with that brilliant, warming smile.

He wasn't sure what she was talking about, and was a bit shocked as she lay down upon her back in the collecting snow.

"What are you doing?"

"I told you," she said. "Come here and join me." She patted the snow at arm's length.

For some reason that he couldn't quite explain—maybe it had something to do with that smile—he did as she suggested.

It was freezing, and he could feel the chilling dampness being absorbed by his pajama bottoms as he lay there.

"What . . . what now?" he asked, his teeth beginning to chatter.

"Do what I do," she said, spreading out her arms and moving them up and down. She was also opening and closing her legs.

She looked over to see him still watching.

"Go on," she said, continuing to move her arms and legs.

He finally started to see the effects of what she was doing, and did the same.

His friend carefully climbed to her feet so as not to disturb what she had made. She reached for him, pulling him up effortlessly from the where he lay.

"Look," she said pointing out what they had made.

The shapes of two angels in the snow.

"We made angels," he said, feeling a smile spreading across the numbness of his face.

"Yes, we did," she answered, reaching down to take his hand in hers.

"I'm very tired," Bentley said, leaning against his friend.

"Then you should probably rest," she said, putting her arm around his trembling shoulders.

"Yes."

"You could lie down right here."

"In the snow?" he asked.

"Why not?" she answered with the cutest of giggles. "It's just like fluffy feathers."

"Fluffy feathers," he repeated, and chuckled as well as he stared at the white around them.

"Would you like me to lie down with you?" she asked him.

He looked at her then, at her delicate face, and he wasn't sure if he'd ever seen anything quite so beautiful. If he had, he certainly couldn't remember it.

"I would like that very much," he said.

She helped him down, the deepening snow accepting them as they lay upon the ground.

"Comfortable?" she asked, putting her arm around him and pulling him against her.

"Yes," he answered, feeling his eyes grow incredibly heavy.

"Good," she said, her mouth very close to his ear. "You should be comfortable when . . ."

Her voice stopped, and he was about to ask her what she meant, what he should be comfortable for. But before he could form the words, he had already fallen deeply into the embrace of sleep atop a bed of the whitest of feathers that continued to drift down from the sky.

Covering him in their downy splendor.

Chapter Eleven

Bentley thought the dust might kill him.

He flipped back the lid on the old steamer trunk, holding his breath as the dust of the huge attic space swirled about him like smoke. Taking a handkerchief from his back pocket, he held it up against his face to filter out the offending particles, as he began to rummage through the nearly overflowing contents of the chest.

His father had loved the masquerade.

Bentley had glorious memories of the costume parties his father would throw at Hawthorne house, everybody in attendance masked and pretending to be somebody or something else. The costumes were spectacular, but his father always showed them all up.

His father always had the best costumes.

The image of a man, clad in layered robes of scarlet, slowly making his entrance into the grand ballroom, filled Bentley's mind, freezing him in the midst of his task.

Bentley remembered how it at all stopped with the man's entrance, the reverie of the guests going eerily silent.

The Red Death, from Edgar Allan Poe's classic tale. It was as if Death himself had paid the party a visit.

He saw it all against the backdrop of his memories: the striking and fearful figure standing in the center of the dance floor, waiting—watching to see if all eyes were upon him—and when it was so . . .

The figure's hand shot up, the red-gloved hand tearing away the bloodred mask that covered his features to reveal . . .

"What in the name of all that's holy are you doing up here?" Pym asked, his head poking up through the attic's trapdoor like some sort of angry mole.

A mole that scared Bentley half to death.

"Pym," he said, taking in a lungful of the dusty air and immediately beginning to choke.

"I was beginning to think we had a problem with rodents," his manservant said. He climbed up into the attic and stood looking around at the vast space, a look of disgust on his face. "One of these days I must put a few months aside to come up here and clean."

Bentley managed to get his coughing under control and continued his search, removing costume after costume from the large trunk.

"Dare I inquire what it is that you are doing?" Pym asked, brushing cobwebs from the sleeves of his black jacket.

"I'm looking for something," Bentley replied, pulling what appeared to be a rolled pirate captain's coat from within the great box. He remembered a particular party with a *Pirates of Penzance* theme and smiled, momentarily distracted.

"Should I bother asking about the particulars?" Pym asked, interrupting the memory.

"Something that will help me in my latest investigation," Bentley explained as he continued his search. He didn't even have to look up from the chest to see the expression of disapproval on the butler's face. He could practically feel it trying to burn through his back.

"What is it, Pym?" he asked, pulling up a yellowed petticoat and laying it gently upon the floor. It had been part of one of his mother's costumes.

"Nothing, sir," Pym answered, the disapproval now clear in his tone.

"Has anybody ever told you that you're absolutely terrible at disguising your true feelings?"

"Whatever are you implying, sir?"

"Your disdain," Bentley answered, pausing in his search. "Your total disapproval of my new purpose."

"Hmmm," Pym said, carefully navigating the packed space to look out the dust-covered circular window.

"I've explained everything to you, yet still you don't seem to grasp the importance of my task."

"I understand its importance to you, sir," Pym said. He reached out and wiped away a portion of the filth so that he could see the world outside. "I'm just concerned about your well-being, whatever your purpose may be."

"Do we have to have the 'I'm not insane' talk again?"

"Not unless you're planning on telling me something I haven't yet heard."

"Good," Bentley said. "I'm tired of that discussion."

"Very good, sir," Pym said, clasping his hands behind his back as he continued to look through the space he had wiped clean on the window.

"A woman has been murdered," Bentley began to elaborate as he leaned deeper into the crate. "Her supposed murderer has confessed to the crime, been tried and sentenced to death."

Pym turned from the window.

"So what is your purpose, then?" the butler asked. "You've said your function is to bring to justice those who have committed heinous acts of murder, but if the murderer is already awaiting execution . . . ?"

Bentley had practically crawled inside the large trunk.

"And that is where the problem lies," he answered, his voice muffled. "The restless spirit of the woman whose life has been taken . . . for some reason yet to be revealed to me . . . believes in her lover's innocence."

Pym strode closer. "But you did say that he confessed."

"Exactly, Pym," Bentley said. "So you understand my quandary."

"I suppose," Pym answered. "You think that something up here will help you solve that quandary?"

"Yes," Bentley said. "I need to speak to the murderer, William Tuttle."

"Speak to him," Pym repeated.

"Yes," Bentley answered, searching all the more frantically now that he was reaching the bottom of the box.

"In prison."

"Yes."

"On death row."

"Yes, Pym," Bentley answered growing more exasperated by the second. "But in order for me to do that, I must first find—"

Bentley let out a sudden cry of delight.

"Huzzah!" He pulled his find up from the near bottom of the chest.

"I'm guessing you found what you were looking for?" Pym asked, coming around to see.

Bentley held up the scarlet cassock and placed it against himself. "I knew my father had dressed as a man of the cloth," the young man told his manservant. "I remember it as part of a literary masquerade. I believe he was Cardinal Richelieu from *The Three Musketeers*."

"And how will this aid you in determining if this William Tuttle is a murderer or not?" Pym asked.

"It won't exactly," Bentley said, looking for the accessories that went with the costume. "But it should help get me through the door in order to speak with him."

"You're going to pretend to be a priest?"

"Exactly," Bentley said smiling at his butler. "And would you mind driving me to the prison? What high ranking man of the cloth drives himself anywhere?"

"But of course," Pym said dryly.

———

The warden's name was Delocroix, and he stank of whiskey and salami.

"William Tuttle," the fat man with watery, red eyes and a pink, sweaty complexion said as he stared at the open file upon his desk. "A waste of tax payers' dollars, is what I say."

Bentley, playing the part of Cardinal Dickenson, smiled beatifically and tilted his head. "I'm not quite sure I understand, Warden," he said.

"Well, Father," the fat man said, leaning back. His chair shrieked in protest as it bent toward the wall. "Trying a man for murder is an expensive endeavor." The warden smiled, and Bentley felt his skin crawl beneath his costume. "And Blackmore Prison is just filled with those serving twenty to life who swore they were innocent right up until sentencing. A trial by a jury of their own peers was needed to determine their guilt."

Bentley folded one hand atop the other and attempted to look holy. Whatever that meant.

"Yes?"

Warden Delocroix came forward in his chair, elbows landing hard upon the desktop.

"Tuttle said that he'd done it the minute he was arrested," the loathsome man said. "He never denied it. A complete waste of the judicial process and all that it entails."

"Ah, I understand now," Bentley said, nodding ever so slowly. He hoped that his request would soon be granted so he could get on with his questioning of William Tuttle and be away from this man. "But he is still one of God's creatures," Bentley continued, playing the part of a very holy man. He was doing his best to remember all the portrayals of priests he'd ever read, and hoped he was at least doing a relatively convincing job. "One of His flock. And a chance to unburden his soul might—"

"Yes, his soul," the fat man grumbled, again picking up the file and thumbing through the information. "I'm not sure that someone like Tuttle even has one."

The fat man looked up, his eyes bulging so much from his large, flabby face that Bentley thought they might shoot out at him.

"Do you know what this friend of your family did?" the warden asked, making reference to Bentley's lie that Tuttle was the friend of a dear cousin on his father's side of the family.

"I'm guessing you're about to tell me." Bentley tried not to sigh, having already heard more than enough from this disgusting individual.

"He killed the woman he supposedly loved with his bare hands," the warden said, holding up his own pudgy hands and pretending to wrap them around something. "According to eyewitnesses, they were holding hands and laughing it up, having a good time at the circus where they both worked, and then less than ten minutes later she was dead."

Delocroix glanced down at the papers in the file again, then fixed

Bentley with his beady, bloodshot eyes. "Tianna Hoops was dead," he said. "Strangled . . . her throat crushed by her lover."

He leaned back again, and the joints and springs in the chair screamed even louder.

"Honestly, would somebody with a soul do something like that, Father?" he asked, waiting for Bentley to reply. "Kill the woman he supposedly loved in cold blood?"

"It's obvious that the man is troubled," Bentley said. "His soul is burdened with sin."

"When asked why he did it, he couldn't even give a reason," the warden said with a scowl. "This one is a real animal that deserves to be put down."

Bentley forced a smile onto his face.

"I would imagine it must be difficult to remain compassionate in a place like this," he said.

"After you've seen what I've seen over the years, the word barely even exists anymore," Warden Delocroix said.

"Understandable," Bentley said as he pushed out his chair and stood up before the warden's desk.

"I would like to see William now," he said.

"Still think that you can save him?" the warden asked, leaning forward, his girth flowing onto the desktop.

"One can only try," Bentley said.

"Huh. Fitzgerald!" he bellowed.

The door opened, and a prison guard in full uniform stepped in.

"Take Cardinal Dickenson to one of the visitor rooms, and then bring in Tuttle."

"Yes, sir, Warden."

"The cardinal here thinks he's going to save Tuttle's immortal soul. What do you think of that, Fitzgerald?"

The prison screw started to laugh. "Good luck with that," he said, looking to his boss.

"Exactly." The warden stared at Bentley. "Good luck with that, Father," the foul man repeated, and smiled grotesquely.

"Right this way, Father," Fitzgerald said, gesturing toward the door. As he was escorted from the office, Bentley could hear Warden Delocroix chuckling to himself.

———

The prison was old and filled with so, so many ghosts.

Bentley followed the guard down the long corridor through the center of the multitiered facility, able to capture glimpses of cells and their imprisoned inhabitants.

And the ghosts that haunted them.

Bentley could see the spirits of those whose lives had been touched, or taken, by the prisoners. One man sat slumped in his cell, surrounded by the victims of his murderous acts. They bore down upon him, and their presence obviously felt—*oppressive.*

Bentley felt eyes upon him and looked up to a cell in the higher tier. A thin man with dark, cruel eyes watched him as he passed. The specter of a woman appeared from behind the man, reaching out with long, spidery fingers to flick the lobe of his right ear. The man jumped suddenly, swearing aloud as he swatted at the air around him.

A long, tormented life was due them all before Death allowed them their freedom.

"Are you coming, Father?" the guard asked, holding open a heavy metal door. Bentley hadn't realized that he had stopped.

"Of course," he said, hurrying to catch up. "So sorry."

The guard held the door for him, allowing him to pass through first.

"Right down here," Fitzgerald said, going around him to the end of a semidarkened hall. He removed keys from inside his uniform pocket and unlocked the door.

He opened the door, and Bentley stepped inside.

"You can have a seat, and I'll be right back with Tuttle."

Bentley thanked him with a smile and sat down at one side of the table as the guard closed the door behind him.

Bentley could feel it in the air inside the room, like a cold draft from a broken window. Death was a presence here. It lived here, waiting to collect its charges.

He wondered if William Tuttle would be one of those taken shortly, or if there would perhaps be a change in plans. Bentley waited, anticipating Tuttle's arrival, nearly jumping from his seat when he heard the door open.

Turning in his seat, he watched Fitzgerald escort the large, shackled man into the room. Bentley first noticed the man's size. There was a powerful air about him, but he could also sense an incredible sadness.

"Who's this?" Tuttle asked, looking at the guard.

"Somebody who wants to talk to you," Fitzgerald answered, bringing his prisoner around to the other side of the table and shackling him in place. "He wants to try to save your soul."

"What if I don't want it to be saved?" Tuttle asked as he sat down heavily in the wooden chair.

"That's probably up to you," the guard said, making sure the prisoner was shackled properly.

"You've got fifteen minutes, Father," the screw said as he left the room, closing the door behind him.

Bentley stared across the table at the big man; Tuttle stared back, studying him.

"Is this something you priests do before somebody gets executed?" William Tuttle asked. "Thought it was all taken care of on the day, right after my last meal." He smiled sadly. "I ain't dying for another week . . . unless they moved it up." He shrugged his huge shoulders. "Fine with me if they did."

Bentley continued to study the man, unfamiliar with the vibe he was getting from him. Tuttle was unlike any other murderers he'd encountered since becoming an avatar of Death.

"What did you do, William?" Bentley asked, watching the man's reaction.

His blocky face screwed up in a strange mixture of sadness and rage.

"I killed the best thing that ever happened to me, that's what I did," he growled, pulling on his restraints.

The ghost of Tianna Hoops materialized beside the man, staring at him with sad, loving eyes. Bentley watched her, fascinated that such love could be felt for the man who had killed her.

"Did you, William?" Bentley asked. "Did you kill her?"

Tuttle's face went red, and he surged up in his chair, pulling on the chains that held him there. Bentley half expected the links to snap and the man to come at him, but Tianna's ghost had floated in closer to Tuttle, stroking his sweating brow and gently kissing the side of his angry face.

His expression softened, and he sat back down in his chair, tears now streaming from his eyes.

"Tell me, William," Bentley asked. "Tell me what happened that evening."

The man was sobbing now, the ghost stroking his face adoringly.

"She was all that I could have asked for," he said. "There was nobody more beautiful than her."

"Take me through what you remember," Bentley told him.

"It was all that I needed, just spending time with her," he said. "I had the day off, and I'd waited around until after the last show . . . for when she was free for the night."

He paused, remembering her.

"She was a trapeze artist," he said smiling. "It was as if she could fly when she was doing her act."

"Tianna," Bentley said softly.

William slowly nodded, remembering his love.

"What did you do that night?" Bentley asked, wanting to understand. He needed to know how this man, who seemed to have loved so very strongly, could have performed such a heinous act. "Where did you go when Tianna was done with her show?"

The man thought for a moment, tears continuing to run down his face and spatter upon the wooden tabletop.

"We stayed at the circus," he said. "Just walking around doing nothing . . . but saying everything." William chuckled, remembering. "She said that she wanted to know everything that there was to know about me . . . my job . . . everything!"

The ghost of the trapeze artist was lovingly holding the man now, her own ethereal tears flowing from her eyes to drift about their heads like wispy clouds.

"Nobody that I'd ever known gave two shakes for a roustabout like me. She wanted to see what I did there . . . know how I did it, so I showed her around, pointing out everything that I was involved with."

He stopped talking, and Bentley could see that the ghost of Tianna Hoops was reacting as well. She was staring at the man who loved her . . . the man who . . .

"We'd made our way to the exhibits," he said, his voice going flat, emotionless. "I guess it was in the Chamber of the Unearthly when . . ."

Bentley leaned forward on the desk.

"When . . . when what, William?"

"When I lost my fucking mind," he said with a ferocious growl, bending his head down to wipe away the tears that dampened his face. "I think I've talked about enough to you," he added.

Tianna had drifted back away from the man, watching him with an accusatory stare.

"Why, William?" Bentley persisted. "Why did you lose your mind?"

He shook his large, blocky head. "I don't know . . . I don't know anything. One minute I'm the happiest palooka on the planet, and the next thing I know, I'm waking up looking down at the thing I had done."

William was clearly remembering it again. The horrible moment.

"I strangled her," he said. Even then the disbelief in his tone was evident. "I killed the greatest thing that ever happened to me."

The man then looked Bentley square in the eyes.

"And I have no idea why I did it," he said, rage and sadness twisting his features into something horribly pathetic. He looked at his large, powerful hands: the weapons that had committed the act.

"It was like I wasn't me . . . like somebody else had done it."

Bentley allowed the words to nestle in his brain, snuggling down into the gray matter, where their potential meaning could begin to grow.

The door to the room opened, and Fitzgerald entered.

"Time's up, Father," the guard said, walking over to William and starting to unshackle him from the table.

"That's fine," Bentley said, leaning back in his chair, continuing to let the information that he'd heard percolate. "We were just about finished."

"Don't you waste any of your blessings of forgiveness on me, Father," William said as Fitzgerald began to escort him from the room. "I'm getting what I deserve . . . going where I deserve . . .

"For what I did, I'm going straight to Hell."

William Tuttle's words echoed in Bentley's mind as he sat there, waiting for Fitzgerald to return.

The guard came back to escort him from the place of punishment and ghosts, even asking him for a special blessing. To keep up appearances, Bentley did what was requested of him, laying a hand upon the guard's head, and muttering something unintelligible beneath his breath, before stepping outside and heading back to the Packard where Pym patiently waited.

"I was beginning to think they'd convinced you to stay for dinner," Pym said from behind the wheel as Bentley climbed into the back of the car.

"No, thank you," Bentley said, completely distracted by his thoughts. "I'm not hungry."

Pym turned in his seat to look at him.

"Please tell me that it was worth the charade, and the trip."

Bentley focused on the man.

"Yes, yes it was," he answered.

"So?"

"More questions than answers, I'm afraid. Take me home, Pym. There's much that I still need to think about," Bentley said, his mind already beginning to wander again.

Chapter Twelve

BEFORE:

The butler had never been so scared.

He'd rushed downstairs, frantically calling Bentley's name, but garnering no response.

He had hoped the boy would return, would come to his senses and come back in from the storm, but alas.

Pym ran into the kitchen and found the back door ajar, snow having already collected upon the floor just inside. Without any hesitation he grabbed his coat from one of the hooks near the door and tugged it on even as he was heading out of the house and into the storm.

The snow was piling up, and in no time at all his soft-shoed feet were cold and saturated, but it didn't stop him from searching out his charge.

"Bentley!" he called over the howling wind, struggling through the yard and into the woods where he'd seen the child disappear. "Bentley . . . where are you, boy?"

Pym stopped to listen, holding a hand up before his eyes to keep the particles of frozen moisture from striking his face. All he could see was white, wherever he looked, the ground and air merging to create a reality of shifting alabaster. He had to look up to the tops of the waving trees to help with his bearings.

It was freezing, and his concern for Bentley and the boy's delicate constitution began to escalate. He almost began to panic.

Almost.

Panic would get him nowhere, Pym decided, tromping down the useless emotion and surging ahead into the forest, squinting through the blowing bits of ice that nearly blinded him.

"Bentley!" he called out again. "I'm becoming quite cross with you, boy!" The snow in the forest was up to his knees in places, and the panic he was trying to keep at bay suddenly surged forth as he looked around his frozen surroundings with not a sign of the child in sight.

What am I going to do? Perhaps he should return to the house, find Mr. Hawthorne and the professor; their combined efforts might . . .

The tip of his shoe caught upon something concealed beneath the drifting snow, and he pitched forward.

"Damn it all!" he cried out, falling into the snow, now even more wet and freezing than he had been before. Pym rolled over, quickly getting to his feet, his flurry of activity revealing what had tripped him, buried beneath the shifting white.

The child's face was almost as pale as the snow that nearly covered it.

"Dear God," Pym whispered, throwing himself on the ground before Bentley's body. He dug his hands and arms beneath the numbing white and hauled the child's frozen body up from the snow.

"That's it, my boy," he found himself saying. "Old Pym has you now . . . that's it." He knelt in the snow, holding Bentley tightly, searching for a sign that the boy still clung to life, but everything was so very, very cold.

Pym touched the child's face; it was like touching marble.

"Bentley," Pym said, leaning toward him. "Can you hear me, son?" He began to pat the boy's cheeks, the gentle furtive strikes turning to out and out slaps.

"Bentley!" he cried, shaking the child. "Can you hear me? Stop this nonsense at once . . . Do you hear me? Bentley!"

The child remained lifeless, not a sign to be seen or heard that life still clung to him in any degree. Hopelessness washed over Pym; all he felt was despair as he knelt in the snow, cradling the boy, the storm howling around them. He stared at Bentley, the color of his skin reminding him of the delicate china baby dolls in the windows of the high-end department stores in the city.

At that moment he was forced to face the horror of a situation that he'd often thought about, but refused to acknowledge.

What if he dies?

With the years of sickness, the question had always been there, but the answer had been avoided when the child bounced back, some new medicine having a miraculous—although temporary—effect.

Each time enough to keep the reality of the question at bay.

What if he dies?

And now here Bentley was, cold and heavy in his arms, and all Pym could do was stare in abject horror as the snow fell heavily around them.

The despair was like a living thing, suddenly surging to life in the center of his chest, rushing up through his body to fill his lungs and escape out into the storm in a cry from his now gaping mouth. The sound was horrible, and he imagined its awfulness calling down the storm in all its fury, the snow falling harder and harder until both he and the boy were covered, swallowed up by the ferocity of nature.

It was something he almost welcomed; the pain he was experiencing was so all-encompassing, he wasn't sure he could survive it.

The tears and sobbing came next, his entire body revolting against the fury of emotions that threatened to decimate him to the core. He buried his face against the cold of the boy's neck and continued to cry.

Despondency gripped his heart and soul, and Pym almost missed the flutter of warmth on the lobe of his ear. Pulling his face back, he again looked upon the child's deathly countenance, still finding no sign of life. He was about to succumb to his misery, believing that he had imagined the heat upon his ear, when he saw something—a flutter of movement beneath the lid one of the child's eyes.

He went rigid, watching with increasing expectation, but saw nothing else for what felt like the passage of a thousand years.

But then there came a sound.

A low, distant moaning from somewhere deep within the boy's chest.

He's alive.

Pym continued to stare, eyes riveted to the youth's face, watching . . . waiting . . .

Bentley's eyelids fluttered, and his pale blue lips curled into a nasty snarl.

The boy still lives.

Pym struggled to stand on legs that had grown numb from the damp and cold. He almost fell back down to the snow, but somehow managed to remain standing. Clutching Bentley tightly to him, he hoped that the life and heat from his own body would somehow transfer to his charge.

"Don't you worry, boy," he said, making his stiffened legs work as he plowed through the collected snow. "We'll get you home and make you warm and well again."

Pym forged on, praying to whatever deity that might be listening to keep the boy alive long enough to get him back to the house. And someone, or something, must have heard his pleas, for suddenly Hawthorne House appeared through the shifting white, beckoning for their return.

"Almost . . . there," Pym grunted.

He was glad to see that Bentley was conscious now, moving in his arms as if wanting to get down, but as Pym reached the large front doors of the estate, he realized that the boy was reaching, beckoning for something behind them.

"My friend," Bentley cried out to the woods as they were swallowed by the storm. "She wants me to come play with her!"

———

The doors to the grand foyer flew open and Pym practically fell inside, Bentley still clutched protectively in his arms.

The warmth of the mansion surrounded them like eager dogs, lapping at the numbness of their exposed flesh.

Bentley was still going on about his friend out there in the snow; obviously some sort of hallucination brought on by hypothermia. But Pym had to wonder, what on earth would have made the boy go out there in the first place?

Not believing for a moment that the boy was safe, the butler began to call for help as he removed Bentley's soaking-wet clothing.

"What the devil is all the yelling about?" Pym heard Mr. Hawthorne angrily ask. He looked up see the man and his wife in the doorway of the drawing room.

"Your son," Pym began, as Mrs. Hawthorne rushed to his side and dropped to her knees, sweeping young Bentley up into her arms. "He was out in the snow . . . I think I found him in time, but . . ."

Mr. Hawthorne stood paralyzed in the doorway.

"Is he . . . ?"

"He's alive," Mrs. Hawthorne said, lovingly touching her son's face. "But barely."

She then looked to her husband, and Pym noticed something almost palpable pass between them.

"It has to be now," she said, and her husband nodded in silent agreement.

A shadow moved in the doorway behind the master of the house, and Pym watched as Professor Romulus appeared.

"Is everything all right?" the man asked, but as he took in the scene in the foyer, his look said he realized it wasn't.

"It's time," Abraham Hawthorne told the professor. "It has to be now."

The professor wore a startled look for a moment, but quickly seemed to understand.

"Very well, then," he said grimly, motioning for them to follow. "Bring the boy to my lab."

Chapter Thirteen

Bentley was exhausted.

Since his return from Blackmore Prison two days ago, the restless spirit of Tianna Hoops had refused to allow him rest.

He sat in the library, surrounded by his favorite works, as well as the favorites of his mother and father, and attempted to close his eyes.

But she was there as well, floating in the sea of blackness, watching him, urging him on, demanding that she be allowed to rest, and that her lover . . .

"What?" he asked the ghost who floated before him as he sat in the leather wingback chair. "What exactly do you want me to do?" He could hear the intensity in his voice from lack of sleep, but was unsure how to proceed. Yes, something most definitely did not seem right in William Tuttle's story, but where to go from there eluded him. And time was running out: the man's execution was scheduled for the end of the week.

"I'm sorry," he told Tianna's ghost. "I wish I could do more . . . I just don't know what—"

The doors to the library came open and Pym entered, holding a serving tray.

"So sorry to interrupt your conversation with yourself, but I took the liberty of making some lunch," the butler announced, walking over to a nearby table and setting the tray down with a clatter.

"I wasn't talking to myself," Bentley muttered.

Pym turned slowly, looking around the room. "Oh?"

Bentley was tired of explaining; he weakly raised a hand and motioned the butler away. "I'm too tired to eat."

"The sandwich will give you strength," Pym said, turning toward Bentley with a plate holding his lunch. "I even cut away the crust the way you like it."

Bentley took the offered plate, resting it upon his pajama-covered thighs. "I don't know what more to do," he muttered, exasperated. His stomach grumbled at the sight of the sandwich, and he picked it up, suddenly ravenous. "I've exhausted every resource."

Pym stood listening, watching him as he took his first bite of sandwich.

"Is she here now?" the butler asked, again looking around. "This ghost making demands of your attentions?"

Bentley nodded, chewing the large bite he'd taken.

"Yes," he said after swallowing. "She hasn't left me alone since I got back . . . She wants something more, but I don't know what. I saw her boyfriend, I heard his story . . . he told me he did it. What more can I do?"

Bentley ate more of his sandwich, his aggravation skyrocketing.

"I wish I'd been given a rule book, or perhaps even some training courses before—"

Interrupted by the ringing of the doorbell, both he and Pym looked toward the entryway into the library.

"Who on earth could that be?" Bentley asked, wiping crumbs from his mouth with the back of his hand.

"I haven't a clue," Pym said, walking from the room. "Excuse me while I go check."

Bentley started on the second half of his sandwich as Tianna floated above his chair. He didn't want to look at her, didn't want to stare into the darkness of her accusatory eyes.

He'd had more than enough of that, thank you very much.

"Leave me alone," he muttered beneath his breath.

"Well, that's a fine how do you do," a female voice suddenly boomed, and he thought the ghost had somehow gained the ability to speak.

But it wasn't the ghost at all—it was a guest, the ringer of the doorbell. His neighbor from down the road.

Gwendolyn Marks.

"Oh, hello, Gwendolyn," Bentley said, setting down what remained of his sandwich.

"That's more like it," the woman said, a too-large smile spreading across her face. "What's cooking, Bentley? Haven't seen you in a dog's age."

Pym appeared in the doorway.

"Miss Marks is here," he announced.

"I'm quite aware of that now, Pym. Thank you."

She had gone over to his lunch tray and was helping herself to some grapes.

"I was starting to worry," she said, popping a grape into her mouth and chewing. "You don't call, you don't write."

"I've been quite busy."

Gwendolyn Marks was the daughter of multimillionaire newspaperman Aloysius Marks. The Marks family lived ten miles west of Hawthorne House and, with the sprawling Crestwood Cemetery separating the two estates, were Bentley's closest living neighbors.

As children, the two were often encouraged to play with each other, but Bentley was never quite comfortable with the brash and forceful young girl who had grown up to be an even more brash and forceful woman.

"I thought you might've croaked," Gwendolyn said, continuing to eat his grapes.

"No," he told her with a shake of his head. "No croaking . . . yet."

The ghost of Tianna Hoops hovered closer to the woman, watching her with curious eyes. Bentley almost said something, but managed to keep his mouth closed.

"What brings you out to the house, Gwendolyn?" he asked, in an attempt at being sociable.

"It's like I said," the young woman said, "I haven't laid eyes on you in a while, and I thought I'd stop by to see how you were doing."

"How . . . nice," Bentley said, watching as the ghost returned to him and floated mere inches from his face. He tried his hardest not to look at her.

"Yeah, I thought so," she said, strolling around the library. "So, read anything interesting lately?" she asked, her hands stroking the bindings of the books in the case before her.

"No," Bentley said. "I've actually been too busy to read."

"That's too bad," she said, strolling back to his lunch tray, where she picked up a folded copy of the *New York Inquisitor*, the paper owned by her family and managed by her father. "I hear that some mighty impressive works of investigative journalism have been published lately."

She tapped the folded newspaper on the palm of her hand, trying to get him to notice.

"Really?" he asked, trying to sound interested.

"That's what I hear," she said, eyes widening as she suddenly seemed to notice the copy of the *Inquisitor* that she was holding. "Hey, wait a sec," she said. "I think one of those amazing pieces might actually be in here."

"You don't say," Bentley said.

She was over to him in a flash, unfolding the paper to find the story.

To find *her* story.

"I started out working an angle on a string of arsons that have been going on in the Bronx since last summer, but Daddy caught wind of me poking around and put the kibosh on the whole story."

"So it's not the arson story?" Bentley asked, scanning the newsprint.

"Naw," she said disgustedly. "Daddy was afraid his little girl might kick up a little too much dust and get herself in too deep with a less-than-reputable element."

"So what did you . . . ?"

"Flower show," she said, poking the bottom of the page.

"Flower show," he repeated.

"Yeah, not as good as arson, or even murder, but I'm working on it," she said. "All I need is for Daddy to let me have my big break, or to at least get the jump on a story so big that he couldn't say no if he wanted to."

She left him where he sat and began to pace around the library again. Gwendolyn had lots of energy, and always had. Bentley remembered how she'd always been this way: inquisitive, eager to uncover a mystery even when there wasn't one present. She had always wanted to be a reporter, just like the ones at her father's newspaper.

Gwendolyn went back for more grapes, only to find that she'd eaten them all.

"It's too bad about the arson story, though," she said, leaning back against the table and crossing her thin, bony ankles. "I did all kinds of research. I figured the firebug was traveling from state to state. Maybe a traveling salesman of some kind . . . maybe selling encyclopedias or vacuum cleaners! Going from town to town, setting fires and then taking off before . . ."

Something clicked then. Bentley practically heard it, like some heavy locking mechanism falling into place.

"The newspaper," he said, the mechanism of his brain—the tumblers—clicking into place.

"Yeah?" she asked.

The ghost of Tianna knew something was happening and slowly drifted closer to him, watching him with expectant eyes.

"There are ways that you can track things," he said, trying not to look at the ghost before him.

"Track things? How?" Gwendolyn asked, the look on her face telling him that she wasn't quite sure what he was going on about.

"If I needed to know where something was . . . say, a stage show, or a carnival? With your amazing connections and reporter's skills, you could probably tell me where it is."

She pushed off from the table, thinking about his statement. "Yeah, that would be kid's stuff. Why? What do you need to find?"

Bentley looked up into the face of the murdered woman—into the face of her ghost—and saw that she was smiling sadly.

She knew.

"Tell me, Gwendolyn," Bentley said, his eyes twinkling. "How do you feel about circuses?"

Chapter Fourteen

BEFORE:

The former sunroom had been transformed.

Carrying the delirious boy in his arms, Pym could only stare at the strange machinery as it hummed and flashed about the room, making the air itself feel charged with electricity.

"Put the boy on the table," Professor Romulus commanded, heading toward one of the machines, examining one of its many dials and turning a succession of knobs.

"What are all these . . ." Pym began, rooted in place, the moaning child in his arms.

"You needn't concern yourself with anything, Pym," Abraham Hawthorne said as he took Bentley's limp body.

They had forbidden him from entering this room since the professor had come to stay with them, and although he'd known that changes were being made, he'd never imagined anything like this.

The butler had no idea what it was he was looking at.

He watched as Bentley's father brought the boy to what looked like an examination table and gently laid him down.

"What are you going to do?" Pym asked, not entirely forgetting his place in the household, but suddenly not caring. He needed to know.

"It's not your concern," Mrs. Hawthorne informed him, moving to stand with her husband.

Bentley moaned and suddenly sat up. "Where is she?" he asked, his eyes wide and glassy. "Where is my friend?" He looked to the large windows that made up one entire wall of the sunroom. The storm was raging even harder now. "She's so cold . . . so cold," he said, staring, eyes wide but not really focused on the here and now.

"What's he going on about?" Abraham Hawthorne asked, going to his son and pushing him back upon the table.

Pym looked to the windows . . . at the storm outside. "He said that he has a friend out there."

The boy started to struggle under his father's hands.

"Where is she?" Bentley asked, attempting to sit up again. "She was out there with me . . . outside in the snow like soft pillows . . ."

"He's delirious," Edwina said, laying a hand upon her son's brow. "He's burning up."

The professor strode away from his machines to approach the examination table. From the pocket of his laboratory coat he produced a stethoscope and listened to the child's chest.

"His heart is weakening," he said with authority, returning the listening tool to his pocket. "Good."

Good?

Pym must have been mistaken—must have misheard.

Stepping toward the scientist, he took hold of his arm. "What did you just say?"

Romulus glared at the offending hand. "Remove your hand at once, sir," he growled. "We haven't the time for this."

Abraham glared. "Pym," he said, voice dripping with authority. "That will be enough."

Pym released the professor's arm, looking to his master.

"But the boy . . ."

"That will be enough, Pym," Abraham repeated even more forcefully, his hand lying flat upon Bentley's chest, holding the boy in place.

Pym hesitated, unsure of what to do. To see his charge, the boy he had practically raised, quite possibly on the brink of death—it was more than he could tolerate.

"Sir, I must insist that I—"

It was the child's mother who spoke next.

"Please, Pym," she said, tears welling in her eyes. "It's for his own good . . . please understand."

He started to protest, but the look in her eyes, the intensity of the love he saw there, was unlike anything he'd ever seen before. And he knew then that whatever they were about to attempt was for the sake of the child.

And how could he deny them that?

He started to walk toward the exit, fighting the urge to stop—to demand that he be allowed to stay—to witness what was going to be done, but . . .

"*Please*," Edwina mouthed.

He fought the compulsion to remain, and stormed out into the hallway where he stopped. Slowly he turned to look back into the solarium, now transformed into some form of wild laboratory.

The boy's father was standing there, a look Pym would never forget etched upon his stony features.

A look that told him something was about to be done.

Something that had never been attempted.

Something that shouldn't be attempted.

And he slammed the doors closed, leaving Pym standing outside.

Waiting.

But for what? And why did the anticipation fill him with such dread?

———

Abraham spun around to face the lab, the doors closed at his back.

"Do it, Professor," he commanded. "Save my boy."

Romulus had slipped on a pair of long, black rubber gloves and was wearing a pair of circular goggles. He approached the child on the table, observing him carefully.

"Things are proceeding as I expected," he said. He reached down with rubber-covered fingers and pried open the child's eyes. The pupils were dilated; the boy's skin was now cast with a deathly gray pallor. "It shouldn't be long now."

Abraham heard his wife gasp, a hand going to her mouth as she stood at the opposite end of the table. He went to her, placing a strong arm around her shoulders.

Professor Romulus was already on the move, practically running across the solarium toward a six-foot-high, metal-framed glass case. Carefully he got beside it and began to wheel it across the room to where the boy lay dying.

"What can we do?" Abraham asked, feeling so anxious he thought he might rip from his skin. He kept looking at his child, his boy lying there—dying upon the table. Seeds of doubt began to germinate within his mind, and he began to curse himself for not seeking out traditional, more conventional methods to save his son.

The words to suggest that they might want to reconsider danced upon the tip of his tongue when he was again caught up in the moment.

"The stasis chamber should be placed close enough to pick up on the death energies that should begin to manifest at the moment of the child's demise," the professor was saying. He reached down to one of the chamber's wheels and locked the container in place.

"Bring me those cables, quickly!" the professor commanded.

Abraham immediately crossed the room, bending down to retrieve a jumble of thick electrical cables and dragging them across the room to Romulus's eager hands.

"The power that will run through these cables will create the field which will hopefully allow us to entrap the entity," the professor explained breathlessly, attaching the ends of the cables to ports on the bottom of the glass container.

"Death," Abraham said to him.

The professor looked up at him. Abraham could see his own haggard face reflected in the dark glass of the circular goggles.

"Excuse me?"

"Death," Abraham repeated. "We're going to trap Death."

The professor seemed to think about that for a moment, as though he might have been unfamiliar with the concept before—

He quickly looked away, securing the last of the cables and then jumping to his feet to examine the box once again.

"Professor," Abraham called out, causing the man to look his way once more. "You can do this . . . you can save my son?"

The professor's goggled eyes looked into the emptiness of the glass cabinet, as if imagining it full.

Filled with Death.

"We are most certainly going to try."

———

"We're going to trap Death."

The child's father forced Romulus to confront what they were about to do.

To seriously look at, and consider, and wonder—*Do we dare? Have we the right to attempt such a thing?*

Theodore Romulus had always had a fascination with death, beginning with the death of his mother from smallpox when he was but a toddler. The woman who had loved him, who had satisfied his every want, had been removed from his life.

Something had taken her from him.

It was at that point, Theodore believed, that he had become aware.

Suddenly conscious of that force, he had begun to see its presence everywhere: in the changing of the seasons, bloodred leaves falling from the trees to dry and wither upon the ground, in the swollen bodies of the forest animals void of life lying by the side of the road, and in the people in his life—those for whom he cared the most—who always left him.

That force of nature had become his obsession, and he'd thrown himself into the study of death, as well as life, for one could not fully understand the existence of one without knowing the other.

Romulus had traveled the world, familiarizing himself with all beliefs and religions regarding these powerful forces in the universe, coming to understand the various interpretations that had formed as civilizations had developed.

It was while studying with a holy man in the hills of Nepal that Romulus's theory about the entities that he would call Death Avatars had begun to take shape.

He had been asked to partake in a kind of farewell ceremony for one of the village elders who was very near death, and he believed that he had glimpsed something as the old man had passed from life.

Was it a trick of the light? Or an aftereffect of the smoke that wafted from the ceremonial pipes being passed around as they sat in a circle around the dying man?

But he was sure that he had glimpsed something as the man had died.

He believed that something had come for the spirit . . . the soul . . . the life-force of the man.

But he needed to be sure, and threw himself into his research, experimenting with cameras and films sensitive to specific kinds of energies. After years of trial and error, Professor Theodore Romulus believed that he was, in fact, successful, and that was what had led him here, to this moment.

The next step in his pursuit of the truth.

"We are most certainly going to try," he said.

The beginning of an all-new adventure.

———

Edwina could not take her eyes from her son, paralyzed by the sight of him dying.

She held tightly to his cold hand, imagining that it was growing colder with every passing moment. This was how it had to be, she told herself, in order for the professor's plan to be put in motion.

She would do anything to allow her son to live, even if it meant allowing him to die.

He seemed so much smaller as he lay there, his body twitching from time to time, his colorless lips moving ever so slightly, the words he spoke barely audible.

Something about . . .

Something about a friend.

———

Bentley floated someplace between here and there.

He could feel the pull of there, the darkness at the bottom of it like a vast pool of nothing, threatening to take him from the moment.

From the here and now.

He was vaguely aware of the activity around him, the professor running about. *Why is he wearing those goggles and rubber gloves?* He could feel his mother's hand in his, and knew that was what held him here, not allowing him to slip beneath the ocean of oblivion.

He could sense his father close by, the man having such a powerful and overbearing presence that one could feel it in the very air when he was near.

Bentley wanted to ask him what was happening, what all the machines were about, for he could hear the click of switches and the hum of electricity as they came to life.

But what were they all for?

The tug of the void finally became something he could no longer fight. He felt himself begin to slip away, to fall, and not even the touch of his mother's hand was enough to stop it.

But all was made right by another touch.

In his other hand he felt it, delicate and fragile like a flower, and he managed to turn his head.

She had found him, smiling so sweetly as she took his hand and promised him that everything was going to be all right.

—

"Professor!" Edwina called out over the infernal humming of the machines.

Abraham rushed to stand with her beside their son, and knew at once what had caused her reaction. There was no doubt in his mind that their child was close to death.

He wasn't sure if the scientist had heard. The man scuttled about, moving from machine to machine, checking—rechecking—before finally acknowledging their presence again and returning to the table where the boy lay.

Dying.

Again the stethoscope appeared, and Romulus checked the child's life signs, as faint as they were, and growing fainter. Abraham and his wife watched this man, this man of science who had become their last hope for their son.

Romulus reacted, having heard—something—through his instrument, pulling the earpieces from his ears and allowing the listening device to hang from his neck.

"Is it now?" Abraham asked, wanting to prepare psychologically, emotionally, for what was about to be attempted.

The professor did not answer, instead pushing past the Hawthornes to get to the machines closest to the glass cabinet. He dropped to his knees, pulling on the cables that snaked across the ground, making sure that they were secure, and then checked the two closest apparatus again before turning to face them.

Abraham was about to speak again, to ask the question that hung tingling and fat from the tip of his tongue, when Professor Romulus grew incredibly still, his head cocking ever so slightly.

It was if he were listening.

And then . . .

Abraham could feel it, and was sure his wife could as well. There was something in the room with them, something that might have been there before but had not made its presence known until . . .

"It's time," Romulus said, his rubber-gloved hand reaching over to the machine closest to the glass case. He flipped a switch.

Abraham was surprised that he could hear it over the clicks, hums, and buzzes of all the other apparatus in the room, but the sound that this simple switch made, turned from off to on, was nearly deafening.

Maybe it had something to do with the weight of its purpose.

Or maybe it had something to do with what it had done—what *they* had done. By throwing that switch, they were defying the laws of nature, rejecting what was supposed to be—what was meant to be.

They were saying no to the forces of entropy.

They were saying, *No, you cannot take our child.*

We will not let you.

The cacophony of sounds in the makeshift lab became as one, all the machines unified in their sound and purpose.

Abraham looked to his wife and saw panic in her eyes, and tried through his own force of will to command her to be strong.

For their son.

Something was happening; the feeling in the room was strange.

Different.

Abraham's every animal instinct began to scream—something was wrong, something felt terribly, terribly wrong, and it wouldn't have surprised him if everybody and everything in the room in which they now stood had flown off, flying every which way as the forces of gravity were canceled, or if the oxygen in the air was suddenly gone, or if all the atoms and such that made up the reality they were most familiar with decided to drift apart and everything that defined their existence was—unmade.

"What is happening, Professor?" Abraham managed, and he was frightened by how scared he sounded.

"It's here," the scientist said, his goggle-covered eyes moving about the room, taking it all in.

As if sensing something as well, Bentley reacted, his thin, sickly body thrashing weakly upon the examination table.

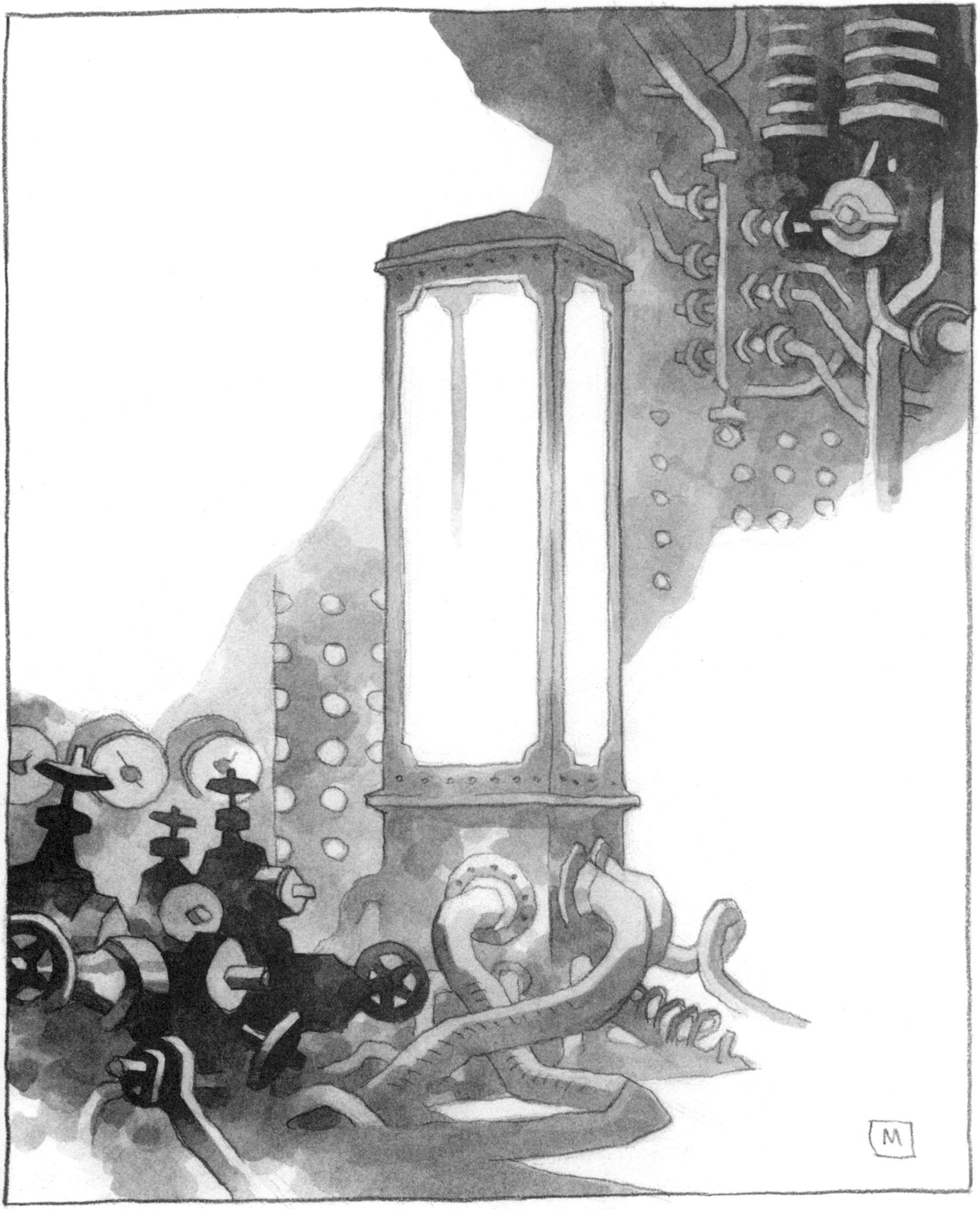

"Don't . . ." he said breathlessly, as if so very, very tired. "Don't . . ."

His mother went to him, holding him down and whispering that everything was going to be all right.

Abraham wanted to believe that, down to the marrow in his bones he truly did, but . . .

The glass case became illuminated by an eerie light, vibrating from within—as if no longer empty.

"The death energy," Professor Romulus whispered, looking from the writhing boy back to the glass case. "It is being collected . . . like metal filings to a magnet."

The case began to rock ever so slightly.

"Don't!" Bentley wailed again, thrashing his sweaty head from side to side. "Don't hurt her!"

Abraham wondered who it was his son was talking about, who could be of such concern to him as he lay there on the brink of death.

And something began to appear inside the glass case, to coalesce before their very eyes from the light and shadow.

Something that appeared . . . almost human.

No matter how much he wanted to disbelieve, Abraham saw it—and knew that the others saw it as well. There was now a child inside the box, her tiny hands slapping the glass in an attempt to get out.

"Please don't hurt her," Bentley begged.

The girl grew angrier, her movements becoming more frantic.

More violent.

"It's true," Professor Romulus said, a touch of wonder in his voice. "It's all true."

"Please don't hurt my friend," Bentley cried out.

And the child inside the box began to scream. Not a scream of fear.

But a scream of anger.

How dare we, Abraham thought.

How dared they, indeed.

Chapter Fifteen

The 1930 Buick Sport Coupe sped down the winding back road, traveling far faster than Bentley cared to go.

"Don't you think you're going too fast?" he asked Gwendolyn, who was smiling from ear to ear, both hands clutching the steering wheel.

"Not at all," she said, eyes fixed on the twists in the road ahead of her. "I could go faster, if you like."

Her smile became insanely wider as she increased the pressure on the gas pedal.

"Gwendolyn," Bentley said, reaching out to grab hold of the dashboard as his eyes grew wider.

"What's the matter, Bent?" she asked. "Am I making you nervous?"

"I just don't think we should be driving this fast on these lonely country roads, is all," he attempted to explain, imagining them coming around a bend, losing control, and wrapping the car around a tree. He briefly wondered if Death would send someone for him.

"Well, you know, you could have driven yourself," Gwendolyn retorted.

"I appreciate your offer to drive," he said. "I truly do, I'm just not too comfortable with traveling at great speeds down roads more equipped to handle horses and buggies than roadsters."

"I get it." She laughed, slowing the vehicle dramatically. "I was just teasing you."

"Of course you were," Bentley responded, removing his hand from the dashboard.

"So do you even know how to drive?" she asked him.

"Of course I do," he answered, offended by the question.

"But you prefer to be chauffeured around?"

"I just prefer not . . . to drive. It makes me nervous."

"You don't say?" Gwendolyn cackled. "Well, I don't mind driving at all . . . in fact, I prefer to be the one behind the wheel. It's all worked out for the best, I'd say."

"Exactly," Bentley agreed. "And seeing as you were also responsible for finding the carnival's current location . . ."

"Exactly," Gwendolyn echoed with a confident smile. "Gave me a chance to put on my reporter's hat for bit and snoop around. Gotta tell ya, wasn't really all that difficult. You just gotta know what rocks to flip over."

"And you certainly did. I don't think I would have ever been able to locate Doctor Nocturne's Circus of Unearthly Wonderment."

"Well, thanks, sport," she said. "And what's up with that, anyway? I never took you for the circus type."

"I've heard some things about this particular amusement and was curious to see for myself," Bentley explained. Although he didn't go on to say that he wanted to see for himself if there was anything to explain William Tuttle's murder of Tianna Hoops.

"Well, it's a good thing I came along when I did," she said. "The circus season is pretty much wrapping up, and this upstate location is the last place they're gonna be before heading back to Florida for the winter."

"Quite fortuitous, I must say," Bentley said.

They were both quiet for a bit, the drone of the country road beneath the car's wheels filling the void until . . .

"Hey, Bentley."

"Yes, Gwendolyn."

"Would you consider this, y'know . . ."

"Consider this what?"

"Y'know."

"No, I don't know."

"Y'know, a date."

"No."

"Oh," she answered abruptly. "I was just checking. I wasn't sure, but I thought that maybe . . ."

"No," he said again, this time stressing the word.

"Good," she said. "Good to know."

And he was glad that she did, for his life was already far too complex to have to consider the needs of a woman, never mind one who fancied herself a reporter.

Death was his mistress now, and a harsh one to boot.

———

They had to endure the suddenly uncomfortable silence for only a few moments longer as the Buick came around a bend to reveal an open patch of land with a circus and sideshow operating upon it.

"Here we are," Gwendolyn muttered, as she slowed the car and turned onto a rutted dirt road that brought them to a large field that had been set aside for cars and the carnival's transport trucks.

Bentley felt a strange charge of electricity as he climbed from the passenger seat of his friend's car, his eyes at once finding the elaborate entrance to the show. DOCTOR NOCTURNE'S CIRCUS OF UNEARTHLY WONDERMENT, the arched sign over the entryway proclaimed. A rather menacing illustration of a gaunt man in a turban and eveningwear smiled down upon them, opening his arms in welcome. Doctor Nocturne, Bentley imagined.

"So, are we going in or are we just going to stand here and admire the sign?" Gwendolyn asked, already striding toward the entrance.

"Oh, yes, of course." Bentley rushed to catch up with her.

They had just passed beneath the arch when he felt spider legs crawling along the back of his neck, and he turned around to see the ghost. Tianna Hoops hovered just outside the entrance, staring forlornly into the place where she had died.

Is it possible for a ghost to be afraid? Bentley wondered. He tried to tell her with his eyes that he was going to seek answers, but she would not look at him—her gaze was transfixed.

"Oh, fried dough!" Gwendolyn exclaimed, slapping his arm so hard that he was almost certain it had left a mark. "Let's get some!"

He followed the woman to the concession stand, where she purchased a plate of the oily dough. She wanted to buy him some as well, but he could only imagine what something like that might do to his rather delicate digestive constitution.

"Suit yourself," she said, digging into the dough with wanton abandon, her upper lip quickly becoming covered with powdered sugar, making her look as though she sported a graying mustache. Bentley stared.

"What?" she asked through a mouthful of hot dough.

He didn't want to embarrass her, but he raised a finger up to his lip.

Gwendolyn brought her own hand up to touch her mouth, and examined the white powder that stuck to her fingers.

"Jeez," she said, wiping the sugar away. "I must look a sight."

He had to agree, but managed to keep his mouth shut. They continued to stroll about the carnival. It was later in the afternoon, and attendance was quite light, making for ready access to anything that might strike their fancy.

"Is there anything specific you're looking to see?" Gwendolyn asked as his eyes carefully scanned the dirt promenade.

"I'll know as soon as I see it," he told her.

The screams of those supposedly enjoying the rides off in the distance followed them as they strolled past many games of chance, the barkers attempting to entice him to play by challenging his manhood.

"That pretty lady looks as though she could use a teddy to hug," a thin, ugly man with an alcoholic's nose suggested as he leaned upon an overly large hammer that would be used to ring a bell in a test of strength. "Whadda ya say, sport? Three swings for two bits . . . heck, I'll even give ya a free one to warm up."

"What do you say, sport?" Gwendolyn chided.

Bentley snarled, ignoring her and the carnival barker, as he continued to look for . . . something. He did not know what it would be, but had a sense that he would once his eyes fell upon it.

A bell clanged noisily behind him, and Bentley cringed as he turned. Gwendolyn had paid her two bits and taken possession of the hammer to win herself that teddy.

"Well, you weren't going to do it," she said, hefting the large hammer in her hands.

He rolled his eyes as he turned away from her, close to resigning himself to the fact that this investigation was going to be a failure.

But then he saw it, and felt that familiar tingle at the base of his spine.

"Hey, what do you see?" Gwendolyn asked, clutching her teddy bear to her chest and eating a candied apple as she struggled to keep up with him.

Bentley didn't answer her. Instead, he moved toward the wheeled carnival wagon, its wooden side covered with posters of various attractions that had performed with the carnival over the years. What had caught his eye was a drawing of a leg, the rest of the image covered up with another poster promoting Mistress Bobbie and her Jungle Cats. Somehow he recognized that exposed leg, and grabbing the corner of the Mistress Bobbie poster, he peeled it back.

THE AMAZING TIANNA, said the poster under Mistress Bobbie's, showing an idyllic interpretation of the performer as she flew through a star-filled constellation on her trapeze.

"There you are," Bentley announced, taking in the details of the poster.

"Who's that?" Gwendolyn asked.

"Someone I've heard about."

"Whatever you heard," said a lone figure that shambled out from behind the wagon toward them, "was probably all true . . . so long as it was about how lovely, nice, and talented she was."

The man was painfully skinny, with a scraggly gray beard and tiny beady eyes. The closer he came, the stronger the smell of alcohol grew.

"Phew!" Gwendolyn whispered as she leaned toward Bentley, waving her hand in front of her face. "Don't light a match near that one, Bent."

Bentley thought the meeting fortuitous—here was someone who had actually known Tianna, and probably William Tuttle as well.

"Damn shame what happened to her," the man said, staggering over to look at the poster, his eyes filling with emotion. "A damn shame." He reached into his back pocket and removed a bottle of clear, strong-smelling liquid. "Excuse me, I have to take my medicine."

"Of course." Bentley stepped back slightly to avoid the overpowering alcohol stink.

"Medicine, my foot," Gwendolyn grumbled.

"So what happened to her?" Bentley asked, ignoring Gwendolyn and watching the man as he swayed before the poster.

"Everything was so good . . . we was all like a family for more years than I can remember. She hadn't been with us that long, but she fit right in . . . her and Tuttle."

Bentley had been right in his assumption. This drunken person had known both Tianna and William.

The man had some more medicine before starting to talk again. "But things started to go south when he bought the whole kit and caboodle."

"Who?" Bentley questioned, feeling that maybe he was onto something.

The old drunk's eyes fixed upon him. "Nocturne," he said, as if his mouth were filled with poison. "Doctor Nocturne bought the carnival from the original owners, and that's when . . . things started to happen."

"What kind of things?" Bentley wanted to know.

The drunk twisted the cover from his bottle, preparing for another swig. "You're a nosey little shit, ain't ya?" he said with a grotesque, wet-sounding cackle. He took a long pull.

"Mishaps . . . accidents . . . murder." He looked at the poster, his eyes welling up near to overflowing. "Call 'em what you will. I tried to tell 'em, but nobody wanted to listen . . . They tossed me out." He began to cry. "Now I'm livin' in a flophouse out on Beaton Street instead'a here with my real family."

He raised the bottle again, eagerly sucking in its numbing contents.

"Why the run of bad luck?" Bentley asked him.

"Bad luck?" the man asked. "It ain't no bad luck. It's the Chamber," he began, and Bentley was certain he was going to go on . . . until two carnival workers took notice of their conversation.

"Hey! Ain't that Charlie Huggston?" one asked the other.

"I believe it is," said the other. "And he ain't supposed to be showing his drunken face around here ever again."

The drunk, now revealed as Charlie Huggston, stumbled back, away from them. "Now, just a minute, fellas," he slurred. "I got every right to . . ."

The large men came at him, each grabbing a bony arm.

"You was warned, Charlie," said one with a sneer.

"Leave the guy alone!" Gwendolyn yelled, dropping the teddy bear onto the ground and advancing toward the men.

"Back off, sweetheart," said one of the goons, "or I'll have to take you over my knee."

It wasn't going well at all, and Bentley quickly considered his options. He was leaning toward taking Gwendolyn by the arm and leading her away.

But she had other plans.

"You think so, you ugly palooka?" she said, balling up her fists.

"Gwendolyn, please!" Bentley said, coming up from behind her to take hold of her elbow.

"You better keep your woman in line," the uglier of the two men warned.

"She is not my woman," Bentley quickly corrected.

"Right, I ain't his woman," she reiterated, barreling down on the ugly man and giving him a swift kick to the kneecap.

The man screeched, releasing Charlie Huggston, who flopped drunkenly to the ground.

"Why, you little bitch!" the man said through gritted teeth. He actually looked as though he might strike the woman, and Bentley was about to do something incredibly stupid, like get between Gwendolyn and the man who wanted to punch her, when a booming voice stopped everybody in their tracks.

"Is there a problem, Mr. Kretch?"

Bentley and Gwendolyn turned to see a statuesque man, dressed in morning clothes and a bejeweled turban, standing behind them, his hands clasped behind his straight back. He bore a striking resemblance to the painted figure presiding over the carnival entrance.

"No problem we can't handle, Doc," Mr. Kretch answered.

The other man reached down and grabbed Charlie, who continued to struggle in his grasp. "We found Charlie here filling the customers' heads with all kinds of nonsense, didn't we, Charlie?" the man asked.

"Let me go!" Charlie slurred. "Don't know what you're talking about, you filthy animal!"

"That will be enough, Mr. Dyre," the man addressed as Doc said. "Kindly release Mr. Huggston."

"But I thought . . ." Mr. Kretch began.

"That will be enough, Mr. Kretch," the man said, nodding for Mr. Dyre to do as he was instructed.

The man released Charlie's arm.

"I didn't say nothin' to nobody, Doc," Charlie began.

"You have been warned, Charlie," the man in the turban said, advancing ever so slightly toward him. "And I would suggest that you heed those warnings and leave this property at once."

It looked as though Charlie wanted to say more, his mouth moving as though he were a fish suffocating upon a dock, but instead he spun around and stumbled off.

"The effects of alcohol can be so unpleasant, especially on a once productive member of society," the man said as he turned his gaze on Bentley and Gwendolyn. "Hello," he said with a smile that seemed to take a very long time to spread across his face. "I am Doctor Nocturne." He offered them a dramatic bow.

"The establishment's namesake," Gwendolyn said, amused by the introduction. "Pleased to meet you."

Bentley studied the man, searching for a sign of . . . what, exactly? He had no idea. He was looking for something, anything, that could prove William Tuttle's innocence before it was too late and allow the ghost of Tianna Hoops to finally be at peace.

"I must apologize for this incident," Nocturne said, his focus primarily upon Gwendolyn. "Something like that should never have occurred." He turned an icy gaze on the two workers.

"We're sorry, boss," Mr. Dyre said quickly. "We thought we was doing what you wanted us to do."

"Yeah." Kretch backed up his friend. "We knew he shouldn'ta been here, and tried to kick him off the premises before he could start any trouble."

"But trouble was started anyway," Doctor Nocturne said, motioning toward them with a delicate hand. "And here we are."

Bentley stepped forward then. "There was no harm done," he said. "I was just admiring this lovely poster." He approached the picture of Tianna. "Mr. Huggston was simply filling me on the tragedy of her death."

He continued to stare at the poster.

"In fact," he said after a moment's pause, "there have been quite a few tragedies here over the last few years." Bentley turned his full attention to the Doctor. "I wonder why that is?"

Nocturne seemed to be studying him now, the jewel in the center of his turban twinkling seductively in the light of the fading sun.

"First you must take into account where the words originated," the carnival's owner said. "He is a disgruntled former employee."

"And a drunk!" Gwendolyn was happy to add, nodding vigorously.

"Yes, one, sadly, with a drinking problem," Doctor Nocturne agreed.

"But one must also remember that this place, this carnival, it is our home . . . a universe unto itself. A microcosm of the world. There are good things and bad things happening all the time . . . life, as well as death."

"Yeah, I can see it," Gwendolyn said, still nodding. "That's pretty deep, Doc."

"It is the truth . . . the Circus of Unearthly Wonderment is my home . . . it is *our* home, and everybody who lives here is family."

He smiled at them, and Bentley felt that spider-legs chill run down the length of his back. Something was—off.

"And just so you do not speak ill of my family . . ."

Nocturne's hands came up, and suddenly two tickets were being presented to them.

"What are these?" Gwendolyn asked, reaching for them.

"Passes," the Doctor said. "Passes for you to enjoy the Chamber of the Unearthly, free of charge."

"Thanks!" Bentley's companion said, relieving the Doctor of the passes. "That's mighty nice of you. Don't you think it's nice, Bentley?"

Bentley continued to study the Doctor, looking for a crack in his facade, something foul leaking out.

"Fabulous," he said. "I think it's fabulous."

—

The Chamber of the Unearthly was a rather dark and rank-smelling structure of winding wooden corridors that emptied into rooms displaying said unearthly objects.

The first objects that Bentley and Gwendolyn found were jars, each containing an oddity, lining a wall.

"Is that a two-headed monkey or is it a baby?" Gwendolyn asked, leaning against the velvet rope that held the audience at a respectable distance from the displays.

"I don't know," Bentley answered, without much interest.

"Well, whichever it is, it's ugly," she commented. "And look at all this other stuff."

Bentley glanced over briefly. There were strange animals floating in yellowish preserving fluids, as well as what appeared to be deformed and amputated body parts. Truly not things he cared to see, but Gwendolyn could not resist the idea of free passes, and one never knew what might be discovered while looking around.

Hadn't William Tuttle said that he and Tianna had been inside the Chamber when—

"Sweet Jesus!" Gwendolyn exclaimed as they rounded a corner on a large and quite powerful-looking beast—a gorilla—wearing a fine, brown suit, sitting in an easy chair and reading a newspaper.

"I see that even gorillas can enjoy your father's publication," Bentley said jokingly. "I would have believed simians more intelligent."

"You know where you can stick that business, buster," she warned, keeping her distance from the beast as he looked up from his reading to fix her with his dark, beady eyes.

"What are you looking at?" she asked the gorilla.

They walked past that exhibit to the next, where a large, hairless man— he didn't even have eyebrows—sat in what appeared to be an electric chair.

Bentley immediately thought of William Tuttle, sitting in the penitentiary awaiting his punishment, unless something was discovered that might prove his innocence.

"Oh, don't you worry none about Mr. Bippo," the hairless man said. "He's perfectly harmless as long as he's got somethin' to read."

"Nice to know," Gwendolyn said, grabbing hold of Bentley's arm. "And what's your story?"

"Story?" the big man asked, shifting his bulk in the elaborate wooden chair. "Yeah, I guess we've all got one."

The gorilla suddenly appeared in the man's space, and Gwendolyn yelped.

"Hey there, Bippo," the man said. "Want to light me up?"

The gorilla in the suit grunted, waddling his strange ape walk over to a large, humming machine on the stage that was covered in dials and switches.

"Want my story, pretty lady?" the hairless man said, gripping the armrests of the chair. "How about this . . . got hit by lightning when I was just a little tyke, and since then . . ."

The gorilla looked over at him before turning some of the knobs and throwing a switch.

Electrical current shot down the length of wires hooked up to the chair, coursing through the man who was seated there, making him shake and groan, his skin beginning to smoke. A strange, cooked-meat smell filled the air.

"The Human Dynamo can't get enough!" the man yelled at the top of his lungs, his teeth actually beginning to smolder in his mouth.

"Let's get the heck out of here," Gwendolyn said, pushing Bentley along.

They moved down even darker, more rickety corridors, glimpsing more displays of questionable validity. They passed an exhibit of strangely malformed bones, which were being called the ossified remains of a gargoyle, as well as an object that might have been an enormous tooth—perhaps one from the mouth of a fire-breathing dragon like the sign professed, but Bentley highly doubted it.

At the end of the corridor was a curtain that Bentley guessed would take them out of the Chamber. He pushed the dusty velvet hanging aside and realized that he was wrong.

They were inside another room . . . another exhibit.

"What now?" Gwendolyn asked, and he could feel her grip tighten upon his arm.

The room was empty except for a large tank that took up nearly one whole side of the small room. A single lightbulb burned in the ceiling, casting strange, shimmering shadows off the greenish water inside the glass container.

"What's in there?" Gwendolyn wanted to know, curiously approaching the front of the tank. A sign on the platform to the right of the exhibit said it contained the last known mermaid in existence.

"A mermaid," Bentley told her, watching her as she stepped toward the tank. The water shimmered and roiled, and he searched for signs of movement—for signs of life.

"I don't see anything inside there," she said, growing closer.

Bentley continued to stare, and for the briefest of moments, he thought he saw something.

Two, dark, soulless eyes.

Staring.

"Let's go, Gwendolyn," Bentley ordered, suddenly having had more than enough of this Chamber of the Unearthly.

She looked away from the tank.

"But I haven't seen the mermaid," she whined.

He did not bother to argue with her, just shook his head in annoyance as he found the exit and stepped out into the early beginnings of twilight.

———

Their drive back to Hawthorne House was mostly silent. Bentley, mind tweaked by the musing of the drunkard, Charlie Huggston, was lost deep in his thoughts, attempting to resurrect every bit of memory.

If there had been other deaths at Doctor Nocturne's carnival, he must know more of them, Bentley decided.

"We're here," Gwendolyn suddenly announced, and he saw that they had pulled up in front of Hawthorne House.

"Oh," Bentley said, pleasantly surprised. "The journey home seemed much shorter." He began to open his door.

"Yeah, probably had something to do with the total silence," Gwendolyn said, obviously annoyed by the time he'd spent ruminating.

"Thank you again for finding the circus and attending with me," he said, being polite.

"You're welcome," she said, smiling, sliding over on the seat closer to him. "Who knows, maybe this is the beginning of something. Y'know, me and you maybe going places and doing things?"

Bentley knew exactly what Gwendolyn was hinting at and decided to nip it in the bud immediately.

"I have very little time these days to socialize, Gwendolyn," he said, pushing open the door of the roadster and quickly climbing from the car, afraid she might pursue him.

He leaned back into the car to finish his words to her. "But if time should ever open up, which I seriously doubt it will, I would consider calling on you . . . and we could maybe go to a place . . . for something . . . to do something."

He hated to give her false hope, but at the moment decided that was for the best—a payment of sorts for the aid she'd provided him.

"Ya think?" she asked, her extra-wide smile beaming.

"I doubt it. But one never knows," he said, slamming the passenger door closed.

Chapter Sixteen

BEFORE:

There was a little girl inside Professor Romulus's box.

Abraham attempted to understand that as he stood there, staring at the petite figure stirring in the glass coffin trimmed with metal and bolts.

"Professor?" Abraham called out over the high-pitched whines and hums of the various machines.

The scientist ran about, checking instruments and gauges. "Everything is holding," Romulus called out excitedly.

The child was angry; Abraham could see it in the way she lashed out at the glass, and by the way her pretty face—though it wasn't so pretty now—screwed up, her mouth opened unusually wide in a silent scream.

A silent scream of rage.

"Professor?" Abraham called out again, wanting the man to see what he saw. How was this possible? Was this so-called entity . . . a child?

"Please," a voice begged.

Abraham managed to tear his eyes from the contents of the box to see his own child, his son, thrashing wildly upon the examination table, his wife struggling to hold him down.

If anything, he seemed stronger as a result of what they had done. *What they had done.*

He looked back to the cage, to the beautiful little girl. For a brief instant he saw something else inside the containment box, and felt his breath catch painfully in his throat.

Something that now hungrily watched his boy.

"Edwina, you must take the boy and go," Abraham ordered.

She was trying to hold the flailing boy still, as Bentley called out to his mysterious friend.

Is that even possible? Abraham wondered. Could their son have somehow befriended the thing they'd captured? He wanted to call it a child, a lovely little girl, but for the memory of what he'd just glimpsed.

His wife was now paying close attention to the box.

"It's just a child," she whispered, forcing her weight down upon her writhing son. "How is it that we've captured a little girl?"

Abraham could hear the panic creeping into the normally strong woman's voice, as she attempted to comprehend what was happening.

"It's not a child," he corrected her firmly. "And this is why you must take Bentley and . . ."

"It's not a child," Professor Romulus repeated, suddenly appearing in the midst of them, his face red and shiny with sweat. "It could never be anything so innocent." He removed his goggles and stared, mesmerized, at the contents of his box.

"She's my friend," Bentley cried out, reaching for the captured little girl.

The entity within the box reacted like metal filings to a magnet, drawn to the side of the box where Bentley's outstretched hands beckoned.

"I don't understand," Edwina cried out, while attempting to keep her son in place. "Why does it look that way?"

"Death is a clever, clever thing," Professor Romulus said. His head suddenly tilted to the right as one of the machines began to make a different, barely audible sound. "It will assume the form of something nonthreatening, to make one's loss of life . . . of one's existence easier to accept."

"I saw it for what it is . . . what it truly is," Abraham interjected, trying to make his wife listen. "And that's why you must take Bentley and leave the solarium before . . ."

Something happened inside the cage.

And it seemed to have somehow affected the machines.

Abraham stopped talking, looking around as the lights dimmed, and the machines began to sound—odd.

Strained.

Edwina screamed. They all looked to the source of her terror, and they saw that the little girl had started to change. They watched as she went from blond haired and fair skinned, dressed in the prettiest of red party dresses, to a thing composed of tattered shadow and fury.

"No!" Romulus yelled as he gazed upon the shifting thing, growing larger and more active within the case. The machines were becoming louder, and the smell of burnt ozone filled the air.

The scientist tore his gaze from the entrapped entity, running to his machines as he continued his rant.

"No! No! No! No!"

The thing trapped in the case had grown in size, its bulk pushing against the glass. Its prison started to shake, rocking from side to side.

"You're hurting her!' Bentley cried out, pushing at his mother and causing her to stumble to one side.

The boy threw himself from the table, landing in a crouch from which he sprang toward the trembling glass case and the writhing nightmare it contained.

Abraham tried to stop his son, stepping into his path, but the boy proved inexplicably quick, darting around his father's outstretched hands to reach the case.

Bentley stood swaying before the container, staring with wild glassy eyes as the entity struggled within.

"I won't let them hurt you anymore," he said to the thing inside.

"Bentley!" Abraham yelled, striding toward where the boy stood. "You don't know what you're doing, boy!"

—

Bentley knew exactly what it was he was doing.

His friend was in trouble, and he had to free her. Pulling back, he made a fist and punched the glass with all his might.

He could hear his father coming up behind him, yelling that he did not understand, but he understood perfectly. This—what they had done to his friend—it should never have happened.

"Bentley!" He heard his father cry out and felt his strong hands grip his shoulders, trying to pull him away, but Bentley was not yet done, and bent himself forward, slipping from his father's clutches.

He knew that his opportunity was waning, and that he would likely not get many more chances. Looking into the case, through the shifting dark-ness trapped inside, he saw his friend there and told her his intentions.

"I'm going to get you out," he said, and again slammed his fist against the glass. "But you need to help me."

Bentley drew back his fist and brought it toward the glass with all that he could muster. Inside the tank, a fist formed as well, coming to meet the impact of the boy's strike from the other side.

The two fists hit on opposite sides of the glass with a sound like the crack of a whip.

"Bentley," he heard his father say so very close to his ear. "What have you done?"

Tiny hairline fractures, like cartoon bolts of lightning, appeared where their fists had met, spreading out across the surface of the glass, moving faster and faster until there wasn't a part of the glass on any of the four sides that wasn't marred by a multitude of fine fissures.

Bentley turned to face his father and smiled dreamily.

"I've helped her," he said as the glass let loose behind him, crashing to the solarium floor in a rain of pieces, releasing what had been captured inside.

"I've set my friend free."

——

Professor Romulus knew that he should run—every instinct told him to flee, to get as far away as was possible.

But he knew he wouldn't be able to escape it. That was the sad truth that he already knew, but he needed something like this—a failure of such magnitude—to drive the point home.

He tried to maintain the machines, but he knew it was only a matter of time before the bulbs blew, and the power that they were attempting to contain was released. The sound of shattering glass from behind made him cringe, as the first of his complex machines exploded in flames, a thick black smoke that smelled of burning rubber leaking out from within, mak-ing him choke.

And the air behind him—the entire sunroom—filled with the most awful sounds.

Angry sounds.

Romulus continued his futile task of trying to maintain the machines, but it was far too late for that. They could no longer do what they had been created for; the power of the universe was now released, unbridled, causing the machines to explode and burn in their ineffectiveness.

The horrible sounds built to a near deafening crescendo, then stopped abruptly as he watched one of the last of his special machines sputter and die.

Professor Romulus could feel its presence close by, the hair at the nape of his neck standing up straight as every primitive sense in his body warned him of imminent danger.

A primal voice inside his skull screamed for him to run, to run and hide and pray to the forces of creation for some kind of mercy, to be spared this inevitable fate.

But he couldn't do it. It was his curse to try to understand, to look into the eye of the unknown and attempt to comprehend it all. If he was to meet his fate, he would do it on his own terms.

The sense of the presence behind him had grown even stronger, like a giant hand pressing down atop his head, wanting to drive him to his knees.

But Romulus would not bend, turning around instead to face what he had foolishly attempted to control.

His brain could not quite comprehend what it was that he was looking at. It was large and looming, looking like a living piece of shadow that had decided upon its independence, but if one looked upon it long enough . . .

At first, the black of it was impenetrable, like the most beautiful of evening skies, far away from the lights of the city.

And the stars inside this vast and endless darkness weren't stars at all, but were the life-forces—the souls—of all who had lived and died since the dawn of life and death.

It wanted to show him how foolish they'd been, how mad they'd been to imagine that they could even begin to hold something of its magnitude.

Looking upon it, Professor Romulus finally understood the true beauty of the cycle of life, and the finale of the process. But he also understood the terror: that Death could take him lovingly in its embrace and lead him blissfully from life, or it could take him begging and screaming into the unknown.

Romulus saw all that as he looked upon the undulating mass that bore down upon him.

"I'm sorry," he said, fighting the urge but not strong enough as he reached out to it, placing his hand and arm inside the body of the infinite.

To touch the unknown in an attempt to know it further.

And Death touched him back.

Professor Romulus cried out, screaming for what seemed like an eternity as his arm—the muscles, tendons, and veins—withered away at the touch of it, becoming nothing more than some shriveled dead thing dangling from his body.

Death wanted to show him more, but the professor could not stand it. Still screaming, he pulled back from the shadowy mass, the terror that he felt fueling his need to flee. His arm hanging uselessly by his side, Romulus ran through the choking smoke, any intellect that might have caused him to stop, ponder, and rationalize now gone as quickly and easily as the flesh and muscle that had once covered his arm.

There was only the animal part of him now, the part that needed to live, the part the made his heart pump madly and his legs propel him away from the thing that scared him to the depths of his soul.

Through shifting smoke his saw it, a world of white just beyond the horror unfolding behind him. He would get to this peaceful place, he told himself as he ran faster, and faster still, as if Death itself were chasing him.

Which indeed it was.

The barrier of glass was just an obstacle, something to be broken, smashed through, in his pursuit to escape. The large window shattered with the impact of his body, an explosion of cold, wind, and snow now rushing into the smoke-choked place of horror he had left behind.

Professor Romulus did not turn around; he continued to run even as the accumulated snow attempted to stop him.

Running until he could run no more.

Swallowed up by the storm.

———

Something had taken Bentley's parents.

His rational brain said it was the ravening fire and the choking smoke, but he knew better.

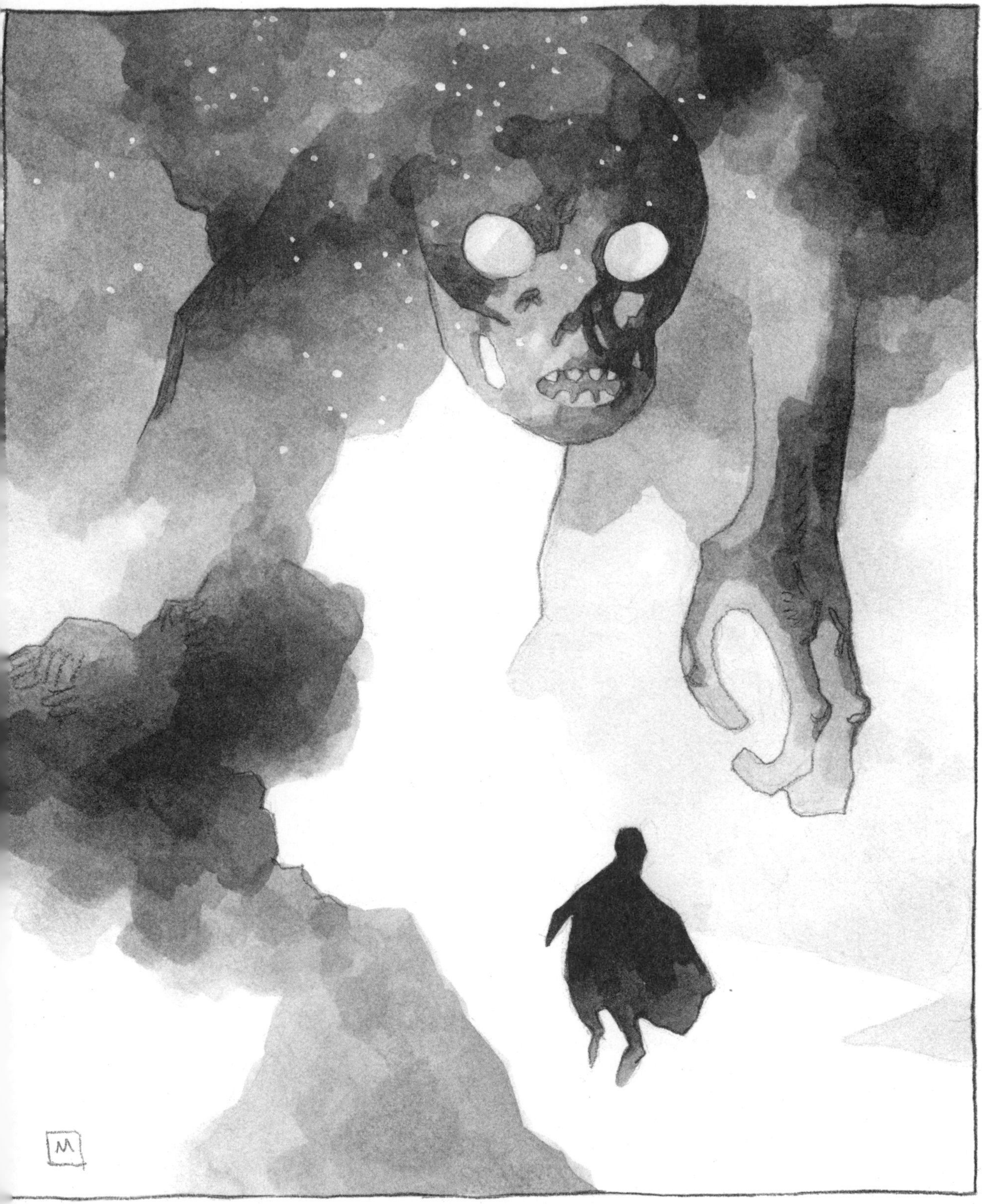

The thing that had been inside the case moved through the solarium, shrieking its anger.

Bentley had thought they were friends, and begged for it to please reconsider, begged for it to spare his parents from its anger.

But its fury was too great, and it reached out to them with claws of rage and darkness and took their lives like fruit plucked from a tree.

Bentley wanted to go with them, to be with them, for was he not partly to blame for what had happened here? If it were not for him, they would never have attempted anything so foolish. The smoke was thicker now, the flames from the machines even larger, fueled by the air rushing in through the broken window.

He tried to recall where he had seen them last, crying out and sounding so very scared as the thing—*his friend*—made them pay for their sins.

Bentley tried to call to them, but the smoke that filled the air took this as an invitation to enter his mouth and nestle comfortably within his lungs, making him cough and choke and crumple to his knees.

Kneeling amid the broken glass, he tried to gather his strength, but there was none to be found, his reserves depleted. How sad it was, he thought as he slumped there amid the burning machinery and the suffocating smoke, for his parents to have gone through all this in an attempt to save his life, and still to have failed.

Bentley managed to raise his gaze for a moment, his hopes of finding at least one of his parents alive dwindling like his strength, when he saw movement.

Something moved within the smoke, coming toward him, and he thought for just a moment that maybe his mother or his father had indeed survived, and that he might live through this as well.

The little girl parted the smoke like heavy curtains, her beautiful face looking down to where he knelt, filled with disappointment.

Bentley now knew what she was—what she truly was—and felt an intense sensation of fear course through his body.

"I'm sorry," he apologized to her, not knowing what else he might be able to do to make amends for what had been done.

"I'm sorry for them all, and for what they tried to do to you."

The look upon his friend's face went from one of severe disappointment to one of resignation, and she opened her arms to him.

And believing himself forgiven, Bentley responded in kind, opening his arms to her, but as he moved to embrace her, he found that she was gone. There was only smoke.

——

Abraham had locked the doors from the inside.

Pym had heard the sounds, the infernal ruckus, and immediately set to work trying to get back into the room. He was certain there was a key someplace, perhaps in the kitchen, where innumerable key rings hung just inside the wall of the basement door, but there wasn't time.

Something was happening inside the solarium-turned-laboratory.

Something that very well might harm the members of the household that he had sworn to serve.

But most important, he needed to make sure the boy was safe.

He pounded upon the door with powerful fists, testing the strength of the lock and wood. Pym then slammed his shoulder as hard as he could, multiple times, feeling just the slightest give, but still the doors held. He tried to ignore the sounds from inside, the screams of terror and pain, the wails of something . . . unnatural.

Pym knew that his physical strength would not be enough to get him inside and quickly searched nearby for aid. At the end of the corridor sat a long-legged wrought-iron planter. He vaguely remembered when the plant that it once held—a fern, he believed—had died, but it had never been replaced. Pym threw himself down the hall, snatched up the heavy decorative piece from the ground, and returned to the doors.

The sounds inside had intensified, and he believed he'd never heard anything quite so horrible. The smell of smoke was strong now, tufts of black leaking out from beneath both doors. There wasn't any more time to waste, even though he knew that there was danger on the other side.

Danger to the boy.

He was suddenly like a madman, grabbing the iron planter by the legs and slamming it repeatedly against the doors. Again and again he struck, watching as the area around the knobs and lock began to chip, and splinter, and he hoped—he prayed—that he would have the strength to continue.

When the screaming stopped, when it all went quiet, Pym experienced an even greater surge of wherewithal, and he intensified his efforts until the wood and knobs broke away, thumping down to the carpeted floor. Tossing the planter away, he threw himself at the broken doors, and felt their final resistance before they flew open into the solarium.

Pym practically fell to the ground, but managed to regain his balance. He stared about the room, taking it all in and wondering how something like this had happened.

Everything was burnt, blackened, and charred. The machines that he'd observed humming and flashing were now just twisted, ash-covered hulks, sitting silently.

But where was the fire? Where was the source of the smoke he'd smelled and observed creeping out from beneath the door?

Pym came further into the room; a blast of freezing wind, flecked with snow, struck his face as he turned toward the glass windows and saw that one had been shattered, letting in the cold, winter environment. For the briefest instant, he felt hope. Hope that his masters had broken the glass to escape whatever had transpired within the room, that all were safe and sound—*but cold*—outside.

The sound turned him around from the broken window. It was so very soft. It could easily have been the wind moving across the two piles of ash that, if one looked at them at just the right angle, might have resembled the remains of two human forms.

Again he heard it, and moved farther into the lab, his senses now fully alert, listening for another sign. The sound came once more, and that was when Pym found him.

It was some kind of miracle—what else could it be? Pym thought as he ran to the boy.

Bentley lay upon the blackened floor, curled up tightly in the fetal position, everything around him burnt beyond recognition. Pym knelt down beside the child and at once began to check him for harm, but the boy was fine.

Perfect, even.

His face, his clothes were barely even dirty.

How this was possible, observing the condition of the room around him, Pym had no idea—and at that moment, he did not feel the urge to question.

As gently as he was able, he picked up the child from the floor—his memory flashing back to the many times he'd done the same picking up Bentley from the floor of his bedroom, surrounded by his many books— and carried him from the room.

Away from the blackened remnants of what had transpired.

Chapter Seventeen

The steak sizzled noisily as it cooked.

Wearing an apron, Pym stood above the cast-iron frying pan holding a fork at the ready to skewer and flip the searing meat.

Bentley was very particular about how his steak was prepared.

Pym actually caught himself smiling with the thought of the young man and what he had done today. Perhaps Miss Marks was just what Bentley needed to draw him from his perpetually morose state, and distract him from his rather bizarre—and quite dangerous—extracurricular activities.

Sensing that the right moment was at hand, Pym stabbed the steak and turned it. Bentley liked his meat cooked medium, not rare, and certainly not medium-rare. Medium. And the young man wasn't the least bit concerned about throwing the costly meat in the bin if it wasn't cooked to his exact specifications.

Although, truth be told, Pym wanted this night's dinner to be something special, a reward for what Bentley had done. He tried to remember the last time his young master had left the house with anyone other than himself. Strangely, the details completely escaped him.

The steak was ready, as were the vegetables: steamed carrots and a side of boiled potatoes. He quickly plated the meal, placed it upon a serving tray, and covered it up for delivery. Normally Pym would have demanded some decorum, ordering the youth to take his meal in the dining room, but tonight he was feeling a bit lax, nearly euphoric with the idea that maybe Bentley would be all right.

That maybe he needn't worry so much about the boy's future.

As he climbed the stairs, he actually found himself humming, something from a Gilbert and Sullivan production he'd seen ages ago. He was surprised that he still remembered the song, never mind how to hum. He reached the second floor and continued on down the hall, a slight spring in his step. Stopping before Bentley's door, he carefully balanced the loaded tray on one arm while knocking softly with the other.

"Come in," Bentley said, but his voice sounded strange.

Pym pushed open the door, and nearly dropped the tray.

Bentley was standing in front of his dresser, looking into the mirror, but it wasn't the young man's reflection that stared back at Pym in the doorway.

He was wearing the mask again.

The skull mask.

"What on earth are you doing?" Pym asked, his voice a whispering hiss, everything he'd thought the boy had achieved this day seeming suddenly far more distant.

"We met a man today," Bentley explained, his voice strangely distorted by the mask. "Someone I need to speak with more . . . no, someone who Grim Death needs to speak with."

"Bentley, please," Pym said, almost begging. He set the tray down. "You've been out all day, doing things . . . normal things."

Bentley didn't turn, continuing to let his skull-adorned reflection speak.

"And what exactly is that supposed to mean?" Bentley asked—*was it really him?* "That since I was out and about with Gwendolyn, my responsibilities to Death have been negated?"

Pym just shrugged. "Have you considered it? Have you thought about maybe just stopping?"

Bentley pulled the skull mask from his face and turned to face the man. "I think about it all the time, but then I remember what my mother and father . . . what Romulus tried to do."

"They tried to help you."

"They certainly did," Bentley acknowledged sadly, approaching Pym. "But now I have to cover the cost."

He stopped before the tray and lifted the cover. "Medium?"

"Exactly the way you like it," Pym told him, watching as the young man pulled out the chair and sat down at the tray.

He grabbed his knife and fork and immediately cut into the meat to test its center. He looked at Pym and smiled before cutting his first bite.

The silence went on for far too long, and Pym was compelled to speak.

"So this person that you met today," he began.

"One Charlie Huggston," Bentley said around a second bite of steak. "An unpleasant drunkard of a man."

"I see," Pym said. "So you're saying that you . . . Grim Death . . ."

"Very good," Bentley complimented the steak, as if Pym weren't even speaking.

"That Grim Death has to question this unpleasant man," Pym continued without missing a beat.

"Exactly," Bentley said, cutting more pieces from his meal. "He seemed to know things about the circus that I think might clear William Tuttle."

"The man who confessed to murdering his girlfriend."

"Yes, exactly."

"Confessed."

"Yes, Pym, I understand he confessed," Bentley said condescendingly. "But there's something—besides the restless and unhappy ghost of his lover—that tells me there's more to it than that."

Pym watched as Bentley looked across the room at something he could not see, but the young man obviously could.

"Of course there is," he responded, matching Bentley's condescending tone.

"And time is of the essence," Bentley said, fussing with his meal. "Tuttle is to be executed by week's end."

And without another word, Pym turned to leave the room.

"Pym?" Bentley called to him.

"Yes?"

"This steak is excellent."

"Thank you, sir." He started to leave again.

"Pym?"

He turned.

"I would like you to drive me tonight," Bentley said, finishing the last bite of steak with some carrots and potato.

"What if I said no?"

Bentley chewed thoughtfully for a few moments. "Then I would need to drive myself," he finally offered.

Pym shuddered at the thought, remembering the last time Bentley had taken a car. "That won't be necessary." He sighed, resigned to his fate.

"Excellent." Bentley rose and crossed the room to retrieve a map from his desk. "I picked this up today when Gwendolyn stopped to fill up," he said, unfolding the map. "You will drive, and I will be your navigator."

"Oh . . . good," Pym said, not quite sure what to say.

"Can't have you having all the fun," the young man said with a smile, "can we?"

———

"The exit for Stewartville should be coming up on our right," Bentley said, holding the flashlight beam steady as he hunched over the map in the large backseat of the sedan.

"If you had told me we would be driving all night, I would have refused to do this," Pym said from behind the wheel, slowing the vehicle down as he prepared to take the next exit.

"Come now, Pym," Bentley said. "You know you don't mean that."

"I certainly do," the manservant said, turning the wheel and taking them down the curving exit. "This is insane, driving all this distance to track down a drunkard who used to work for the circus you're investigating. You're not even sure if he's here."

"I'll find him," Bentley said. "He mentioned living in a flophouse on Beaton Street . . . and it won't be me who questions him." He put the map down on the seat. "Beaton should be just beyond the center of town," he said as he reached for the skull mask inside of his coat. He stared at it for a moment, his eyes caressing the grotesque contours, imagining a voice deep in back of his mind whispering, *Put me on.*

He slipped the mask over his head.

"Dear God," Pym said from the driver's seat. "Do you have to put that on now? It nearly scared me half to death when I looked in the rearview."

"Sorry," Bentley said, his voice taking on a more gravelly tone now that he was wearing the visage of Grim Death. "This looks like the town center. Look for something seedy." He leaned forward to peer out the curved windshield. "There!" he said, pointing. "The Pinnacle Hotel. Does that look like it fits the description of a flophouse?"

"I would rather sleep in the car, if that's enough of an answer for you," Pym said, looking at the old, six-story brick structure as they drove slowly by.

"Find a side street and park," Bentley ordered, "preferably someplace in shadow."

Pym turned the car around at the next intersection, then found a spot on the same side of the street as the Pinnacle. "How about I park it right here?" he asked.

"This is good," Bentley said, looking out all the windows to see if there was anybody about. It was quiet on the streets of Stewartville, not a soul to be found at this late hour, which was good when one did not want to be noticed.

He put the slouch hat on top of his mask-covered head, pulling it down low enough to cast a shadow across the upper part of his face. "I'll return as soon as I have the information I seek," he said, in a menacing tone he'd been practicing for effect.

"And what if he doesn't have any?" Pym asked, turning slightly in his seat.

"Excuse me?" Bentley asked.

"What if this man . . . this drunkard and former employee of the circus, doesn't have anything . . . or isn't home . . . or moved out this afternoon?"

Bentley wasn't quite sure how to answer.

"I . . ." he began.

"This could all be for nothing," Pym said, obviously annoyed—yet again.

Bentley caught a flurry of movement from the corner of his eye and glanced over to see that the ghost of Tianna Hoops had joined him on the long backseat, staring ahead longingly, waiting . . . waiting for answers.

Waiting for him to bring her peace.

"If I don't find answers here, I'll have to look someplace else," Bentley said, opening the car door and slinking out onto the sidewalk. "I'll return as quickly as I can . . . Be ready, in case of trouble."

"Trouble?" he heard Pym question as he pushed the door closed, cutting off any further comments from the butler.

———

Skulking down the alleyway, Grim Death stayed close to the pockets of shadow, swimming in and out of the darkness like a shark coursing through the vast ocean in search of prey. Ahead of him, he saw a flickering entrance sign, on the verge of extinction. He approached cautiously, quickly glancing about him before grabbing the knob and pulling open the door.

A fat man lay sprawled on the floor of the tiled back foyer, the stink of cheap liquor wafting from his every pore. His eyes opened wide at the sight of the grim visage staring at him through the open doorway.

"Oh, sweet Jesus," the man slurred, squirming upon the floor, trying fruitlessly to get up, his feet and legs sliding on the slick surface. "I don't want to die! I ain't ready yet! I'll quit the booze . . . I promise!"

Grim Death thought quickly, deciding to use the unique situation to his advantage. "What is your name, child of the earthly plain?" he asked in his creepiest voice as he stepped into the hallway, allowing the door to slam closed behind him.

"Otis," the drunken man cried. He was still trying to stand, refusing to look at the deathly visage before him.

Grim Death reached down and grabbed the man under one of his flabby arms, helping him to stand. It was not an easy task, and Grim Death found that he almost joined Otis on the floor.

"Stand up, Otis!" he commanded the drunk, managing to prop the man against the locked door into the hotel proper.

"Do you live in this place?" Grim Death asked.

"I promise," Otis muttered, his eyes locked shut. "I promise I'll never take another drop. I promise, if you don't take me, I'll remain sober till the day I die."

"Which will be today . . ."

Otis shrieked and wailed, almost sliding back down onto the floor, but Grim Death caught his arm, preventing his fall.

"Unless . . ."

Otis stopped his carrying on, opened his bleary eyes, and looked into the face of Death.

"Unless what?" he asked, the alcohol smell from his mouth so strong that Bentley was surprised it didn't melt his mask.

"Unless you assist me," Grim Death said.

"What I gotta do?" Otis asked, raring to go.

"Do you live here, Otis?"

The drunken fat man nodded eagerly.

"Then you will open this door, and we will enter together."

"Okay," Otis said, starting to fish through his pockets, looking for his key. Change and bits of junk spilled out onto the floor of the foyer. "I know my key is in here somewhere."

"And do you know others who live in this building, Otis?"

The drunken man looked up, his hand filled with items from his pocket.

"Yeah, I guess," he said. "You lookin' for somebody . . . other than me, that is?"

"Would you rather I just leave with you?" Grim Death asked.

"No! No! No!" Otis objected. "Who you lookin' for?"

"Charlie Huggston." Grim Death watched as the fat man's eyes grew wide with recognition.

"You're lookin' for Charlie?" he asked incredulously, his hand still loaded with junk from his pockets.

Grim Death saw what he was looking for and reached out to pick up the key and hand it to Otis. "Yes."

Otis took the key with a trembling hand.

"He lives up on four," he said.

"Thank you," Grim Death said. "Open the door."

Otis turned, and after three or four tries managed to get the key in the lock and open the door.

"He's kind of a jerk," he added, pulling the key from the lock and returning it to his pocket.

"I'll be the judge of that," Grim Death answered, moving toward the stairs. "Four, you said?"

"Four-oh-three," Otis confirmed.

"You've been very helpful, Otis," Grim Death said, as he began to climb the stairs.

"Does that mean you ain't gonna take me?" he asked, a tremble of joy evident in his drunken slur.

"Not tonight."

"Then when?" Otis called out.

"When it's your time," Grim Death told him.

"What the hell is that supposed to mean?" he heard Otis mutter beneath his breath, as he continued his climb to the fourth floor.

——

Bentley found himself just a bit winded. He paused on the landing of the fourth floor before continuing on to the door marked 403 in tarnished brass numbers.

He would have preferred to knock, but when wearing the visage of Grim Death, rules of etiquette were all but suspended. He felt a surge of power go through him, something that he only experienced when wearing the mask, hat, and coat of Death's agent. He slammed his shoulder hard into the door, feeling the cheap lock give way, and the door swung into the room.

And Grim Death entered.

The entry went unnoticed, for Charlie Huggston lay on his mattress, clad only in his boxers, snoring, an empty glass bottle on the floor beside the bed.

Pushing the door closed behind him, Grim Death approached the bed, standing over the sleeping man.

"Charles Huggston."

The man continued to sleep.

"Charles Huggston!" he said, a little bit louder.

And still the man continued to sleep.

Grim Death reached down, grabbed the man by the front of his yellowed T-shirt, and twisted it in his fist. "Charles Huggston!" He gave the man a violent shake. "Grim Death would have words with you!"

Huggston's eyes snapped open blearily and blinked.

"AHHHHHHHHHHHHH!" he began to scream, as Grim Death muffled the cries with a gloved hand.

"Be silent!" he commanded. "Or I will silence you."

The man went quiet, looking up with fear-filled eyes.

"Do we understand each other?" Grim Death asked.

Charlie nodded.

Grim Death removed his hand.

"Who the hell are you supposed to be?" Charlie Huggston asked, a tremble of terror evident in his voice.

"I am an agent of Death, seeking answers," Grim Death said as he loomed above the man.

"Answers?" Charlie asked. "What kinda answers . . . I don't know nothin'!"

"Doctor Nocturne's Circus of Unearthly Wonderment," Grim Death growled. "Something is . . . *wrong* there."

"Besides them being no good sons of bitches for letting me go?" Charlie complained.

Grim Death slowly nodded, the action urging the man to continue.

"I don't know," he said, seeming apprehensive. "There were things, I guess." He reached over the side of the bed and grabbed the discarded bottle lying there. "You mind?" Without waiting for an answer, Charlie tipped the bottle back for any moisture that remained inside.

"What kind of things?" Bentley asked, as Charlie looked down the neck of the bottle, as if expecting it to suddenly fill up again.

"I don't know . . . things . . . bad luck and stuff. People getting hurt . . . doing things to each other, and . . ."

He angrily tossed the bottle onto the floor and threw his scrawny bare legs over the side of the bed, bending down to rifle through the newspapers and dirty clothes that covered the ground. "I think I've got another bottle somewhere," he muttered beneath his stinking breath.

"And why do you think that is?" Grim Death attempted to cajole. "What do you blame for this . . . bad luck?"

Under a pile of filthy clothes, Charlie discovered a half-empty bottle of something dark and smiled from ear to ear. "There you are," he said almost lovingly, unscrewing the cap, never taking his eyes from the bottle.

"What caused the bad luck, Charlie?" Grim Death demanded.

He was bringing the bottle to his mouth and stopped, thinking. What he thought about filled him with fear; Grim Death could see it on the drunkard's face.

"The Chamber," he said, and made a face. "There's something about the Chamber that . . ."

The man never got the chance to finish his statement. The window to the right of where he knelt exploded inward in a shower of glass and wooden framing, as something large and stinking of the wild forced its way inside.

Grim Death jumped back as he was pelted by razor-sharp shards of glass, throwing the arm of his trench coat up to protect his face. Whatever it was that had forced its way inside decided to deal with him first, charging forward with a bestial grunt and throwing him savagely back against the far wall as if he were a rag doll.

Charlie was making a mad dash for the door, screaming like a lunatic, when the beast grabbed him. The old man continued to scream, certainly sober now, as the powerful, manlike animal hauled him up from his feet and raised him above its head.

Through bleary eyes, Grim Death watched in horror—finally recognizing the gorilla invader as it savagely brought a still screaming Charlie Huggston down upon its raised, stubby knee, nearly breaking the old man in two.

Grim Death knew this animal—this killer—having seen him that very afternoon calmly reading a newspaper in the Chamber of the Unearthly, but there was nothing calm about him now. Mr. Bippo, still wearing its brown, specially tailored suit, repeatedly slammed Charlie Huggston's body down upon the wood floor to make certain he was dead, and when that was most definitely the case, it tossed the broken body of the man aside.

The gorilla turned its attention to Grim Death, and silently charged at him. There was a look in the beast's eyes, something strangely calm— almost dreamy.

Realizing that he needed to do something or he would share in Charlie Huggston's fate, Grim Death jammed his hands into the pockets of his coat and produced the twin Colt revolvers that had once belonged to his father. Aiming at the moving target, he fired twice, striking the great ape in the shoulder of its suit coat and causing the beast to recoil.

Still, it did not make a sound. It did not roar or cry out in pain. It re-mained eerily silent, with that strange look in its dark gaze.

Grim Death was about to fire again when the gorilla spun away, gal-loping toward the broken window, and leapt outside onto the fire escape and over the side.

Grim Death hesitated for only a moment, weapons aimed at the shat-tered widow. There was a part of him that was terrified, that wanted to leave the blood-spattered room immediately and flee to the safety of his home. But there was another part.

A newer part.

This part overrode the fear, clamping it down and propelling him for-ward to action. This part—this frightening part—had a purpose, a job that it wanted to see through to the end as an agent of Death itself.

Grim Death appeared upon the metal fire escape, peering down into the alley below. There was a truck parked in the alleyway, and the gorilla was making its way toward it.

Seeing an opportunity that he couldn't allow to escape, Grim Death opened fire with his twin pistols, striking the gorilla once again, this time in the leg, causing the animal to fall to the rubbish-strewn street.

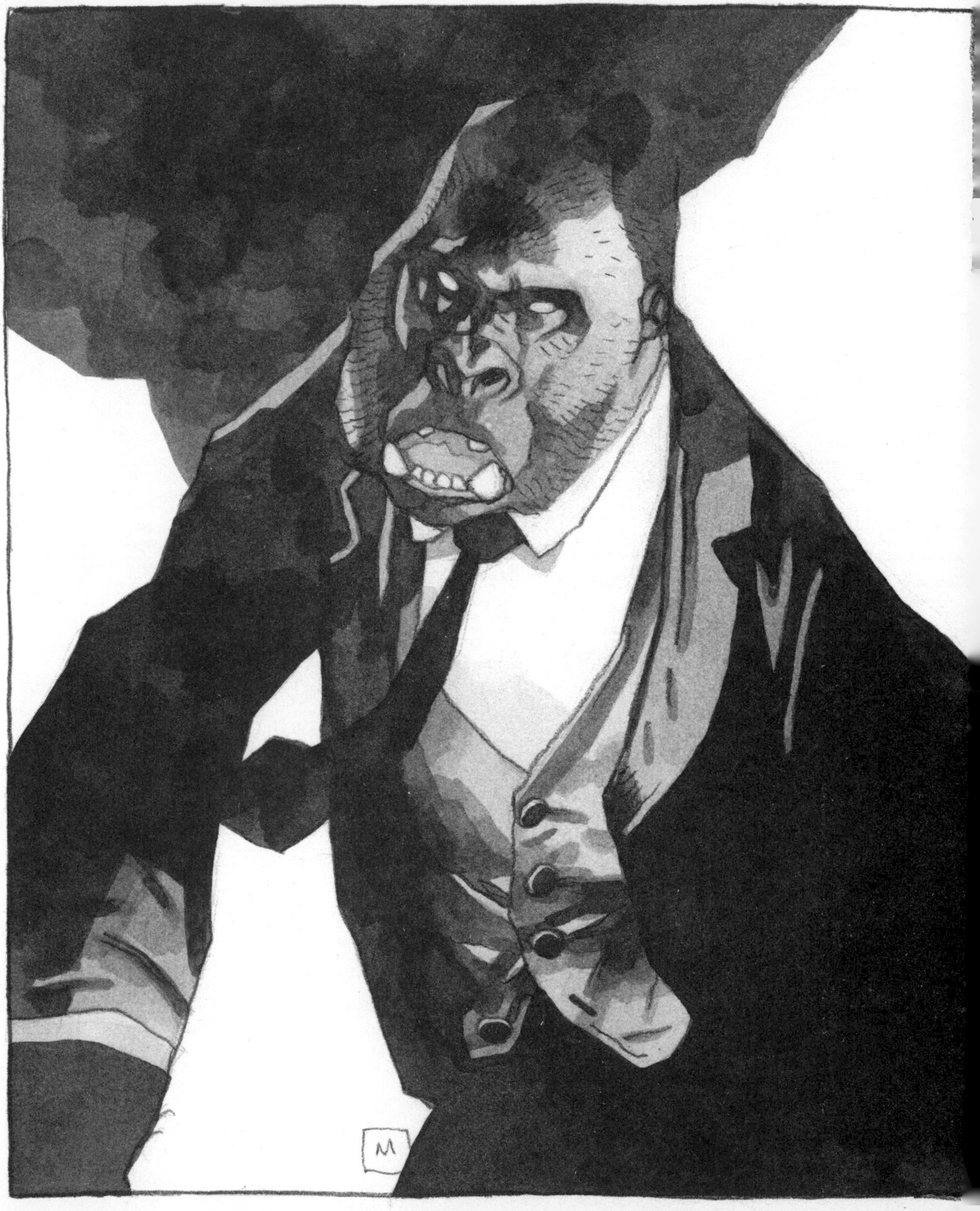

"Stay where you are, beast!" Grim Death ordered as he started down the fire escape, not really sure why he was talking to an animal. He doubted the beast could understand. What he really wanted was to have a talk with whoever was driving that truck.

He was just about to the last flight of metal stairs when the door to the truck swung open, and a large bald man climbed out from the driver's seat.

The Human Dynamo looked up at him, freezing him on the landing. There was that familiar stare again . . . exactly what he had seen when he looked into the eyes of the gentleman gorilla.

Grim Death aimed his weapons.

"You and I will talk," he said, putting on his creepy voice.

The Human Dynamo barely reacted, lumbering toward the fire escape and bending down to place the flat of his hand upon the bottom step.

At first Grim Death had no idea what the man was doing, but then he saw the bluish sparks of electricity leaping from the man's fingertips to the iron of the steps . . .

And felt the numbing jolt of thousands of volts as they coursed through his body, making him perform a kind of crazy jig before pitching forward into space.

Succumbing to the pull of darkness.

Chapter Eighteen

BEFORE:

Bentley awakened from a deathlike sleep, feeling more alive than he had in a very long time.

He wasn't exactly sure how, but he was certain he had been changed. Perhaps something had been taken away—or maybe even added.

But he was different, that he could tell.

He wanted to jump from his bed and find his parents, to tell them that they needn't worry about him being sick anymore, that he was better now and Death would not be coming for him anytime soon.

How long was it before he remembered they were gone? He made it down the hall and halfway down the stairs, where he found Pym standing at the bottom.

"Bentley," the man said, obviously very glad to see him, but something was wrong.

And then the boy remembered the solarium laboratory, and what his parents and Professor Romulus had tried to do—and the end result.

"They're gone," he said, his voice cracking as he descended to the grand foyer in his pajamas, "and they're not coming back."

And he dropped to his knees right there, and Pym came to him, taking him in his arms and promising that he would take care of him no matter what.

There was great comfort in those words, a comfort that he carried with him through those darkest of days.

Bentley had awakened on the day of his parents' burial. Pym insisted that he return to bed at once, to continue his recuperation, but Bentley would hear none of it.

He needed to be there, to say his final good-bye.

The sun was shining brightly but delivered no warmth on the cold winter's day. There was a large turnout, important people in government and industry. They approached him, saying how sorry they were for his loss, but after a while he stopped listening, instead trying to truly understand what had happened that day at the house.

What had Professor Romulus and his parents really done when they'd trapped his friend? And why did he have the sense that things were far from over?

That what his parents and the professor had attempted would have lasting repercussions for him?

It was when he started to see the ghosts that he knew he was right.

———

The first time he saw a ghost was at the cemetery, as the remains of his parents were being laid to rest.

At first he believed them to be other mourners, people who had come to visit the graves of their loved ones and grieve, but then he saw the way they moved, the way they floated above the ground.

It was then that he realized what they were, and actually believed for a little while that he was losing his mind.

But slowly, eventually, he came to understand.

Years passed, and still he continued to see them.

Bentley saw them everywhere he went: riding into the city, sitting beside him during a matinee at the picture show, walking in Central Park. The ghosts were always with him.

But never as much as they were back at Hawthorne House.

It became just a matter of fact that he was never alone. No matter where he went on the grand estate, there was always somebody nearby—haunting him, or whatever it was that they were doing.

And their numbers were growing.

Bentley was never sure exactly what had compelled him one late-summer evening. He'd attempted to communicate with the spirits before, but they did not respond, no matter how hard he tried to get them to interact.

But on that hot summer night, Bentley felt driven. It was getting so bad that no matter where his eyes fell, one of them was there. He needed to know . . . wanted to know . . .

Why? Why were they there . . . Why were they still on the earthly plane? Why were they bothering *him*, of all people?

And on that night, as he sat in one of the estate's drawing rooms, with the French doors open and a warm, late August breeze causing the curtains to flutter, he decided it was time.

He asked them yet again, "Please . . . why?"

Maybe it had something to do with his age, finally being in the right place in life where he could act on their behalf. Or maybe it was because this time he had asked nicely, begged them please. Bentley wasn't sure.

Whatever the reason, they came to him in droves, and he could not hold them back. One after another they flowed at him—touching him with their preternatural coldness—telling him their tales of woe.

And leaving a little bit of themselves behind.

He tried to scream, to cry out, but it was simply too much for him to handle as he sat there inundated with the spirits of the dead and their stories.

As they came at him, some so eager that they forced their way upon him two and three at a time, Bentley Hawthorne saw the connection.

Suddenly he knew why they haunted him, haunted his home.

At last, he understood.

All of them, each and every one, had died as a result of a weapon . . . A pistol, rifle, or bomb had cut their lives short.

A weapon made in the factory of the Hawthorne family munitions business. It all became painfully clear to him as the hundreds, if not thousands, of ghosts crowded the room before him and beyond.

They all had died because of his legacy.

They all had died because of something he was now responsible for.

It took him a while to recover, and in that time he thought many thoughts, and eventually came to a conclusion as to how to make things right.

Exhausted by the experience, Bentley left the study, walking the halls of the great manor until he finally reached his destination, determined to share his decision with the one who had been like family to him since before the death of his parents.

"Pym," he cried, throwing open the door to his manservant's room.

The butler shot up in bed, eyes wide with shock.

"Bentley, what is it?" he asked. "Bad dreams again, sir?" He started to get out of bed, grabbing for his robe. "Let me warm some milk for you, and—"

"No need, Pym," Bentley said proudly, still standing in the doorway. "I've figured it out."

"Figured it out, sir?" Pym asked, slipping into his heavy robe. "What have you—?"

"Why they're here," Bentley said, turning around to see a small legion in the hallway behind him. "Why the ghosts are still with us."

"Ah yes, the ghosts," Pym said. "Still about, I imagine?"

"Yes, yes, they are," Bentley said, watching as some flowed into the butler's room. "And I think I know what I need to do to put them to rest."

"Very good, sir," Pym said. "Now, let's go downstairs to the kitchen where I will prepare you that milk, and maybe . . ."

"I'm going to shut it down, Pym," Bentley said.

"Shut it down, sir?"

Bentley nodded. "All the death it creates . . . all the innocent lives that are lost because of what's made there."

Pym looked at him strangely, the idea of what he was talking about finally permeating. "Are you talking about the factory, sir?" he asked. "Hawthorne Munitions?"

Bentley nodded ever so slowly.

"You can't be serious," Pym said, a look of shock appearing on his tired face.

"I'm completely serious, Pym," Bentley said. "We're shutting it down, so it can't cause any more harm."

"But, sir, I don't think . . ."

"It's already decided," Bentley said with finality, looking at the ghosts that now gathered around him. "Hawthorne Munitions will be closing as soon as possible."

They both stood there in the deafening silence of the early morning, and Bentley wasn't sure if he remembered ever feeling quite so right.

So serene.

"Pym," he said, seeing the butler's face fill with the hope that he'd changed his mind and come to his senses.

"Yes, sir?"

"Could we have pancakes?"

"Pancakes?"

"Yes, I'd like to celebrate."

Chapter Nineteen

Bentley swam in a sea of novocaine, enfolded in its embrace of total numbness.

At first there was no pain, but gradually . . .

"Unggh," he said oh so eloquently as he opened his eyes, looking out through the eyeholes of the skull mask he wore to see the shape of the Human Dynamo pacing stiffly back and forth before him.

Grim Death noticed at once the strangeness in his movements, that weird look that he'd also seen in the gorilla's eyes. It told him something . . .

But what?

The Dynamo lunged, grabbing the mask on Bentley's face and tearing it away. The hairless man then stared with that strange, bottomless gaze, tilting his head from side to side.

And then the Dynamo spoke, and remembering how the hairless man had spoken to himself and Gwendolyn in the Chamber . . . Bentley knew it too was totally wrong.

"You," the Dynamo said. "Something told me you would be trouble when I saw you . . . you and that pretty little girlfriend of yours."

The Dynamo sneered, and his eyes lit with pent-up internal energy, a bluish flash eerily illuminating the sclera of his wide eyes.

Bentley tried to move, to get to the other pocket of his coat for his second gun, but the Dynamo lunged forward, his hand filled with hissing sparks.

"I thought we'd catch both of you at the pretty little thing's house," he growled, snakes of electrical current slithering around the corners of his awful smile.

At first Bentley was confused by the words, but suddenly realized that the Dynamo was talking about Gwendolyn, and that she was in danger.

"But I guess we'll just deal with you here," the Dynamo said as he reached for Bentley. "While my other puppets deal with the girl."

Bentley attempted to move, to squirm away from the electrical man's grasp, but he knew that his actions weren't enough, and prepared for the feeling of thousands of volts coursing through his body, boiling his blood and cooking his internal workings.

His thoughts briefly went to William Tuttle, how he and the circus roustabout were going to be sharing a similar experience . . .

The first bullet ricocheted off the concrete just in front of the electrical man, causing him to hesitate and allowing Bentley the moment he'd been hoping for.

Pym rushed around the corner of the alley waving a pistol of his own, commanding the hairless, electrical man to step back and away.

Bentley was already on the move as the Dynamo raised a hand, the crackling volts of electricity collecting in his palm like a humming swarm of angry bees. He wasn't sure why he did it, but Bentley snatched his skull mask from the bottom of the fire escape stairs and pulled it on over his face before throwing himself wantonly at his foe, connecting with the bald man's midsection, driving him back and to the floor of the alley.

The Dynamo hadn't even a moment to react before Grim Death had pulled his other Colt .45 from the pocket of his coat, and even though there was a powerful part of him that wanted to kill this man, he was able to restrain his bloodlust, instead brutally striking the man's wide forehead with the butt of his pistol, driving his bald head down onto the ground.

"Stay down," Grim Death growled, looming above him with gun in hand. "You will tell me . . . things."

And that was when Bentley noticed something incredibly strange. The Dynamo was blinking his eyes furiously, almost as if he was waking up from a dream.

"Bentley," Pym said coming up alongside him.

"Don't call me that," he snapped. "Grim Death . . . when I'm like this, I'm Grim Death."

"Of course you are," Pym replied coldly. "Maybe next time I'll just stay in the car and let Grim Death handle the whole thing."

He ignored the butler's anger, choosing instead to focus upon the strangeness happening below him.

The Dynamo stiffened as he looked around, his eyes growing steadily wider with disbelief. As he gazed upon the skulled visage looming above him, the look turned to sheer, undiluted terror.

"Where am I?" the Dynamo asked fearfully. "What's going on?"

He tried to get up, but Grim Death pointed the barrel of his gun at the Dynamo's face, forcing him back to the ground.

"Who sent you here?" Grim Death demanded.

The Dynamo's mouth worked, but little that he said was comprehensible. He was scared beyond reason, and Grim Death could see it. It was all in the eyes: the electrical man's eyes were completely different than they had been moments earlier.

"Please," the Dynamo begged. He started to roll over in an attempt to curl himself into a ball when he saw the injured animal.

The gorilla lay shivering just beyond the truck.

"Bippo?" the Dynamo called out. "Is that you, boy? What in God's name is going on?"

The man started to crawl toward his friend, and Grim Death allowed it.

"Yes, what is going on here, Bent—Grim Death?" Pym asked.

Grim Death wasn't sure exactly, but something was beginning to slowly, inexplicably take shape.

"You!" Grim Death barked, striding over to the man, who now cradled the injured gorilla.

"He's hurt," the Dynamo said. "We need to get him some help."

"Never mind that," Grim Death commanded. "You say you don't remember any of this . . . If that's the case, what's the last thing you *do* remember?" He aimed his pistol again for effect.

The Dynamo was still afraid—and why wouldn't he be, with a skull-faced figure holding a Colt .45 on him?

"The last thing I . . . I remember?" he stammered. "I was closing up for the night . . . I was closing up the Chamber." He paused, remembering.

"What?" Grim Death demanded, jabbing the weapon at him.

"That's when I heard the singing," the Dynamo said. "The singing . . . and then I don't remember a thing."

The gorilla moaned fitfully, and the Dynamo held him tighter.

"You gotta help him," the man said. "Please . . . he's hurt."

Grim Death ignored the man's pleas, turning toward his accomplice and his transportation.

"We need to get home," he said, already on the move to where he remembered the car was parked.

"But . . ." Pym began.

"Gwendolyn might be in danger."

———

Slumping in the backseat of the car, he pulled the skull mask from his face and laid it on the seat beside him.

Bentley sighed, feeling the beginning of exhaustion brought on by his massive adrenaline surge back in the alley.

"Would you mind explaining what happened back there?" Pym demanded from the driver's seat.

Bentley looked toward the rearview mirror, at his butler's bulging eyes.

"Things have just begun to come into focus," Bentley said cryptically, his brain already putting the bizarre picture together from the scattered puzzle pieces of the story.

"And what the hell is that supposed to mean?" Pym cursed, pounding the steering wheel in his frustration. "A man with electricity leaking from his body . . . a gorilla, Bentley? Really? A gorilla in a suit? If I hadn't seen it with my own two eyes, smelled the scent of gunpowder . . . If I didn't still feel the weight of the pistol in my pocket, I would think this all some sort of fever-induced nightmare."

"I know, Pym," Bentley said, attempting to rouse himself, his eyes drifting down to the mask on the seat beside him—staring up at him.

Did it just whisper for me to put it on?

"But this is the world my life has become since Death itself . . ."

"No!" Pym said, and again he pounded the steering wheel as he sped down the darkened back roads toward the highway, and home. "It is not your world—it is *our* world," Pym explained his frustration. "No matter what you think your fate to be, my being by your side should always be a given. I swore an oath to your father and mother a very long time ago when they brought a sickly baby, weighing no more than three pounds—who was never expected to see his first birthday—home from the hospital."

"I didn't mean to insult your dedication to me, and . . ."

"Don't interrupt, sir," Pym snapped. "It's rude."

Bentley fell silent, allowing the butler his rant.

"But live you did, and I would like to think I had some small part in that."

Pym paused, and Bentley wasn't sure if he should attempt to explain himself further or . . .

"You are a crucial part of my life, Bentley, and as much as you might struggle with it, I am part of yours," Pym continued. "You and I are intertwined, and I'm afraid this is how it's going to be."

Pym went silent, continuing to drive far above the speed limit on their journey back.

"May I speak?" Bentley asked quietly.

"Yes," Pym answered, clearing his throat. "I believe I'm finished."

"Would you care to know what I'm thinking in regard to this current situation?"

"I thought you'd never ask."

"My suspicion about something being wrong at Doctor Nocturne's Circus of Unearthly Wonderment is a correct one. I believe there's someone, or something, capable of controlling the minds of those in the employ of the Circus, and I believe that it is connected somehow to the Chamber of the Unearthly, where our assailants tonight worked and where William Tuttle last remembered being before the murder of Tianna Hoops."

"Mind control?" Pym said. "Normally I would consider such a thing nonsense, but you were attacked tonight by a man who shot electricity from his hands and a gorilla in a three-piece suit."

"I certainly was."

"And Miss Gwendolyn?" Pym asked. "How does she fit into all this?"

"By being unlucky enough to have been with me when I asked too many questions today at the circus."

"So you think they may have sent others to silence her in case . . ."

"That's exactly what I believe."

There were no further words, just the sound of the car's steady acceleration as they raced to the Marks estate.

Chapter Twenty

BEFORE:

The ghosts were still there.

He found it odd that they hadn't accepted his offering and moved on. In fact, there seemed to be more than there had been before.

Bentley didn't understand; he'd done what he'd promised, closing Hawthorne Munitions' doors as a way of offering up penance for being somewhat responsible for their untimely passing.

But the ghosts of the dead remained, meandering about as if they'd grown used to their earthbound environment.

Perhaps closing the factory had not been enough, he thought, wondering what more he could do to somehow appease the multitude that haunted him, and his home.

Their number grew continuously, and he wondered what would happen when all the space in the Hawthorne mansion was taken up.

And that was when Bentley had the most wonderful idea.

If the ghosts of those killed by weaponry produced by the Hawthorne family business insisted on remaining about, haunting him, he would give them their own space. And perhaps, once they got tired of his generous act, they would feel they could move on to the next phase of their journey.

Pym had not accepted the news well, believing that the young man had truly lost his faculties after the death of his parents. But Bentley had been insistent, hiring the best architects and contractors to add on to the already sprawling mansion and surrounding land, even going so far as to contact Europe's greatest psychic medium, Madame Marie-Claire Cornellion, to help him formulate and design what might be best for the spirits he hoped to house.

Madame Cornellion was specific in her ideas, the designs strange and confusing to the architects and builders: stairs that led up to solid walls, doors that opened onto rooms so small that a mouse might have found them cramped. Rooms that were not created for human occupancy.

But were perfect for ghosts.

And as the new wings were completed, and the places where the spirits could reside were finished, what Bentley had planned for the restless dead came to be.

The ghosts gravitated to their new dwellings, and a kind of balance appeared to have been struck. The ghosts remained, but they seemed to enjoy their new residences. Madame Cornellion even returned for a visit to see how he and the spirits were making out, and was quite impressed by how well the restless dead were adjusting to their new homes.

But she sensed in Bentley something wild—something untamed that she could not identify, and left the young man with a cryptic warning to approach the future cautiously, that something was coming that would change Bentley's life dramatically.

Pym scoffed at the predictions of the future, and then grew hopeful that perhaps it meant that Bentley might meet somebody special, settle down, and give up the foolish belief that wandering spirits haunted their ever-growing estate.

Bentley knew how his friend and manservant felt, but it did little to change his views of the ghosts, which he'd grown rather fond of. Madame Cornellion's warning was always at the back of his mind, peeking around a darkened corner of his consciousness, but as the years passed and nothing dramatic occurred, he grew less and less concerned.

It wasn't long after his twenty-second birthday that his destiny came calling.

He had been reading in the burnt-out remains of the solarium. For some reason, even with all the construction workers about, adding to the estate, he did not make it a point to have that place restored. He could not quite identify why he liked it the way it was. A reminder of an event that had changed his life.

And altered his world.

He was about to learn by exactly how much.

Sitting in the charred and blackened space reading through the latest work by T. S. Elliot, he noticed the apparition of a woman walking through a wall on the far side of the room. It didn't faze him in the least, barely causing him to look up from his reading, for ghosts were commonplace in Hawthorne House.

He sensed her presence close by, a cold air wafting toward him, and looked up to see her standing there.

"Hello," he said, not expecting any notice of his greeting, for that was the way of the ghosts in his home.

But her eyes focused upon him, and he felt a sudden jolt of surprise as he realized she had heard him.

She was an older woman, dressed in what appeared to be a flowing blue nightgown. There was a nasty laceration on the side of her head, an ectoplasmic bleed draining out into the air around her.

Bentley stared into her eyes and felt her looking back at him.

"Are you lost?" he asked her, thinking that maybe she had lost her way and needed to be shown the places in the sprawling house that she could go.

She continued to stare at him, waiting.

"Do you need something?" he asked her, and in her gaze he swore he found that she did. "Do you need something . . . of me?"

Bentley wasn't sure why he did it, but he found himself rising to his feet and walking toward the ghost of the woman. His eyes were drawn to the leaking wound on the side of her head. He lifted a hand up toward it, allowing the ghostly drainage to waft around it.

There was a sudden tug upon his fingers, an unknown current that pulled his hand toward the woman's head and into her ghostly skull.

And that was when he saw it. Her life, as well as her death.

Bentley stood transfixed as images of the woman's existence flashed before his mind's eye, staccato flashes of everything that made her who she was, leading up to the final, horrific moment when . . .

She had been murdered. Her skull bashed in, in some violent act. The vision was blurry, and he couldn't quite make it out, or the person responsible, but he saw enough to know it was murder.

And he knew deep down in his gut that whoever was responsible had not yet been brought to justice.

Bentley pulled his hand back from within the apparition's ghostly skull, his fingers numb as if he'd placed them in icy water. He stared at the woman, who stared back intensely, beckoning.

Compelling him to act.

But how?

"They're always pretty insistent."

A strange, croaking voice suddenly spoke from so close, it practically came from inside Bentley's skull. The young man nearly leapt from his skin.

"Who's there?" he demanded, clutching his frozen hand to his chest as he looked about the burned-out room for signs of the intruder. "Show yourself!"

There came a fluttering of wings, and from out of a patch of deep darkness flew a large, black bird: a raven, to be more specific.

Bentley watched the animal as it touched down on a section of charred mantel across from him.

"Happy?" it asked, tilting its head and fixing him in one of its dark, copper-colored eyes.

Bentley looked around again, expecting to find a person.

"There's no one else here besides you and me . . . well, and that poor soul standing beside you," the bird informed him.

Bentley looked from the raven to the ghostly woman.

"You can see her?"

"Clear as day," the bird answered. *"The name's Roderick, by the way, and now that it's time, I've been sent to offer you some guidance."*

"It's time?" Bentley asked. "What do you mean, it's time?"

"It's time for you to pay up," Roderick said. *"It's time for you to do the job that's been assigned to you."*

"Job? I don't know of any job?"

"Seriously?" The bird tilted his head from left to right. *"You didn't think that after what your folks and that mad scientist pulled a few years back there wouldn't be repercussions?"*

"Repercussions?" Bentley repeated. "My parents perished in that incident, and Professor Romulus . . . he went missing, as if he fell off the face of the planet."

"And you thought you were going to get off scot-free?" Roderick asked, leaning forward from the mantel.

"I didn't . . ."

"*But you did,*" the raven corrected. "*You're alive, aren't you?*"

Bentley stared. "I . . ." he began, then stopped, not having a clue as to where this bizarre discussion was going.

"*You're alive because of what my boss saw in you,*" Roderick said.

"Your boss?"

"*That's right,*" the bird said, starting to waddle up and down the blackened wood mantel. "*Normally he would have just taken everybody in the room, there one minute, gone the next, but he saw potential in you . . . something that he could use to make up for what your parents had done.*"

"Your boss," Bentley began. "Who . . . ?"

"*Seriously, kid?*" Roderick asked. "*C'mon, nobody is that dumb.*"

The bird made a strange sound that might have been a laugh.

"*The boss thinks it's time for you to pay the piper,*" Roderick continued, "*and he sent me along to help guide you down the proper path.*"

Bentley finally understood about whom the bird was talking—his boss—and was terrified. He'd seen the faces of the entity that his parents and Romulus had attempted to trap. One was that of a beautiful little girl, and the other a ragged thing of rage and nightmare.

Bentley had known them both, and had always suspected that it had left a little bit of itself behind when it had embraced him.

"The proper path," he said. "I have no idea what that even means."

"*You've been given a gift,*" Roderick said, "*the ability to see those who have left their physical bodies behind in death. But with that gift comes a job.*"

Bentley found himself staring at the ghostly old woman, realizing that she was there for a very specific reason.

She was indeed there for him, and for what he could do for her.

"Tell me about this job," he said, a feeling of dread gripping his heart. "Tell me what Death wants me to do."

"*Some of those who have died were taken before it was their time,*" Roderick said. "*Lives snuffed out by others who do not respect the sanctity of life.*" The raven fluttered his wings, puffing up his ebony feathers. "*It will be your purpose . . . your job, to avenge those who have had their lives so brutally torn away.*"

"How?" Bentley asked.

"*They'll show you what they remember,*" the bird explained. "*The act that stole away their precious lives . . . and you will be as Death, and reap payment from those responsible . . . or something like that."*

"I will be Death?" Bentley asked, incredulously.

The bird nodded. *"But not just any Death. You won't be gentle, or loving, or quiet. You will be the Death that they deserve."*

"A murderer's Death," Bentley said, feeling something totally unnatural awaken in the pit of his soul.

"A grim Death," Roderick said, and began to squawk noisily, loud enough to wake the dead.

Chapter Twenty-one

Gwendolyn had been thinking quite a bit about the sickly young man with the pale skin and nervous disposition.

Why, she hadn't a clue. There was just something about Bentley Hawthorne that she couldn't quite put her finger on.

Was she attracted to him? Was that it? She couldn't say. It wasn't as simple as like or dislike . . . there was just something unnamable that drew her to him.

She'd been practicing writing her married name—if she and Bentley ever managed to somehow, miraculously come together—in one of her notepads, *Gwendolyn Anne Hawthorne*, when she first heard the sound.

Gwendolyn set her pen down and listened.

Her father was out at the club, attending one of his frequent work dinners, and not wanting to be bothered, she had sent the help home for the evening.

It was supposed to be a quiet night of reflection on why she was so attracted to somebody who obviously wasn't attracted to her—in fact, she wasn't even sure if Bentley liked girls. She wasn't sure if he liked anybody, or anything—except for his butler. It was obvious that the two of them were close.

But it seemed that a quiet night wasn't in the cards.

There was somebody moving around downstairs, there was no doubt in her mind, and she quickly set her notepad and pen down on her bed and kicked off her shoes so she could move silently across the room.

Gwendolyn carefully opened her door and stuck her head out into the hall to listen. There was most definitely somebody, or a group of some-bodies, moving around on the first floor below.

Not hesitating for an instant, she darted from her room and silently pad-ded down the corridor to her father's. Turning the knob, she quickly en-tered the room and went right to the closet. Gwendolyn knew where her father, an avid hunter for as long as she could recall, kept his favorite gun, as well as its ammunition. Grabbing the hunting rifle from the wall rack in the walk-in closet, she quickly rummaged for bullets. She listened for sounds of the intruders coming closer as she loaded the gun. There was a part of her that wanted to lock the door of her father's bedroom and hide herself away, but there was another part—the part her father often said he associated with her deceased mother—that was infuriated by someone dar-ing to enter her home uninvited. Anyone rude enough to do such a thing deserved what they got.

With a surge of anger, she walked toward the door, rifle in hand. Silently she cursed her father for not being home, and at the same time thanked him for the early morning pheasant-hunting sessions during which he'd taught her how to use a gun.

Gwendolyn stepped out into the dark hallway, heading for the stairs, but stopped with a gasp as she saw the figure ascending. She raised her gun. "I'd stop right there, if I were you," she warned.

The figure continued to slowly ascend, gradually stepping into a patch of moonlight streaming in from the high windows in the foyer.

"I'm warning you," she yelled, stepping forward for a closer shot and aiming down the length of the barrel at her target.

The figure entered the moonlight, and she felt her heart turn to ice.

"Christ on a bicycle," she mumbled, not believing her eyes.

The clown was holding a knife and smiling as he continued to climb. Never a fan of clowns to begin with, she thought he was one of the most terrifying she had ever seen, with bright red hair sticking up from either side of his bald white head, enormous red-encircled lips, and huge teeth that would have given Seabiscuit a run for his money.

And he was almost at the top of the stairs.

"You thought you were so pretty," the clown said, in a strange, mono-tone voice. "You were trying to show me how pretty you were, weren't you? Rubbing my face in the fact that you had a cute boyfriend . . . Well, I had a cute boyfriend, too."

Gwendolyn backed up, still aiming the gun, but the clown's words confused her. He was speaking as though they'd met before, and nothing could have been further from the truth.

"Don't come any closer," she warned the clown.

A creak from the other end of the corridor caused her to take her gaze from the approaching nightmare.

Coming from her room was another nightmare: another clown, only much smaller—a dwarf.

"Not so pretty now that you're scared," said the small clown, in that same weird monotone. He was holding what looked like a meat cleaver as he waddled down the corridor from her room.

Gwendolyn didn't know whom to aim at first, her brain in a total panic over the nightmare she was facing.

"Where's your boyfriend now?" asked the dwarf clown as he switched the cleaver from one white-gloved hand to the other.

"Thought he'd be here with you," finished the other clown, who had reached the top of the stairs. "No matter. We'll wait here after I've finished with you so we don't miss him."

The clown at the top of the stairs lunged without warning, and she aimed the best that she could at the moving target, firing a shot but missing the multicolored nightmare coming at her.

The dwarf charged silently, and she was able to fire another shot, striking the tiny figure in the leg and causing him to collapse to the hallway floor. The other clown struck her head-on as she attempted to bring her rifle around again. The grinning attacker pushed her back against the hallway wall with incredible force, causing her to drop the rifle.

The clown smiled, and she found herself looking into his vague, glassy eyes as he brought the knife up to show her.

"I'm gonna carve that pretty face off your skull," he said, as she struggled to be free of his clutches, finally slamming her knee up between the clown's legs and connecting with his family jewels.

The clown didn't even seem to feel it. He leaned in closer, bringing the knife blade up toward her cheek.

There was no mistaking the sound of the front door slamming open, and she thought for sure it was her father, returned home to save her.

The clown paused to look toward the noise, and she made her move, pushing her attacker away with all her might and running toward the banister.

"A little help up here!" Gwendolyn screamed, peering down into the foyer, desperate for a friendly face.

The face she saw looked anything but friendly.

It was a skull.

What was that about a quiet evening?

———

Bentley hoped he wasn't too late.

Pym had stopped the car in a patch of shadow not far from the Marks estate so they wouldn't be seen. That would be all they needed, for Gwendolyn to see Bentley wearing the guise of Grim Death. Her reporter's hunger for news would be voracious.

"Be careful, sir!" Pym had said as Grim Death had leapt from the car and run down the long driveway toward the darkened house.

He ran past a beat-up old truck hidden in the shadow alongside the mansion. That wasn't good—the chances of the attackers being inside the home seemed even more certain.

Grim Death headed directly for the front door; something inside him, gnawing in his gut like a hungry weasel, told him that subtlety and stealth would be out of the question. Gwendolyn would be in need of help immediately.

Guns in hand, he reached the door, pulling back his leg and delivering a tremendous kick to the center of the double doors. They flew open, and he heard a familiar voice cry out, "A little help up here!"

He looked up to the second floor to see the young woman staring down at him, her expression going from one of supreme relief to one of complete horror.

He was going to reassure her, to tell her that everything was going to be all right, but a clown wielding a butcher knife appeared from behind her and instead he was forced to violence.

The clown was going to cut Gwendolyn's throat, and even though there was a chance that she might be hit, Grim Death had no choice but to act. He aimed his Colt and fired at the clown, striking the white-faced nightmare in the hand that held the knife in an explosion of crimson.

Grim Death was already on the move, running up the stairs, ready to fire again if necessary. What he found shocked him, stopped him at the top of the stairs.

"Miss Marks, don't!" he warned her.

Gwendolyn had picked up a rifle from somewhere and was aiming at the clown who clutched his bloody hand as he knelt upon the floor. Grim Death also noticed that there was another, smaller clown rocking to and fro in pain as a puddle of blood formed on the expensive carpet beneath him.

Suddenly ignoring the clowns, Gwendolyn took aim at him.

"Who the hell are you?" she demanded.

He lowered his pistol to put her at ease, hoping that she wouldn't take it as an invitation to shoot.

"I'm a friend," he said. "I've come to help."

"You look about as much of a friend as these two," she said, moving the barrel of the hunting rifle down to the clown with the damaged hand, and then at the dwarf, before pointing it back at him.

"If I was with them, would I have shot my own teammate?" he asked, hoping that she would see he meant her no harm.

"I should finish them both off," she said with a snarl, and he watched as tears began to glisten on her flushed cheeks.

"I wouldn't do that." He stepped closer, but stopped as she again aimed the rifle at his chest.

"That's close enough," she said. "And why shouldn't I shoot them both dead? They came into my house and tried to hurt me."

"Because I don't believe they know what they're doing," he said. "I believe that they're being controlled by some strange, unknown force."

He watched her face twist up in confusion.

"What are you saying?" Gwendolyn asked. "That they're not in their right minds?"

"Something like that," Grim Death said.

And as if on cue, the clown at her feet sprang up with a scream, and still clutching his bloody hand to his chest, pushed her out of the way and ran to his partner.

Gwendolyn fell back, but still held on to her gun, raising it up to aim and fire. Grim Death would not see an innocent life taken; he ran across the hallway and pushed the barrel down so she fired into the floor.

"What the heck!" Gwendolyn bellowed angrily.

The larger clown picked up the smaller like a mother cradling her child, and ran toward the railing, jumping over the side.

"Holy crap, they've killed themselves," Gwendolyn said as she and Grim Death rushed to the railing.

The clowns had landed awkwardly, but had survived the fall, both now running and limping grotesquely, leaving a dark crimson trail of blood as they made their way toward the open doors to escape.

"They're getting away," Gwendolyn yelled.

"They are no longer a concern," Grim Death said. "The control over them has been broken."

He felt the hard barrel of the rifle poke him in the back.

"Give me one good reason why I shouldn't hold you for the police," she said.

Grim Death slowly turned. The gun remained pointed at his heart.

"Because there is no time for that," he said. "A ghost's cries for justice must be answered."

She looked at him hard, and so that she did not see too much he lowered the brim of his hat.

"The innocent dead must be avenged."

"Who the heck are you?" Gwendolyn asked, lowering the rifle, attempting to move closer to him.

Grim Death evaded her approach, heading for the stairs.

"The guilty will evade punishment no longer," he said as he descended the steps.

He could feel her eyes on his back.

"You didn't answer my question," she called to him.

He stopped in the doorway and turned to look up at her.

"Who are you?"

"I am the punishment that the guilty deserve," he said before darting out the door to lose himself in the shadows of the night.

"I am Grim Death."

━━━

"I thought I heard gunfire, and then a truck sped away from the property," Pym said as Grim Death slid into the backseat of the car. "I was tempted to give chase, but . . ."

"There's no need, Pym," Grim Death said as he pulled the skull mask over his head to reveal Bentley beneath. "I'm very aware of where they're going."

Bentley paused, feeling a sudden exhaustion begin to wash over him, but he did not—could not—succumb. There was still work to be done, the murdered innocent avenged.

And perhaps an execution averted.

"It's where we're going," Bentley said. "We still have a murderer to punish for their sins."

"The circus," Pym said.

Bentley nodded.

"The circus."

Chapter Twenty-two

BEFORE:

The dead woman's ghost remained, going everywhere he did.

Bentley was used to the dead—they were always a presence at Hawthorne house—but this was different. This ghost wanted him—haunted him.

And he wasn't quite sure what he should do.

The bird, Roderick, had told him what Death had intended for him, but what did that mean? How was he to avenge those whose lives had been stolen too soon?

It totally perplexed him, but the constant presence of the old woman's spirit was beginning to wear on him.

"Maybe you could tell me?" Bentley said to the ghost. He was in the kitchen in search of a glass of warm milk. Pym had gone to the market, leaving Bentley alone to fend for himself, which was fine. He wasn't an invalid, despite what his manservant thought.

He took the glass bottle from the icebox under the watchful eyes of the ghostly woman, whose head continued to bleed into the ether.

"I know I'm supposed to help you, but how, exactly?" Bentley asked. He found a pot after a brief search of the cabinets, poured some milk into it, and placed it on one of the stove burners.

"Shouldn't I go to the police?" he asked, putting the bottle of milk back in the icebox. "That's what my rational mind tells me to do. To go to the police and inform them of your murder."

The ghost continued to watch him mournfully, blood leaking from the break in her skull.

He wasn't sure how long he watched her, his eyes following the trails of ethereal blood as it drifted into the air to gradually dissipate. It was a sudden hissing that finally broke his trance, and he spun around toward the stove to see that the milk had completely boiled away.

"Damn it all!" he hissed, instinctively grabbing the pot handle—and burning himself on the superheated metal.

"Gahhhhhhh!" he cried out as the pot dropped from his injured hand and crashed to the floor.

Bentley experienced a surge of anger and frustration, turning his ferocious stare on the hovering ghost.

"What do you want from me?" he screamed. "Do you want me to solve your murder for you? Is that it? Do you want me to bring your murderer to justice?"

He went to the sink, turning on the cold water and running his blistering hand beneath the numbing torrent.

"I'm sorry, but have you given me a good look?" he asked, turning away from the sink to address the ghost again. "Do I look like I'm capable of avenging anyone?"

The ghost was suddenly gone, and it startled him not to see her floating there. She had become a constant reminder of late.

"Where . . . ?" he began, looking around.

The clicking sound startled him, and he looked to see the cellar door slowly swinging open as if touched by a gentle breeze.

There was not a hint of wind in the kitchen, not even the slightest draft.

He stared at the open door, noticing a faint flickering luminescence as if something were attempting to entice him closer.

It worked. He turned off the water and wrapped his blistered hand in a dishtowel as he cautiously walked toward the cellar door. He peered down into the darkness, catching sight of a glowing shape as it disappeared around the corner, moving deeper into the darkness of the cellar beyond.

Bentley reached out to put the light on, and found that it did not work.

It was almost enough to keep him out of the cellar.

Almost.

He started down the steps carefully, worried that he might stumble and fall and break something fragile. These had been concerns for the majority of his life and were hard to forget, even though he'd miraculously regained his health since the incident that had claimed his parents.

Again he thought of Roderick, and what the raven had told him of Death's desires for him, and shuddered.

At the bottom of the stairs he waited, allowing his eyes to adjust to the gloom. It was larger down here than he remembered, only having been down as far as mid-steps, his father having expressly forbidden him from venturing any farther.

Bentley saw the greenish glow at the far end of the room and found himself moving toward it. He walked carefully, not wanting to smash his shin on anything hidden in his path, but managed to get quite far, the greenish glow seemingly always just out of reach.

"Hello? Is that you?" he asked, curious if it was the old woman leading him, a response to his harsh words earlier in the kitchen. "Do you want me to follow you?"

The ground beneath his feet changed from concrete to loose dirt and rock, and he knew he had come to the farthest reaches of the cellar.

Bentley reached out in the darkness, his hands brushing against damp stone walls. He blinked furiously as his eyes attempted to adjust and find the source that had brought him down there.

Placing the flat of his hand against the wall, he felt his way farther and farther down toward the end of the vast, unfinished basement. Cobwebs stroked his face in the darkness and he reacted with revulsion, pulling the tickling strands away. Hand still pressed against the rough rock of the wall, he stopped, searching the void before him. Finally, ready to give up, Bentley had started to turn back toward the stairs when he saw the light again.

A green orb danced in the air, and for a moment he considered whether perhaps he'd been following some sort of bug. But by the way that it hung there, he knew it was waiting for him.

"Is that you?" he called out to the orb. "Give me some sort of sign that it is, and that you want me to follow you."

In response, the orb went dark, returning the vastness ahead to total blackness. He'd been moving again, and stopped, and again considered that he might have been mistaken about the green orb's origin. Then there was a sudden flash of orange light, as if someone had struck a match, and he saw that a lantern resting on the dirt floor ahead had been lit. The light was warm, dispelling the deep pockets of shadow around it, and Bentley quickly made his way toward it.

The flame danced within the oil lamp's glass enclosure, and he wondered how it had been lit. Bending down, he picked it up and saw that he had reached the end of the vast cellar space, the light from the lantern illuminating a craggy rock wall before him.

"All right," he said, hefting the lantern and moving it around to light the end of the basement. "Now what am I supposed to do?"

The orb had returned, floating before an area of the wall as if trying to capture his attention. Bentley brought the lantern closer to examine where the green circle of unearthly light danced. From what he could see it was all rough rock, and he reached out to touch it.

The rock moved in with a click, and a section of the wall silently swung open into a tunnel.

"Dear God," Bentley said, not believing his eyes. He held the lantern aloft and saw that the tunnel went on for a great distance, gradually descending up ahead.

The green orb beckoned for him to follow, and he did.

The tunnel went on for miles, and he came to realize that the lantern he used to light his way must have been used by somebody else as they made this very same journey.

But who?

He again thought of his father's masquerade parties, and how the liquor—which was illegal at the time—had seemed to flow like water. Maybe this was how the unlawful drink had made its way into their home?

The passage hewn into the rock went on, and Bentley wondered where it would eventually take him. In his mind he suddenly saw a cartoonish image of Hell, a red-suited and bearded Satan waiting for him behind a desk, smiling at his approach.

Bentley stifled a shudder as he continued on his journey.

He had no idea how long he'd walked, time having somehow lost cohesion the farther he traveled, and had begun to worry that perhaps this wasn't the best of ideas, when the passage suddenly came to an end at a large, metal door.

Lifting his lantern, he illuminated the heavy obstruction, and reached out to the door's handle, giving it a solid tug.

Locked.

He pulled on it again just to be sure, and yielded the same result.

"Now what?" he muttered, frustrated that he might have traveled all this way for nothing.

But the green orb remained before him and seemed to be growing in size.

"Do you have a way in?" Bentley asked as the swirling sphere of greenish light more than doubled in size and began to take on a strange, almost human form.

He gasped as the apparition became more defined, and he knew at once who it was who now manifested before him.

"Father," Bentley whispered as the specter took shape.

The emotions that he suddenly experienced were overwhelming, and he threw himself toward the spirit shape, to put his arms around him, but alas . . .

Bentley went through the man's form, feeling a deep coldness that permeated to core of his bones.

Sadly, Bentley turned back to the ghost.

"I'm sorry," he said, attempting to hide the quaver in his voice. "I know how you felt about public displays of affection."

The ghost watched him with unblinking eyes.

"Are you . . . are you well?" Bentley asked.

The ghost continued to stare.

"And Mother?"

The ghost of his father showed nothing, turning away from him and passing through the metal door.

"Wait!" Bentley cried, going after the ghost, but coming abruptly to a stop when he could go no farther. He stood staring at the metal obstruction, and was seriously considering knocking on the door when he heard the door's locking mechanism click loudly like a gunshot, making him jump back.

Bentley reached out, taking hold of the cold metal handle, and gave it a tug. The door swung open with a mournful creak, and Bentley found his father waiting for him on the other side.

He was surprised by how happy he was to find his father still there.

"I thought you'd gone," Bentley said, passing through the doorway into another short corridor.

His father turned and floated away, turning sharply at the end of the passage. Bentley followed, curious as to where he would find himself now.

Around the corner, Bentley found his father passing through yet another door, with the sound of it being unlocked following immediately after. Bentley pulled that door open as well, and was startled to see that it led out onto a metal catwalk. Carefully he stepped out onto the walkway, and the realization hit him.

He lifted the lantern, illuminating what he could and confirming his suspicions. He knew where he was.

He was at the shuttered Hawthorne Munitions factory.

The light barely touched the floor below, but Bentley could see the numerous crates stacked about and wondered what they might contain. He believed the building had been emptied of all product and machinery weeks after the factory's closure, all of it sold for scrap or to rival businesses.

His father waited for him on the floor below.

Bentley found the stairs and started down.

"What is all this?" he asked the ghost of the man who had sired him. Abraham just drifted there, his face lax and emotionless. "Is there something you want me to see here?"

"*We thought it would be appropriate for him to be the one who brought you here*," a familiar voice said, startling Bentley.

He raised the lantern to illuminate the form of Roderick, perched atop one of the wooden crates. The bird flapped his wings and ruffled his feathers.

"How did you get in here?" Bentley asked.

"*I have my ways*," the raven said, looking around. "*So you were asking how you were going to go about doing your new job.*"

Bentley approached one of the crates.

"What's in the boxes?" he asked.

"*The tools of your trade*," Roderick announced.

Bentley found a crowbar nearby and set the lantern down upon the floor. He went to work on the crate lid, prying it open with a whining creak. Discarding the lid, he retrieved the lantern and held it over the contents of the box.

"Guns," Bentley said, looking at the contents.

"*All kinds*," Roderick said. "*Rifles, pistols, and even some explosives.*"

"But I thought all of this stuff was removed when—"

"*It was your father's secret stash . . . prototypes and product kept off the books just in case there was a little bit of money to be made on the side, if you know what I mean.*"

Bentley looked to his father.

"But that's . . . illegal."

"*Yeah,*" the bird croaked. "*Your father was no angel . . . were ya, Abraham?*"

The ghost just silently floated in the air.

"Stop that," Bentley demanded. "He is . . . he *was* a good man."

"*You keep telling yourself that, kid,*" Roderick said. "*The guns and such will give you the means to extract payment that's due.*"

"Payment due?" Bentley repeated. He reached down into the crate and slowly removed a pistol. "You mean kill, don't you?"

The bird cocked his head. "*If you want to think of it in such crude terms. Certainly.*"

Bentley looked at the Colt .45 in his hand, feeling the weight of its potential for death.

"I've never . . ." he began, suddenly repulsed by the object he held. He tossed it to the floor. "I couldn't possibly do that . . . There has to be another way." He looked to the bird. "There has to be another way."

Roderick flapped his wings. "*Afraid not, kid.*"

"But I don't even know how to fire a gun," Bentley complained, "never mind kill somebody. Maybe I'm just not the person that your boss—"

"*Our boss,*" the bird interrupted.

"All right, our boss . . . maybe I'm not the person that our boss needs."

"*No, you're just the guy,*" the raven confirmed. "*You just need a little bit of training, is all.*" He turned his head toward Abraham's ghost.

The spirit reacted as if to some unspoken command, drifting toward his son.

"What . . . what is he doing?" Bentley asked, beginning to back up as the ghost increased his speed.

"*He's gonna teach you a few things,*" Roderick said as the ghost reached out to take hold of Bentley's face, his fingers disappearing inside the terrified young man's skull.

And teach him his father did.

Chapter Twenty-three

There was a flurry of activity as the circus was slowly taken down, dismantled piece by piece to be loaded onto trucks and transported to their next location, wherever that might be.

Grim Death stood in the shadows, having made Pym park their car off the road so it would not be noticed. He'd suspected the circus would be on the move this evening, especially after the failure of those sent to deal with Gwendolyn in her home.

He wondered if they had returned with stories of him—of the mysterious skull-faced benefactor who had appeared out of thin air to save the woman from attack.

Under the skull mask, Bentley smiled. He was finding himself more and more amused by these costumed antics, and wondered whether that was a good thing, or bad.

It would be something to ponder at a later date, after first dealing with the murderer who hid behind the typically joyful façade of the circus. Grim Death stayed in the shadows, moving from one patch of darkness to the next to avoid being seen.

The booths for the games of chance were almost down, the roustabouts working at a furious pace to dismantle every aspect of the amusement city in preparation for erecting it in some other place soon after. At this pace, the circus would be gone by sunup, leaving behind not a clue that it had ever been there.

Grim Death knew where he needed to go, where he was most likely to find the perpetrator of the multiple heinous acts. A big man leading an elephant passed him as he waited in the shadow. The pachyderm turned its enormous head and fluttered its ears as it passed, as if sensing him standing there.

As if sensing something dangerous.

The animal protested, trumpeting its disquiet, but the roustabout just told it to behave and continued to lead the animal across the circus grounds to the trucks waiting to transport the great beasts to their next destination.

The coast clear, Grim Death emerged from concealment to stand before Doctor Nocturne's Chamber of the Unearthly. The building remained untouched. It was if the wooden structure had been imbued with some sort of sentience; the large wooden face, obviously depicting Doctor Nocturne, scrutinized Grim Death as he cautiously approached. Ascending the wooden stairs, he passed through the open mouth of Nocturne to get inside.

Instinct told him to prepare himself, and he plunged his hand deep into his pocket for one of the guns waiting there. He gripped the heavy metal in his hand and felt a kind of confidence flood through him as he entered the cool, musky-smelling darkness of the Chamber.

He heard it immediately upon passing the wooden lectern where a barker would have stood to draw people into the exhibit: a strange, strange sound.

A song, really.

And he was pulled along as if taken by the hand.

The darkness inside the chamber welcomed him, dancing to the song as it drew him along, past the display of dragon's bones and shrunken heads, past the malformed babies floating happily in their jars of yellow preservative.

The song carried him along like a warm ocean current.

He'd only been to the ocean once in his life; after seeing a picture of the Atlantic City boardwalk in one of his mother's magazines, a young Bentley had asked if they could go there someday.

He remembered the looks on his parents' faces; concern from his mother, and a kind of relieved happiness from his father. Bentley had wondered about those looks—seeing them often in recollection—and determined that they were likely a response to how he'd been as a child. He'd never asked to go anywhere, had been perfectly content to stay in his room reading, or exploring the wooded fringes of the grounds. His illness kept him close to home. For him to ask to actually go someplace, away from the protection of Hawthorne House—it must have been quite startling to his parents.

His mother would have preferred he stay at home, where he would be safe—where the harsh world outside could not harm him. But his father . . . his father seemed overjoyed at the idea that his sickly homebody of a son actually wanted to venture outside the protection of the house.

Moving through the darkness, past the unearthly displays, Bentley remembered the excitement of his excursion to New Jersey, as well as the absolute terror.

The fear became pronounced, as if being pulled up from somewhere deep inside him, like an infection drawn to the surface by a warm cloth. It was the strange sound—the lilting song—filling the Chamber that was causing it.

It pulled his fear up from the depths, making him remember how afraid he'd been when he'd first seen it, standing upon the boardwalk.

As far as the eye could see, its blackish-blue mass writhing and seething and crashing upon the shore, calling to him in a loud roaring voice, *Come to me, and I will show you how small and insignificant you are. Come to me, and I will pull you into my embrace and force you to see the terrors hidden beneath me.*

Bentley remembered his fear of the ocean. It was as clear at that very moment as if he had been transported back through time. He wanted to run as he'd run that day, to hide away in the hotel room, trembling with fear, until his father finally gave up and took him home.

He wanted to turn and run, but the song drew him onward, deeper into the chamber.

Into the heart of the unearthly.

━━━

The strange, haunting song pulled him along, past the empty displays for the gorilla that believed he was a man and the Human Dynamo. Briefly Bentley thought about the pair, and whether they would return to the circus, but the song distracted him.

The song told him not to worry, to clear his mind.

He moved past the displays, walking drunkenly through the room toward his destination.

There was only the song now.

At the end of the room, a dusty velvet curtain hung, and he quickened his steps toward it, reaching out with trembling hands to grip the red, sultry obstruction and rip it aside.

As the curtain tore away, the song abruptly stopped, and Bentley found himself slowly able to think again.

In this section of the room, he found who he was looking for.

Doctor Nocturne was in the process of packing up the room's only exhibit, hooking up the tank of dark, murky water to a system of pulleys that would lift and lower it onto a wheeled cart for transport.

Nocturne looked at the skull-masked man standing just inside the curtained-off area.

"The exhibit, I'm afraid, is closed," Nocturne said, his words slurring as they left his mouth. The Doctor then turned away, as if he'd been talking to some random rube, and went about checking to make sure that the tank was secure.

Grim Death produced the twin Colts from his coat pockets.

"It's time you paid for your crimes, Doctor Nocturne," Grim Death growled. "And the cost will be most dear."

The Doctor seemed to not hear him at all, muttering to himself as he made sure the hoist's straps and buckles were tightened.

Grim Death walked closer.

"Face your penance for crimes against the innocent, villain!" Grim Death announced, gripping the twin Colts tightly.

The Doctor continued with his work, almost as if in some sort of trance. And then Bentley remembered the strange song, and how he'd lost all focus when he'd heard it. He wondered if the Doctor could somehow be under the influence of . . .

Something moved within the tank, splashing about and startling him. Bentley found himself pointing his guns toward the activity. A horrific sight peered out at him through the filthy water: a face, and clawed, webbed hands pressed against the glass.

What in the name of all that's holy . . . ? Bentley thought as the creature watched him with round, bulging eyes filled with a cunning intelligence.

The sign had said it was the last living mermaid, but Bentley saw none of the seductive beauty associated with those mythical creatures. The thing that stared at him from behind the glass of the water-filled tank was more sea monster than seductress.

The mermaid seemed to react to his revulsion, thick lips pulling back to reveal nearly transparent needle-sharp teeth. She turned her unblinking gaze to Doctor Nocturne, who continued to work on the bindings, unfazed by what was occurring around him. The mermaid swam toward the end of the tank, looking at the man as he worked, and then opened her mouth.

The song was hers, and it froze Grim Death in place and filled him with an increasing fear. And as he watched the Doctor react to the sound, Bentley slowly began to understand what was happening here.

And how his assumptions had been wrong.

The Doctor stared at the mermaid as she sang her song, his mouth moving as if the two were somehow communicating.

And then Nocturne turned his attention to Grim Death, the expression upon his face filled with a sudden rage.

"You escaped me already tonight," the Doctor said, his voice now strangely flat, as were his eyes, something familiar from Grim Death's conflict with the Human Dynamo and the ape.

"But I'm not going to let it happen again."

As the enthralled owner came toward him, Grim Death suddenly came to realize what the threat at the Circus of Unearthly Wonderment actually was.

And it wasn't Doctor Nocturne.

———

From the pocket of his long waistcoat, Doctor Nocturne produced a knife, snapping open the blade as he stalked toward Grim Death.

The mermaid continued to sing her song, the strange sounds making their way inside Bentley's head, like long, pointed fingers sinking into his brain. He raised his pistols to thwart the Doctor's eventual attack, but something suddenly told him—

No.

With no control of his own, Bentley lowered his guns as the Doctor awkwardly stepped closer. A smile appeared upon his slackened face.

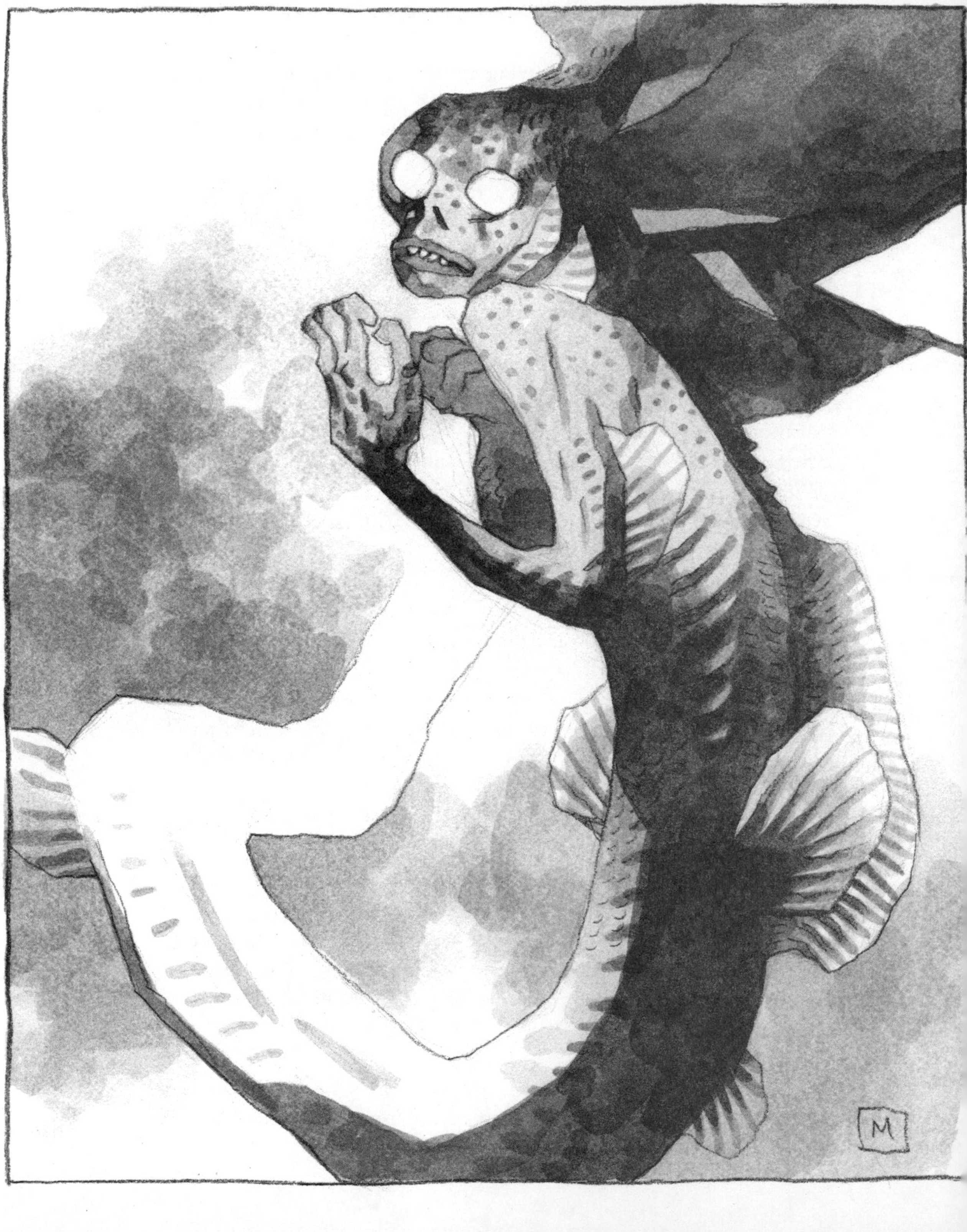
M

Bentley was able to turn his gaze toward the mermaid—the siren—as she watched from the protection of her tank. She wore the same smile he could see reflected upon the face of Doctor Nocturne, the man she now controlled with her strange song.

"What are you?" he managed to ask, attempting to raise his guns, but with little effect.

She would not have it.

The siren pressed her face to the thick glass of her tank, hair like sea-weed billowing out around her oddly shaped head. Her lips moved, and the song became even louder. It was as if she were singing directly into his skull; images that he could not understand began to appear there. Memories.

Memories that were not his own.

She was answering his question with her song.

What are you?

He saw the ocean, vast and terrifying, and cried out as it swept over him, dragging him down in its cold embrace. Beneath the waves he struggled to breathe, then found that the air was present and gulped it greedily as the memories played out.

She had been content in the ocean's deepest depths, alone but search-ing for any clues that others of her ilk might still live. Her curiosity and search brought her closer to the surface, and unfortunately into the hands of mankind.

Bentley experienced the panic she had felt when the fishing nets en-snared her, hauling her up from the sea's watery embrace to the surface and the lands of the air-breathing apes.

The terror was like nothing he'd ever experienced, feeling as she felt as she lay there upon the deck of the fishing boat, suffocating in the air. He saw the crew as they looked as her, their expressions of fear and hor-ror, and something far worse.

Greed.

These were the first humans she'd encountered, and they colored her perceptions of the entire species.

She believed she would die there upon the wooden deck of the trawler, but the humans saw that she was struggling and threw buckets of water on her, eventually untangling her aquatic form from the netting and placing her within a water-filled metal bin used for the storage of fish. They kept her alive, but for what reason she did not know.

It was while she was held within the box that she realized the first of her gifts. She learned that she could see into these creatures' minds, understand their thoughts and intentions, and she saw that she was to be sold into captivity.

Too weak to fight her way back to the sea, she was transported to the land.

The memories grew disjointed—fragmented—as she clung to life. Sold to the highest bidder, she was barely alive as she was transported from one sideshow to the next. She was mere hours away from death when she was ensconced within her latest home in the Chamber of the Unearthly. This would be the last of the indignities she would suffer, she believed, feeling her life slipping away as she lay within the seawater-filled tank.

Bentley felt her despair, experiencing her want to die in order to be free of the torture that her life had become.

But it was all suddenly different—she heard *his* thoughts, felt *his* inherent goodness.

Bentley saw the man through the brackish waters and glass of her tank: William Tuttle, a roustabout for the circus, his big heart overflowing with compassion.

He saw her as more than just a thing pulled from the sea.

Bentley suddenly experienced waves of emotion, and knew that the stranger from the sea had come to love the big, friendly man, looking forward to when he'd come to the chamber to tinker with the filtering apparatus on her tank, or to make sure that she was being fed properly.

He cared for her—the only one in this strange, quite horrible surface world who had.

She loved him, and she believed he felt the same.

It was while experiencing this love that she learned of another ability of her species. Being able to see into the minds of these creatures was one thing, but she came to learn that her voice—her song—could put them into her thrall, allowing her to enter their minds and control their actions.

The images that followed showed her gradual control over her new talent, and how she had no fear of using it, especially when it pertained to William Tuttle.

Heaven help anybody who dared insult her love in any way, for they would feel the bite of her wrath. For the simplest of offenses, circus workers had been gravely injured, and some had even lost their lives.

Bentley felt her joy at the power she now wielded. For the first time in oh so long, she was in control.

But it was all about to come crashing down.

The images—the memories—that followed were painful, sharp, like jagged glass slicing away pieces of his brain. It was excruciating to experience them, and he saw that she had been brought to the brink of madness over what had transpired.

For the first time, the images appearing inside his head—the memories of the sea siren—were vaguely familiar. Bentley had experienced similar memories, but from a different point of view.

He'd seen them through the eyes of a murdered trapeze artist.

William Tuttle came into the Chamber of the Unearthly, and Bentley felt the happiness that came with the big man's visits.

But this time he wasn't alone.

Bentley felt the happiness turn to hurt, and then to anger as sharp as a shark's tooth.

He had brought somebody with him, a female, and the way the two were acting . . .

She had looked inside his skull, and did not like what she found.

William had feelings for this female . . . feelings he should have held only for her.

She watched them with hurt- and hate-filled eyes. William didn't even look in her direction, the two of them whispering and laughing to themselves as they strolled around the dark wooden structure.

She couldn't stand it—all the rage built up inside, roiling at her core until she could bear it no more and released her fury in a siren's song.

Viciously, she took hold of William's mind and body, making sure the violation was as painful as it could be. And, still burning with unspeakable rage, she turned that anger on the female.

How dare she think she could have him?

She marveled at how powerful his body was as she took control, allowing her fury to guide her actions, smiling with his face as he wrapped his strong, large hands around the female's throat. The way the woman's mouth moved as his fingers squeezed, the mermaid was reminded of the suffocating fish that she'd shared a metal locker with on board the boat that had pulled her from the sea.

The female was dead long before the siren released William from her control, the betrayal and anger that she was feeling desperate to come out. Satisfied by the act of murder, she now wanted to watch the man suffer. Freeing his mind from her clutches, she watched from her tank as he emerged from the darkness that had engulfed him to see what he had done.

What *she* had done.

What she saw then satisfied her sick and twisted desire to see the man suffer, and she took great pleasure from the horror and pain that he felt as he gazed down upon the murdered female, unaware of what had occurred but knowing that he had somehow been responsible.

The siren let her hold upon Bentley's brain relax ever so slightly. He had been standing rigidly stiff, his hands down by his sides. His eyes were locked upon her gruesome visage. The remnants of what it was like to be her were still with him. Bentley felt the misery of her existence and her anger toward this world, and how she wanted everyone to pay for her pain.

Killing all who hurt her—one at a time, if necessary.

"You'll need to pay for your crimes," he said to her, having no control over the words that flowed from his mouth. They weren't his words, per se, but the words of the one he now served.

She seemed to understand his pledge, swirling around inside her tank, flipping her massive fishlike tail to splash water upon the wooden floor in response.

And the siren sang again, louder and stronger, for all to hear. Doctor Nocturne, suddenly mere inches from him, plunged the blade of his knife into the meat of Grim Death's upper body.

Chapter Twenty-four

Pym worried about the boy.

Even though he was, for all intents and purposes, an adult, the butler still found himself fretting over the young man whom he'd watched and helped grow up over the years.

Pym stood before his mirror, brushing his thinning black hair over the roundness of his skull before slipping into the black jacket that was part of the uniform of his chosen profession.

He did this every morning at the start of his day, looking himself straight in the eye and telling himself to have a good day. It was something his father had taught him, and something he had done in his service to the elder Hawthornes throughout the years.

Seeing that he was indeed ready, he turned from his reflection and was leaving the room to head down to the kitchen when his eye caught something outside through the window.

Pym went to the window, surprised to see Bentley's back as he disappeared into the thickness of the late-fall woods. Memories of a child lost in a snowstorm echoed in his mind, and he had to wonder where the young man might be going at such an early hour. Normally, Bentley rose closer to noontime than six.

He knew that he should leave the young man alone. Whatever Bentley was doing out in the woods was none of his business.

Pym went to the kitchen and stood in its center, perfectly still, unable to remember what it was that he was going to do at that very moment.

It was the boy . . . Bentley. Concern for him was all-encompassing.

Pym went to the mudroom off the kitchen, grabbed the pea coat hanging by its hook, and put it on. His curiosity as to what Bentley was up to was overpowering, and he found himself leaving the mansion to follow a path at the back of the property that would take him into the wooded area, to where he'd seen Bentley going moments ago.

He thought about calling out, but part of him wanted to see what it was that the young man was doing, what could possibly have brought him out here to the middle of the forest at this early hour.

It was cold, the first hint that winter would soon be knocking at the door. Pym's breath plumed around his face as he walked farther and farther into the woods. The path had disappeared a while back, and he felt himself growing a bit concerned about how far into the wilderness Bentley had gone. His mind immediately began to wander, and he thought of the young man's mental state. He'd always been a delicate child, both physically and mentally, but as of late there had seemed to be a dark cloud following him. The constant construction on Hawthorne House had seemed to alleviate some of his ennui, but that soon began to falter once the newness of the act had worn off. Lately, the darkness had been more than present; Bentley would disappear into the basement for hours at a time, eventually coming up silent and somber.

Pym often wondered how strong Bentley was mentally, recalling that more than one Hawthorne in the thick family tree had taken their own lives after losing bouts with their inner darkness.

The gunshot came from close by, and Pym gasped aloud, imagining his boy—Bentley Hawthorne—lying dead upon a bed of leaves in the thick, dark wood.

He started to run, unsure of exactly where he was going, but knowing he needed to find the boy. The shot had sounded close, so he hoped that he was running in the right direction.

"Bentley!" he cried out as he ran. "Bentley, where are you?"

The silence of the forest was deafening, and he felt the sense of panic and desperation growing in his gut the longer the quiet went on.

"Bentley!"

Pym almost fell headfirst over a small ridge, the toe of his dress shoe catching upon a thick root that had pushed its way up from beneath a patch of olive-green moss. He managed to halt his fall, grabbing hold of the rough bark of a tree, and saw his charge below the ridge.

"Bentley," he cried out again, maneuvering through the undergrowth and carefully going over the ridge to the forest floor below.

Bentley lay upon the ground, perfectly still, gun in hand.

Pym's mind was afire with the possibilities of the situation. Perhaps he was still alive, the shot not being fatal.

Or maybe the butler was indeed too late.

There was blood on the leaves nearby, but it took a moment for the knowledge to register that Bentley was not alone.

The young man lay on the ground beside the body of a large buck, its impressive rack of antlers resembling the twisted branches of an ancient tree.

Bentley lay perfectly still beside the body of the dead animal. It appeared to have been shot twice, once in the side and once in the center of its head.

"I didn't think I could do it," Bentley said, lying beside the corpse of the animal, looking up into the gray October sky.

"Sir?"

"Kill it," Bentley said. "I didn't think I could kill anything, but I was wrong."

"It appears to have been shot twice," Pym said, his eyes going to the two wounds. "But I heard only one shot."

"He'd been shot by a hunter," Bentley said, still looking up at the sky. "It was a bad shot, nicked a lung. The poor thing was suffering, dying slowly."

"How did you know . . . ?"

"This was my first test," Bentley said. "To see if I could pull the trigger . . . to see if I could follow orders."

"Somebody ordered you to do this?" Pym asked.

Bentley sat up, looking at the gun in his hand.

"This was all about mercy," Bentley told him. "To end a living thing's suffering. I wonder if the others will be as easy."

"Others?" Pym asked, feeling an icy sensation wriggle down the length of his spine.

Bentley looked at him, gun still in hand.

"Those will be different," he said, getting up from the ground beside the buck and starting to walk away from Pym, toward home.

"They will be about vengeance."

Chapter Twenty-five

The blade was incredibly sharp, the point easily passing through the material of Bentley's trench coat, his shirt, his undershirt, and into the flesh beneath.

Bentley wanted to cry out, but the siren refused to let him, her wailing song holding him tightly and making him suffer. That was what it was all about for the sad creature now: the suffering.

She wanted the world, and everybody in it, to suffer as she had.

Through the eyeholes in his mask he was able to look into the slack face of Doctor Nocturne. Briefly, in between the pulsing waves of excruciating pain that he felt screaming through his upper body, Bentley had to wonder how long the man had been under the sea siren's control. Did he even know what had been lost to him? Was he even aware that he, and probably a good number of the circus performers, were under the creature's thrall?

The Doctor pulled the knife back, the blade coming free of the wound with a soft sucking sound. Bentley knew what was coming next. The following thrust would be closer to his heart, and that would be when he would actually begin to die. He watched, still frozen in place as the song of the siren wafted over him. It was like being encased in ice, everything coldly numb and rigid. The Doctor's movements were stiff, halting; Bentley could practically see the strings of the monstrous marionette taut in the air above the older, turban-wearing man as he was manipulated by the siren.

The Doctor shuffled a little bit closer and drew his arm back, preparing for his next, likely fatal, thrust.

Bentley could feel the siren's pleasure in this, her enjoyment in the fact that he knew that his death was only moments away. The surface world had made her cruel, and he wondered, if she had never come above and intermingled with humanity, would she still have transformed into a monster?

The blade was moving now, slicing through the air as easily as it had passed through his clothes and the soft flesh beneath. Bentley became hyperactively aware of everything at that moment, the sights, smells, and sounds of the circus exhibit; he would have sworn that he could hear the knife as it cut the air on course to his rapidly beating heart. He tried to fight the siren's hold, to ignore the strangely beautiful sound that held him tightly in place, but it was to no avail. The song of the siren was deadly to the human ear, and he doubted that there was anything human that could overcome it.

Anything human—that was the key.

Bentley felt a stirring, and at first did not recognize it, believing it to be yet another wave of emotions and feelings that his body was going through as it prepared to be murdered.

But then he remembered.

It was the same feeling from all those years ago, when he had stood within the solarium, its air choked with smoke, the ashes of his parents on the floor. It was the same feeling he'd had when she . . . when *it* had come to him, and held him in its arms, and he became more than just a sick little boy.

Death had chosen him. Death had made him something more than he had been before. Death had made him one of its messengers.

Death had brought him here.

Nothing human could overcome the wail of the siren's song.

But Bentley hadn't really been human for quite some time.

He had Death inside him, and not just figuratively. Bentley believed that he actually had a piece of the force that was called Death as part of his makeup. It sat inside him, mostly quiet, but when it was aroused, during moments such as this, it was a force to be reckoned with, and quite terrifying.

Bentley felt it stir, transforming from an old dog sitting comfortably curled up by the warmth of the fire to a wild creature waiting to pounce.

Ready to feed.

He could practically hear it now, in a voice like the softest crushed velvet, whispering in his ear, *This is where I come in.*

Nothing human.

He felt like an observer in his own body, looking out through the holes of the skull mask as something else took control.

Bentley Hawthorne was temporarily pushed aside, and something—Grim Death, for lack of any better name—took control.

The knife blade was still on the way, coming straight toward his heart. Grim Death observed this, and decided that this was something that would not occur. It heard the siren's song, and wrinkled up the face behind the mask in distaste, and shrugged off its preternatural influence, returning control to its host's limbs.

Able to move his arms again, Grim Death glanced down at the Doctor's foot and pulled the trigger once on the Colt .45. The toe of the boot exploded in a shower of bone, leather, and blood, and the man pitched sideways with a grunt, the blade of the knife suddenly off course.

The siren's song was suddenly interrupted, changing into something that sounded an awful lot like a guttural cry of pain.

Grim Death wondered then if the pain of what had happened to the Doctor's foot had somehow made its way back to the sea creature. He certainly hoped so—a taste of her own medicine, so to speak.

The song began again, louder and stronger, and the Doctor flailed as he attempted to maintain some sort of balance. He dropped heavily down to one knee, but managed to hold on to his knife.

Grim Death was tempted to take the man, to put a bullet into his face and end his life, but that wouldn't be right. The Doctor was in some ways an innocent, under the control of a powerful force that he could not fight. The fact that he had been responsible for bringing this foul thing into the circus family shed some shadow of guilt over him, but that was neither here nor there at the moment.

Deciding that he would not kill him, Grim Death lashed out with the barrel of one of his pistols, slapping the older man across the face and knocking the turban from atop his head. The Doctor went down in a twitching heap as the siren attempted to regain control.

Grim Death watched the creature in her tank, stepping toward her watery home and clutching the pistols in each hand. She saw him approaching and increased the intensity of her song, the water swirling from her furious activity, but he just shook his head as he stood before the glass.

"It is over," Grim Death said, lifting one of the guns to fire into the glass.

There was suddenly noise from behind him, and he turned to catch a glimpse of a wave of humanity: all the workers of the circus within reach of her wails, now under her control, surging toward him.

Over? Grim Death pondered as the ocean of flesh landed upon him, driving him down to the ground in its writhing and violent intensity.

Not quite yet.

Chapter Twenty-six

BEFORE:

Even though his father had designed and owned a business that manufactured all manner of weaponry, Bentley had never even held a gun.

Until of late.

"*So, how did it feel?*" Roderick asked from his perch atop a dusty crate.

Bentley stood, aiming down the barrel of the pistol at the makeshift targets he'd set up on the floor of the deserted factory. He breathed in, and then slowly—calmly—exhaled and pulled the trigger. The shot went a little wide, missing the target by a few inches.

"Damn it," he hissed beneath his breath.

"*Do you think you can do it?*" The bird continued with his line of questioning.

Bentley aimed again and fired another shot, this time hitting his target.

"Do I think I can do what?" Bentley asked, turning to address the bird. "Do I think I can shoot someone if I have to?"

"*Well?*" the bird asked with an odd cock of his head.

"If that's what's expected of me I guess I really don't have much of a choice, do I?" Bentley said as he turned back to the targets.

"*They won't be standing still, y'know,*" Roderick said, "*or even made of wood.*"

"I'm aware of that." He aimed again.

"*There could even be some attempts to fight back,*" the bird went on, "*maybe even some crying and begging.*"

Bentley fired off a shot, followed by another. He could still feel the cold presence of his father's spirit inside him, the man's knowledge of weapons and marksmanship somehow left behind for him to utilize.

"*Can you handle that?*" Roderick asked.

"Again, what choice do I have?"

"*We've all got choices, kid,*" the raven answered. "*Some just garner better re-sults than others.*"

"I can imagine." Bentley fired three more shots, hitting his targets every time, a little voice inside his head thanking his father for his skills.

"*People don't need to murder, y'see, that's a choice,*" Roderick squawked.

"They could live out their lives, all well and good, and never have to hear from the likes of you."

Bentley ejected the empty clip from the gun and fished another from his pocket.

"But some choose to take a life that's not theirs to take . . . to take a life that has not lived out its full potential. And that just pisses off the boss."

"And that's where I come in," Bentley said, dropping the gun to his side.

"And that's your choice," the raven said with a cock of his head.

"But is it really?"

"Well," Roderick said, taking flight and landing upon a metal railing above where Bentley practiced his marksmanship. *"Let's look at this. The boss picked you."*

"The boss chose me only because of what my parents tried to do."

"True," Roderick said. *"But I think he likes you."*

Bentley remembered the shrieking horror inside the glass cabinet.

"I'm sure he does."

"Look at what he's done for you," Roderick continued. *"He doesn't do that kinda stuff for everybody."*

"But now he wants me to murder for him."

"Kill for him," the bird quickly corrected. *"There's a difference. These are people who have given up the right to live."*

"But I'm still murdering somebody," Bentley said, looking at the gun in his hand.

"You've got permission from the highest authority to do it," Roderick said. *"And there's the difference. You are a representative of Death himself . . . an extension of his power . . . an avatar, so to speak."*

"I'll be the death that they deserve," Bentley said with a slight, sad chuckle.

"Exactly." The bird fluttered his ebony feathers. *"A grim death."*

"Grim death," Bentley repeated. "Even with this," he said, lifting the gun. "Really not feeling like a representative—an avatar—of Death."

"Not now," Roderick said. *"Got to look the part to feel it."*

"Look the part?" Bentley questioned. "I don't understand what—"

"C'mon," the raven said, taking flight and heading into the secret passage that would take them back to Hawthorne House. *"I'll show you."*

Chapter Twenty-seven

The innocent swarmed atop him.

He needed to remind himself of that—that they were indeed innocent of their actions—as they tried to kill him.

The siren sang on, her song permeating the circus workers' minds, taking over and making them want to murder. The knife wound in his arm made it difficult to fight back, but he managed as best he could, trying to injure as few as possible.

They were not responsible, after all.

He fired into the leg of one of his attackers, followed by a shot that entered the upper arm of another. They cried out as the bullets hit them, the sudden pain breaking the siren's connection and leaving the ones he had shot useless and bleeding upon the floor.

But there were others.

They continued to flow into the room, dragged by the siren's song.

Grim Death watched as they came through the curtain and into the cramped space. He lunged, throwing his full weight into them and driving them back out into the main area where the Human Dynamo and the fancy gorilla had performed. He continued to fire his pistols, delivering one flesh wound after another, until he was completely out of bullets, and then he continued to fight them off by any means that he was able.

Death had made him strong, but every human body had a breaking point, and Bentley was certainly close to reaching his. The wound in his shoulder bled and throbbed painfully as he threw punch after punch, lashing out with feet, knees, and elbows in an attempt to immobilize his attackers.

The ugly man with the alcoholic's nose who worked the test of strength game came at him with his overly large hammer, attempting to brain him into oblivion. Grim Death saw this as an opportunity and drove his fist solidly into the man's red, bumpy nose, then relieved him of the giant hammer.

The hammer was exactly what Grim Death needed, giving him stopping power as well as reach.

The circus workers paused momentarily, watching him with dead expressions. Grim Death could feel the siren through the glassy, emotionless eyes of those she controlled, watching for an opportunity to end his life.

"No matter how many you control," Grim Death growled, "it's only a matter of time before I get back to you."

The words seemed to inflame her all the more; the circus workers reacted in unison and rushed at him. He swung the hammer at the first, letting the weight of the enormous bludgeon do must of the work. The hammer was potentially dangerous, and he needed to be careful in how he wielded it. The sound of the hammer connecting savagely with flesh, followed by the crunch of breaking bone, became like a strange symphony of violence, but they kept on coming, and he kept on swinging his instrument and taking them down.

Bentley's body was experiencing the effects of these efforts, and he cursed—*was it he, or the essence of the deathly force that resided within him?*—the inadequacies of the human design.

The siren must've somehow sensed this, calling upon even more of the circus folk, as well as rousing those who had fallen to his gunshots and hammer. They were swarming him again, their hands reaching, clutching, and grabbing at his clothes, attempting to drag him down, but he continued to swing the ponderous bludgeon.

Grim Death felt the painful burn in his arms, followed by the excruciating ache of cramping as he wielded his tool of mayhem. He backed up toward the stage where the Human Dynamo's electrical contraptions sat silently. Perhaps if he were to put the stage and the heavy metal devices at his back, he thought, trying to come up with some way—any way—he might outlast the perpetual onslaught driven by the siren's song.

The song was still trying for him, coming in through the canals of his ears and attempting to convince him to give up, to put down the hammer and succumb to the inevitable, but Grim Death would hear nothing of it—in fact, he would not listen. The only song he heard was the music made by his efforts at seeking justice for the lovely trapeze artist struck down by the intense jealousy of a monster from the deepest seas, and for the man who sat on death row awaiting punishment for a crime he did not commit.

The mind-controlled mob rushed him once more, and he backed away, his back striking the strange machinery used to feed the Human Dynamo his electrical sustenance. The machine came to life as he bumped up against it, humming and whirring as he continued his fight, swinging the hammer that seemed to be growing heavier by the second.

But he couldn't think of such things. He had to forge on, no matter the limitations of human physiology.

No matter the limitations that were starting to affect his performance.

Grim Death became more savage in his response as the circus workers' numbers again seemed to increase. His mind raced to find a solution to his predicament, knowing that his time was growing short, and that if something was not done soon, the mob would drag him down off the stage and tear him limb from limb.

As if they could somehow read his thoughts, their efforts to end him became all the more frantic.

From the corner of his eye he caught movement, and came to the realization that the new intensity of the circus workers might be more than just an effort to take him down, but also might serve as a distraction.

The curtain at the back had parted, and the limping form of Doctor Nocturne could be seen laboring with something, maneuvering and pulling something that seemed to be of great weight and size.

And as he swung his hammer, breaking bone and bruising flesh, Grim Death saw what was happening. The Doctor was attempting to remove the siren's home: the water-filled tank had finally been loaded and secured upon a wheeled dolly, and was being taken from the Chamber of the Unearthly.

The siren was escaping.

Chapter Twenty-eight

BEFORE:

R oderick led him to the top floor of Hawthorne House and to the ceiling hatch that led into the sprawling attic.

Bentley hadn't ventured up into the cluttered storage space for years, but at the bird's urging, found the ladder and climbed the wooden rungs up to the opening.

"What am I to be looking for up here?" Bentley asked, reaching up with both hands to push the hatch aside.

"*You'll know when you see it,*" the raven croaked from atop a railing.

Bentley slid the hatch across the floor and was immediately caught in a storm of dust.

"*C'mon,*" the bird urged as Bentley sneezed violently and coughed. "*Get up there, and let's get this taken care of.*"

Bentley caught his breath, then clambered up into the space, the floorboards creaking noisily beneath his weight.

"Okay, I'm up," he said, eyes squinting as they attempted to adjust to the semidarkness, a circular window across from where he stood providing some light for him to see by.

Roderick flew up through the opening, landing atop a dress mannequin.

"*Yes, you are,*" the bird said.

"So?"

"*So what?*"

"What am I supposed to find?" Bentley asked, annoyed. He started to walk about the space. There was stuff as far as the eye could see, things that had been left there well before he was born, and probably before his father as well. The attic was the catchall for the Hawthorne family. Pym had threatened to clean it out numerous times, but nothing ever seemed to come of it.

"*Keep looking,*" Roderick said. "*It'll find you.*"

Bentley stopped, suddenly unnerved.

"What do you mean by that?"

The bird seemed to laugh, a strange gargling sound of amusement. "*Your new identity—it's been up here waiting for you for quite some time.*"

"My new identity?" Bentley asked, carefully shuffling across the wooden floor. "I don't understand what—"

His feet struck something quite large and solid, and he almost fell atop it.

"*You will,*" Roderick said.

Bentley started to hear the sound almost at once. At first he thought it might be the wind, softly blowing outside the window, but the location didn't seem right.

The sound—the whispering—seemed to be coming from much closer by.

Bentley's eyes went down to the large steamer trunk he'd almost fallen upon. The whispering sound seemed to be coming from inside.

But that couldn't be. Could it?

Bending down, he searched for the latches to open the trunk.

"Is it in here?" Bentley asked, flipping the latches. "Is what I'm looking for in here, Roderick?"

The raven was silent as Bentley threw back the heavy lid to reveal a trunk filled with costumes. The years of masquerade parties thrown by his parents rushed through his mind, as his eyes fell upon the various pieces of costuming.

The whispering was more distinct now but muffled, almost as if . . .

His hand went down toward the first layer of costumes, and he proceeded to pick it up and search beneath. The sound grew distinctly louder. Part of him was terrified by what he might find beneath an admiral's jacket or a geisha's robe, but a stronger part, fueled by curiosity, kept him searching as the whispering grew louder.

"Is this it?" Bentley asked Roderick, sensing that he was close, his hands growing more frantic as they dug through the layers of costumes. "Is this what I'm supposed to find?"

The voice from behind startled him.

"Bentley? Is that you? What in the name of all that's holy are you doing up here?" Pym asked as he climbed up into the attic.

"Roderick, answer me!" Bentley demanded, ignoring his manservant. "Is this it?"

His hands landed on something cold and rigid, and an electric tingle passed through his fingers and up his arm.

"Oh!" Bentley said, pulling back, but then plunging his hands back into the trunk.

"What are you doing?" Pym asked, coming up behind him. "Who's Roderick?"

Pym was holding a flashlight and moved the beam around.

"The bird," Bentley said as his searching hands found what it was that he was looking for—he was sure of it—and carefully began to withdraw it from beneath layers of costumes. "The bird said that my new identity—"

"The bird?" Pym asked. "What bird are you talking about, Bentley? Are we feeling well today, or . . . ?"

Bentley wished that Pym would be quiet. The whispering . . . the voice sounded as though it was trying to say something as he extracted the item from beneath the costumes and accessories.

"*Oh,*" Bentley said as he looked upon it.

"What is it?" Pym asked, shining a beam of light from his flashlight on the thing now being held in Bentley's hands.

It was the face of Death . . . the Red Death, to be precise.

Bentley held the mask before him in the beam of Pym's flashlight. He remembered how his father had worn the mask as part of his costume at one of his masquerades. It grinned at him, empty eye sockets filled with sucking blackness. The mask had been painted a deep bloodred, but over the years the paint had started to crack and fleck.

Bentley rubbed his thumb over the bumpy surface, breaking away the paint to reveal the more natural color of a skull beneath.

"What do you intend to do with that?" Pym asked, horrified, but Bentley wasn't listening to his manservant, was instead devoting his full attention to the skull mask in his hand and what it was saying to him.

Put me on, and assume your new identity as my avatar, it softly whispered.

"Bentley?" Pym asked again. "What do you . . . ?"

He did what the mask told him to do, sliding it over his face. "Putting it on," Bentley said, turning to look at Pym in his new guise. "Assuming my new identity."

Assume your identity as Grim Death.

Chapter Twenty-nine

octor Nocturne, the toes on one foot shot away and bleeding profusely, doggedly maneuvered the incredibly heavy, awkward, water-filled tank as the sea siren swam excitedly in circles within her brackish habitat.

She continued to sing, controlling each and every person inside the Chamber.

Except for Bentley—except for Grim Death.

He kept an eye on the escaping siren, wanting to do everything in his power to prevent her escape, but the mob that wanted him dead required his full attention as well.

A muscular man in a striped shirt that reeked of tobacco took hold of the hammer's handle, using all of his might to try to pull it from Grim Death's grasp and allow the others to fall upon him.

Kicking out, he struck the kneecap of his muscular attacker, driving the man down to the floor where he was at once covered by five more vying for possession of Grim Death's weapon. He chanced a quick look and saw that Doctor Nocturne had managed to maneuver the cart holding the tank out of the smaller room and was now attempting to pull and roll it toward a nearly hidden side door.

No, Grim Death thought as his attackers tore at his clothes, ripping at his mask to pull it away. His true visage revealed, he felt a momentary lapse in strength, truly experiencing the weight of those who were trying to drag him down and tear him apart.

But he couldn't allow that to happen.

Bentley cried out, a burst of strength allowing him to wrench his hammer from those who would take it away. He did not know how much longer he could continue—he had to do something to stop the mindless horde that swarmed upon him.

But what?

He listened to the song again, feeling the slight tingle of the alien sounds as they attempted to permeate his brain, and knew that something like that—with such rage, hate, and power—could not be allowed to escape out into the world.

It had to be stopped. *She* had to be stopped.

He allowed her song into his head—allowed *her* into his head—and told her that this was the end for her. That she must pay the price for her affront to life.

The siren swam about crazily in her tank, her movement—as well as the movement of Doctor Nocturne as he dragged her habitat across the floor—causing the water splash over the side and spatter upon the floor, forming great puddles.

He could feel her inside his mind, flexing her claws and digging into the soft gray matter there. She told him that he wasn't strong enough, that her hate was a greater force than anything in the surface world above, and that she would make all who came in contact with her pay.

The world would know her hurt.

Bentley could not allow this, but he continued to struggle against the hordes that were trying to take him down. He did not know how much more he had left in him, but suspected it was not much. Through the slack faces of his attackers, he could see her smugness, the idea that she had won against him and the force he represented reflected in their glassy eyes.

Bentley felt himself falter, one knee crashing down painfully to the floor. Their hands were on his weapon, preventing him from swinging. *This is it*, he thought as he felt their burgeoning weight upon him. This was when he failed his employer.

And then he saw her, through the writhing, clawing, struggling bodies: Tianna Hoops, the spirit of the murdered trapeze artist, standing just inside the door as Doctor Nocturne continued to haul the tank and the evil it contained.

Bentley's eyes met hers, and he felt her anger, her disappointment. He tried to show her that he was sorry, that he had tried, but . . .

You promised, her intense, ghostly stare said to him. *You promised to avenge me, and save my love.*

And he had.

Bentley felt himself being forced to the floor, Tianna's ghostly stare of disappointment burned into his psyche. He had a job to do . . . and a promise to uphold. He then saw William Tuttle, alone in his jail cell awaiting his fate, and knew that he couldn't allow it to end this way.

Legs straining against the weight of combined bodies, he braced his feet and let the hammer's shaft slip through his fingers until the head was almost touching the floor. Summoning all his strength, he twisted his body in such a way as to send the hammer and shaft smashing into the legs and lower bodies of those attacking him, knocking a good many to the floor and allowing him a moment.

A moment.

It was all he would need.

"I promised," he said to the ghost of Tianna as he raised the hammer above his head and fixed Doctor Nocturne and the water-filled tank in his gaze as they were just about at the door.

Bentley aimed and let the hammer fly, its heavy wooden head spinning crazily through the air on a direct course to it target. The horde groped at him crazily, still under the control of the siren's song, and as he was dragged to the floor he saw that his aim was true.

Tianna Hoops smiled.

The wooden hammer struck the center of the tank in an explosion of glass and gushing water. The siren, forced out in the torrent of water escaping through the jagged hole, psychically shrieked as she landed upon the floor.

Everyone in the Chamber stopped what they were doing, their hands shooting up to their heads in obvious agony. Bentley winced, feeling the siren squirming around inside his brain. A tickling sensation beneath his nose caused him to reach up to wipe away the trickle; his gloved hand came away stained with blood.

The siren flopped upon the wooden floor, gasping through her gills for the water she needed to breathe. Bentley started toward the fallen abomination, splashing through the inches of water that now covered the floor. He needed to finish what he'd started.

The circus workers went suddenly rigid as he passed, a weakened version of the siren's wail beginning to resonate through the air once again. He didn't have the strength to fight them anymore, and tensed as they came at him, splashing through the water upon the floor.

Bentley could still feel the siren inside his head, enraged beyond description as she suffocated. The mob blocked his path, preventing him from going any farther as they converged upon him. From the corner of his eye he saw something attempting to get his attention. Bentley turned his head to see the ghost of Tianna Hoops standing upon the stage beside the still functioning electrical device used by the Human Dynamo.

The ghost stood beside it, staring intensely. He didn't understand until he started toward her, toward the stage and the device.

Water splashed at his feet.

He looked from the humming machine to the ghost of Tianna. She nodded ever so slightly, as if agreeing with the idea that was suddenly inside his head.

An idea that he needed to act on immediately, before the siren could be saved. Doctor Nocturne had gone to her, lifting her pale, serpentine body from the floor to take her somewhere to be immersed in life-giving water again.

Bentley could not allow this to happen. He charged the stage and leapt upon it. The mind-controlled horde followed, and even though the siren's song was weak, they still obeyed her commands.

But that was about to end now, he thought as he stood behind the humming device. He pushed it with all his might, sending the heavy piece of machinery tumbling from the stage, dragging sparking cables and wires behind it as it crashed down, sending thousands of volts of electricity coursing through the water pooled upon the Chamber floor.

The possessed mob went suddenly rigid, dancing crazily as electricity coursed through their bodies. Bentley saw that Doctor Nocturne had gone completely stiff, the siren in his arms rigid as well. Not wanting to harm the innocent, he darted across the stage to the electrical panel, which sparked and smoked, and carefully pulled the shut off lever, cutting the current from the damaged machine.

The circus mob dropped to the flooded floor, unconscious. Bentley looked across the room to where the ghost of Tianna Hoops now stood over the twitching form of the siren.

Bentley jumped down from the stage and started toward the creature. Stopping briefly, he picked up the skull mask from the floor and slipped it over his face before continuing to the siren.

Before finishing the job he had come there to do.

Chapter Thirty

BEFORE:

Bentley slowly placed the slouch hat on top of his head.

"Well? What do you think?" he asked, his voice slightly muffled by the mask that he wore, as he turned to look at his reflection in the mirror of his bedroom.

He was actually startled by what he saw, not seeing himself reflected there, but somebody else.

Grim Death.

After he'd worn the mask for a bit, getting used to the feeling of it upon his face, the image of the guise he would take slowly manifested before his mind's eye: black trench coat, leather gloves, black slacks and shoes, topped off with a slouch hat.

And then, of course, there were the guns.

Still staring at his reflection, he slipped his hands into the pockets of the trench coat and removed the twin Colts. He pointed them at the deathly visage staring back from the mirror.

"Bentley, I . . ." Pym began.

He could hear the concern in the manservant's voice. Bentley knew how insane this all sounded when spelled out—hell, he even found it to be so—but there was no changing the reality of the situation.

No matter how bizarre.

Death had drafted him into its service, and he had no choice but to answer the call.

Bentley sighed, lowering the guns as he turned from the mirror.

"What?" he asked, doing all he could to keep the annoyance from his tone, but doing a very poor job.

Pym seemed speechless, mouth moving as he searched for the words.

"I know what you're going to say," Bentley said as he removed the fedora and skull mask. "That this is insane . . . that I've lost my mind."

"Well . . . have you considered the possibility?" Pym asked.

"Seriously, Pym?" Bentley said, crossing the room to plop into an overstuffed chair in the room's corner. "There isn't a moment of every day that I don't question it," he said. "Wonder what it would be like to totally ignore it and go about my day."

Pym listened, his expression disturbed.

"But then they catch my eye," he said. "And I see their pain . . . I feel their pain."

Bentley stared across the room to the ghostly shape of the older woman with the seeping head wound who had been there since the realization of his purpose. She was still patiently waiting for him.

She would be his first.

"And I realize that something has to be done."

Bentley looked away from the ghost and back to Pym.

"That somebody needs to act for them . . . somebody must avenge them."

"But why you?" the butler pleaded. "Why can't it be left to law enforcement and . . ."

"In some cases that's exactly what happens," Bentley explained. "But with others . . ." He looked back to the ghost of the old woman, who continued to stare at him pleadingly. "The perpetrator will get away with it."

"And why is that your concern?" Pym asked.

"Because I've been chosen, Pym," Bentley said. "Due to the sins committed by my parents, I've been selected for a special purpose."

Pym slowly blinked, folding his hands in front of himself.

"If you say so, sir."

"Cheer up, Pym," Bentley said, attempting to add a bit of levity to the moment. "You always said that I should find a hobby. Well, here it is."

"I was thinking more along the lines of collecting stamps," the butler replied.

"Yes, well, Death had other plans for me," he said, turning his gaze back to the woman. She was standing closer now, as if aware of what he was finally going to do.

It was time.

Bentley stood up, gazing at the skull mask in his hand. "Tonight, my purpose begins."

"And that means what exactly?" Pym asked.

"We've already gone over this, Pym," Bentley said. "The spirit of the murdered victim will be—"

"Yes," Pym interrupted. "They will be avenged. The perpetrator responsible shall be made to pay for his crime."

"Exactly," Bentley said. "See, you were listening."

"Oh, yes, I certainly was," Pym said angrily. "I wanted to get every single detail so when the police come calling, I can maybe convince them that you're not in your right mind and that they'll take you to Bellevue Psychiatric instead of prison."

Bentley glared. The words were hurtful, but he could understand where the butler's concern was coming from. If only the man could see what Bentley saw.

"I'm leaving," Bentley said, starting for the door. The ghost of the older woman with the gaping head wound evaporated like steam on a mirror.

"Will you be taking a car?" Pym asked.

"How else would I make my way into the city?" Bentley said, stopping in the doorway.

Pym hadn't turned around, his back to him.

"Your skill as a driver—" he began.

"Is more than adequate," Bentley finished, starting through the door into the hall.

"Do you know where you need to go?" Pym asked, back still to him.

"Yes."

Pym slowly turned, walking across the room toward him.

"I'll bring the car around," he said, passing him in the hall, as he proceeded down the stairs.

Bentley followed close behind, with purpose.

Chapter Thirty-one

The workers had started to return to some level of consciousness as soon as Bentley had finished the act he'd been sent there to do, and he left the circus grounds before they could recover, clinging to the shadows as he made his way to where Pym had left the car.

His guns had been emptied, so he'd picked up the giant hammer again and smashed the sea creature's skull into oblivion. Grim Death had experienced no joy in committing the act, actually feeling a moment's worth of pity for the creature taken from the sea and displayed as some twisted oddity for two bits a peek.

But it had committed the most heinous of crimes, and needed to pay recompense.

He felt a moment of panic as he stood in the darkness, searching for the car. Had Pym left him? He began to ponder. It would serve him right for what he'd put the poor man through. He was just about convinced that this was indeed what had occurred when the ghost of Tianna Hoops appeared in the distance, the eerie glow from her body shedding light upon the car hidden in the deep shadows of some trees.

He made his way toward the car, feeling the heavy weight of exhaustion and injury attempting to drag him down. *I'll rest in the car*, he told himself as he approached from the back.

Pym was outside the car, pacing furiously as he approached.

"Bentley!" Pym said, coming toward him. "Are you all right?"

He still had the mask on, and raised a hand to halt his butler's approach. He then removed the mask.

"A little sore, Pym," he said. "But I'll be fine."

"After how long in the hospital?" Pym asked, ignoring Bentley's hand and coming to support him as he almost slumped to the ground. "Two weeks, maybe?"

"I just need to rest," Bentley said, allowing Pym to hold him up. "But you need to drive."

———

He was about to tell his manservant to take him home, but the ghost of the trapeze artist had other ideas. She was suddenly there—the look upon her ghostly features even more intense than it had been before. He wanted to ask what was wrong, but she acted, her spectral fingers sliding through the mask and into his skull.

Showing him what was happening at the prison.

"Right to a hospital," Pym said, opening the back door to help him to sit.

Bentley saw Warden Delocroix taking papers from a filing cabinet and going to his desk, his perceptions suddenly changing to show him what paperwork the man was completing. It was the execution orders for William Tuttle, and from what Bentley could see, the event was scheduled for tonight.

For some reason the execution had been changed—moved up.

"No, I have to get to Blackmore before . . ."

He thought of William Tuttle, an innocent man dying for an act he did not commit. He couldn't allow it to happen.

Pym began, "Couldn't this wait until—"

"No," Bentley said sharply. "It has to be now . . . tonight. The execution . . ."

Tianna appeared beside him, her tears drifting in the darkness inside the car.

"I can't allow an innocent man to die," Bentley told his butler. "Please, Pym," he implored. "Get me there as quickly as you can."

Pym silently did as he was asked, climbing into the driver's seat and pulling the car out from the darkness at the side of the road, tires squealing as they gripped the road.

Bentley could feel Tianna's ghostly eyes upon him. He didn't want to look at her, but he also didn't want to lie. He'd already promised that he would save her love.

But now he wasn't sure he would be able to fulfill that promise, and couldn't bear to meet her mournful gaze.

"Faster, Pym," Bentley said tiredly from the back, skull mask clutched in his hand.

"Time is of the essence."

Chapter Thirty-two

BEFORE:

The old woman's name was Beverly Chambeau. A wealthy woman, from a wealthy family. She was a good woman, donating to many charitable organizations and causes.

She hadn't deserved to die the way she did.

Beverly had lived in Manhattan, in a penthouse on the Upper East Side, with her son, Phillip.

The man who had murdered her.

Pym had begrudgingly dropped Bentley near a back alley off Madison Avenue, letting him slip from the backseat of the car in order to find access to the building.

Standing in the darkness, attired in the full guise of Grim Death, Bentley waited for some kind of inspiration. Something that would tell him how to proceed.

There was a part of him that protested what he was about to do, a tiny voice inside his skull attempting to make him reflect on the insanity of his actions. As if Pym wasn't enough, now he had to deal with a voice inside his head.

Staying close to the wall of the building, he approached a back door, grabbing hold of the knob and attempting to turn it.

Locked.

Of course it was locked, he thought, frustrated. They couldn't have just anybody gaining access to the building.

He was actually thinking of just finding Pym and heading home when he noticed the ghost of the old woman, Beverly Chambeau, standing not too far off down the alley.

"Yes, I know," he told her. "I'm working on it."

Her arm moved ever so slightly, a finger starting to extend. As if pointing.

Grim Death moved closer. *She is pointing . . . but to what?*

The coal shoot had been left ajar, probably after the last delivery of the season. It wasn't the easiest way in, but it *was* a way in, and beggars couldn't be choosers.

He squatted down, pushing up the flap to reveal the shoot that led down to the bin, and wedged his body through the opening, going down the slide into the filthy black coal.

Climbing from the bin, he found himself in the building's cellar. It was almost as crowded as his own, with old pieces of furniture as far as the eye could see. He walked closer, checking out the pieces. They didn't appear to be all that old, or in that bad of condition. Odd that they would be down here.

Grim Death went to the small set of stairs that led up to the building's foyer. It was deathly quiet there, and he waited to be sure he was alone before heading toward the staircase that would take him upstairs to the first floor of the townhouse.

He'd seen this place inside his head, and was familiar with where things were, even in the pitch darkness. He needed to find Phillip, and maneuvered his way through the shadows as he searched.

An explanation of why all the furniture was down in the basement became apparent, as the first floor was rife with new pieces. The woman's son had seen fit to redecorate after her sad demise.

Now that everything belonged to him.

Being in contact with Beverly's spirit, Bentley had learned that the woman had had terminal cancer, that she would have been dead from the horrid, wasting disease in less than a year. It was this knowledge that had led her to a very important decision. She intended to give it all away, her entire fortune, to the most needy of the city. It was when she shared this information with her son that things took the most awful of turns.

Phillip did not care for his mother's idea, preferring instead for the money, and all that it entailed, to stay in his possession. He tried to convince her otherwise, but she would hear nothing of it, explaining to him that he would be taken care of, but life was going to be a little bit harder for him after she was gone.

It was when she explained that she was going to the lawyers the next day, to begin the process of changing over her will, that Phillip realized he couldn't allow her to do this.

That he couldn't allow her to change the kind of life he'd grown accustomed to. It was a matter of his survival.

So he decided upon the unthinkable.

Bentley stood in the center of the newly refurnished living room, the smell of fresh paint and wallpaper glue hanging heavily in the air. He listened as he stood there in the darkness, deciding that Phillip was not home.

Moving through the shadows, he approached the second staircase. This was where the act had been performed. Where the son had sealed his fate.

Bentley saw it, felt it as it had happened.

They'd had another heated discussion, and she'd said that the matter was closed, that she was going to see the family lawyers in the morning.

Bentley saw the way he watched her as she carefully descended the winding, marble staircase. She had become less sure on her feet, so was being extra cautious, holding on tightly to the railing as she descended.

Phillip had zeroed in on this weakness and decided that this was how he would do it.

How he would ensure for himself the life he'd grown accustomed to.

Bentley watched him descend behind her, coming in close. She heard his approach and started to turn, never expecting that he would—

He pushed her. It wasn't hard, but it was enough.

Bentley experienced the horror and crushing sadness she felt as she realized what her son had done, followed by a terrible feeling of weightlessness as she fell back, and then the agony of impact, the shattering of her skull as it connected with the unyielding marble stairs.

Beverly lived for a little while as she lay prone upon the stairs, gazing up at her son as he gradually became less defined, finally turning to black as unconsciousness claimed her.

And Death took her hand.

Beverly's ghost was there beside him now, staring at the spot where she'd been found the following morning. She remembered, as did Bentley, the crocodile tears Phillip had cried as the ambulance drivers came to remove her stiffening body.

It was all a horrible accident, they were led to believe. She had been un-steady on her feet these days, due to her worsening illness.

The authorities didn't give it a second look.

And Phillip's life continued on as it had, undisturbed.

But that was about to change.

Chapter Thirty-three

Blackmore Prison seemed like a ship, its windows and lights about the premises shining, floating in a sea of undulating fog.

"Sir, please," Pym begged. "How will you gain entrance?"

Bentley sat slumped in the backseat, peering out the window at the prison.

"Do you know when the execution was to occur? And how will you . . ."

How? He hated the word just then—it stuck in his craw. *How?* He had no idea, but he did know he had to get in, he had to somehow save William Tuttle before . . .

How? He wanted to pull out his two guns and perforate the word with bullets.

He grabbed the back-door handle to exit, then stopped.

"Think about this, sir, if you're caught . . ."

Before opening the door, he did just that, remembering he'd left his mask, and he slipped it on over his face.

"An innocent life, Pym. I must—"

"But you don't know, Bentley," Pym practically begged. "He might already be gone."

Bentley thought about this for a moment, but it didn't change a thing.

"I still need to go," he said, opening the back door of the vehicle and slipping outside. The fog was thick, like smoke, hiding his foot as it touched the ground.

Bentley leaned into the car to speak to his manservant.

"You can go if you like, just in case I . . ."

Pym couldn't look at him. He sat clutching the steering wheel in both hands and staring ahead.

"I'll wait for you, sir," he said. "But please hurry . . . and do be careful."

"Careful as mice," Bentley told him, never quite understanding the phrase, having seen many a mouse caught in traps that had been set in the basement of Hawthorne House. They didn't seem careful at all.

He pushed the door closed with a click, not wanting to slam it, and headed into a wooded area before he reached the high fence that surrounded the foreboding property. The guardhouse was lit not too far off in the distance, and he thought that he could see the head of the guard inside.

Bentley waited in the darkness and the fog—for what, he wasn't quite sure. Inspiration, perhaps? For an idea of how he could get inside undetected, and somehow save William Tuttle? He didn't even have his priest's disguise with him, and even if he did, how . . . ?

There was that word again, and Bentley felt the cold foot of despair suddenly upon his neck, trying to push him down, down, down.

"*And here we are,*" said a familiar voice. Familiar, but still Bentley gasped.

"Roderick?" he whispered through his mask, looking around for the large black bird.

"*Yeah, it's me,*" the raven answered.

Bentley found him perched upon the branch of an oak, looking out over the high fence at the prison beyond.

"*So, what are you gonna do?*" the bird asked. He did what looked like a little dance, moving up and down the thick tree limb and bobbing his head.

Bentley stared at the prison again: nothing had changed. It still appeared quite impenetrable. "I don't know. But I have to get in."

"*Or not,*" Roderick offered.

Bentley looked to the bird.

Roderick bent down from his perch to address him. "*Look at it this way, you've done what you could,*" he offered. "*You got the creep that was truly responsible for the trapeze artist's death . . . I think the boss would be pleased with that.*"

The bird looked away from him, back to the prison.

"*I think you could go back to the mansion and call it a night.*"

Bentley thought about the suggestion, imagining slipping into a hot bath and soaking for days, followed by at least a week of sleep. That would be truly glorious.

But then he thought of William Tuttle, sitting in his cold, dark cell, being eaten up by guilt for something he didn't even remember doing as he waited to die.

"I could," Bentley said, already missing the hot bath. "But I can't."

"*What do you mean, you can't?*" the raven questioned with a severe cock of his black head.

"William Tuttle is innocent," Bentley said. "It was that creature . . . that siren that killed Tianna Hoops. William Tuttle loved her . . . he would have never done such a thing."

"*Doesn't change the fact that he was convicted and sits in there waiting to die.*"

"If anything, he should know," Bentley said.

"*Know what?*"

"That he didn't do it. That he didn't kill her."

"*But he's still going to die,*" Roderick croaked the sad knowledge.

"Yes," Bentley said. "But at least he'll know that he had nothing to do with hurting her. It's not much, but it's something."

"*So you're still planning on getting in there then,*" Roderick said.

"Yeah," Bentley answered. "I have to."

They were both silent and staring, Bentley waiting for that moment of inspiration when everything would suddenly make sense. It didn't come, and he was about ask the bird if he had anything to contribute, when . . .

The mist began to thicken, rising up from the grounds around the prison, so thick and churning that it nearly suffocated the light emanating from the monolithic structure.

"Is that you?" Bentley asked as the fog continued to grow.

"*Let's just say the boss is happy with your response,*" Roderick said.

Through the expanding blanket of mist Bentley observed the pinpricks of light flicker, like the stars in the sky suddenly blinking out from existence as if God had temporarily forgotten about them, but then remembered.

Bentley looked to the bird again.

"You?"

"*Not this time,*" the raven said.

And Bentley felt a sudden, sickening feeling as he realized what had likely caused the lights to dim.

It wasn't the stars that had gone out, but a life.

An innocent life.

"I'm too late, then," he said, looking to the bird.

"*For this, yeah,*" Roderick agreed. "*But not for what's next.*"

Bentley was confused, and was about to demand that the bird explain, but the raven was gone.

He looked around for Roderick, the thickness of the mist absorbing the sounds that would have come from the flapping of the raven's wings. He caught a glimpse of the black bird as he flew toward the prison entrance.

And Bentley felt he had no choice but to follow.

Chapter Thirty-four

BEFORE:

Bentley had been dozing but jerked awake at the sound of the door to the townhouse opening. He quickly retrieved the skull mask from where it rested on his knee and slipped it on to meet the man he had come to punish.

The mask clung to his skin. Becoming his face.

Bentley had become Grim Death for the man who had murdered his mother.

Phillip Chambeau let himself into his home.

His home.

He liked the sound of that and smiled, the warm alcohol buzz that he was feeling making the experience all the more pleasant. He'd had a good night, though he had been required to shed a few crocodile tears when condolences for his dear, departed mother were offered.

His mother being gone brought another smile, as he came into the apartment, tossing his keys upon a small table. Phillip had tolerated his mother for so many years, and when she became sick, he had believed that with just a little more patience, he'd finally be free of her.

But then she had started with her ideas about charity and helping the needy, before and after she was gone.

He shook his head in disgust as he removed his overcoat and threw it across a chair just beyond the entranceway.

The idea of all that money—*all his money*—going into the pockets of some filthy beggar was enough to send him over the edge.

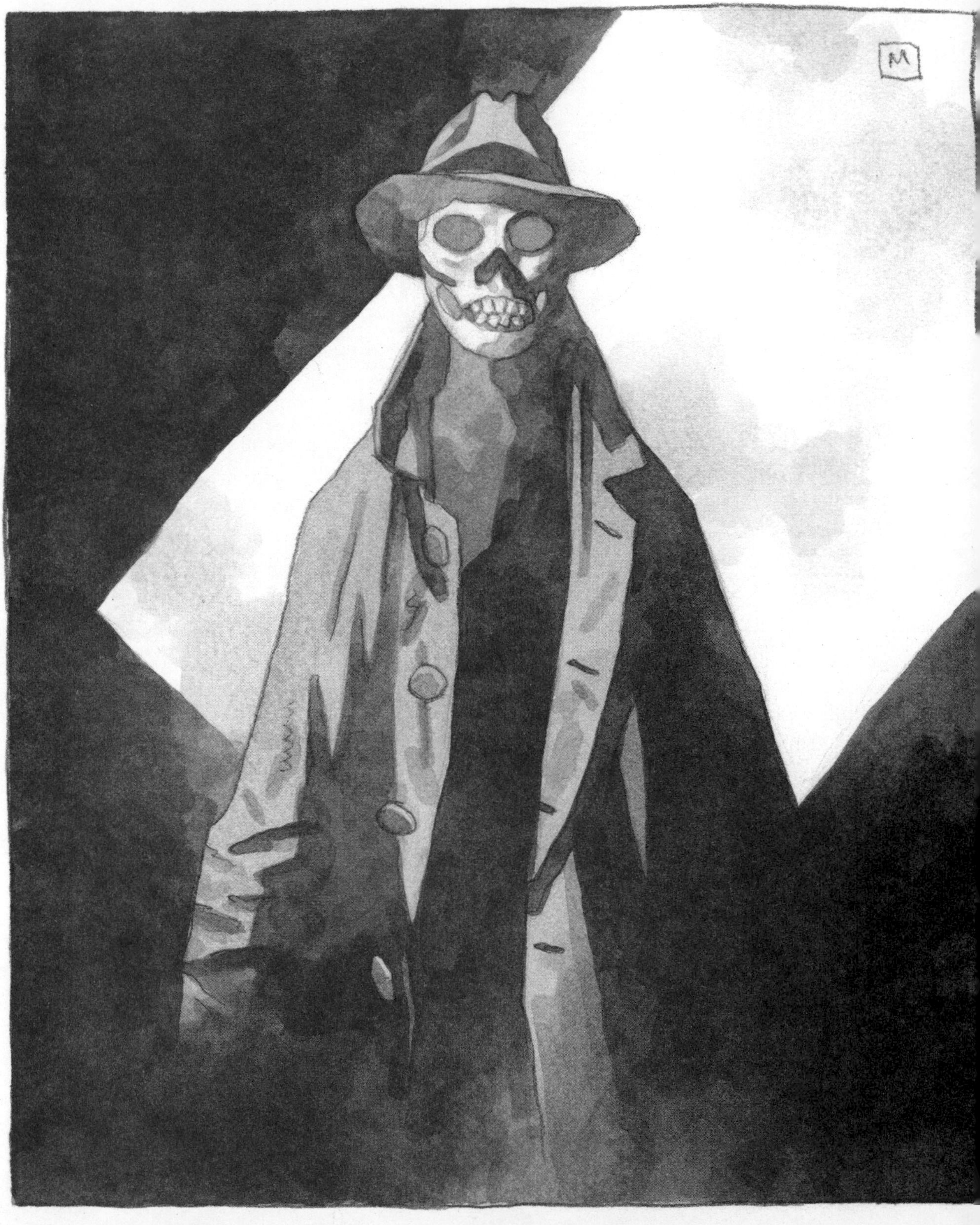

And he guessed it had.

He started up the stairs to his bedroom, feeling the weight of the evening pressing down upon him. As he reached the point on the stairs where his mother had hit her head after he'd pushed her, he felt a stabbing chill at the nape of his neck, and stopped. He saw her again as she hit, sliding down the remainder of the steps, leaving a trail of scarlet on the marble behind her.

"You stupid, stupid cow," Phillip muttered, as he had that night when he'd done the deed, standing over her body as he watched her die.

She'd left him no choice really, he thought, turning back to continue his ascent up to bed. What was he supposed to do without the money he'd grown accustomed to? Get a job? The thought was both terrifying and hilarious.

Phillip started to laugh, lifting his gaze to the top of the darkened staircase. The laughter came to a sudden, choking halt when he saw the figure standing there.

"Who . . . ?" he began, but didn't have the chance—the figure's arm shot out, grabbing Phillip by the tie as he recoiled backward, shoes precariously balanced at the edge of the marble steps.

"Phillip Chambeau," the skull-faced intruder said in a voice ragged and raw, halting his fall backward by holding the red fabric of his silk tie. "Payment for your cruel act has come due."

"Wait!" Phillip screamed, knowing full well what his fearsome attacker was talking about, but hoping for a way to escape his fate. "This is all some terrible misunderstanding . . . please, let me up and I'll explain!"

It was then that he thought he saw something, white and shimmering—like smoke—and for the briefest moment, he thought it had taken a nearly human shape.

And that it had appeared as his—

"Your mother has a message for you," the deathly visage said as he released Phillip's tie and let him fall backward down the steps.

"She always thought you were a snake."

Chapter Thirty-five

The unusually thick mist had found its way inside the prison as well.

Bentley was at first confused by what was happening, the dreamlike quality of it all making him doubt the moment.

Was he actually asleep? Dozing in the back of the car as Pym drove?

He stood still, turning to look at the guardhouse, where the prison's security detail stood. They appeared dazed, frozen by the moment, staring out dreamily as the dense fog billowed and roiled around their feet and legs.

They hadn't even given him a look as he passed.

The sound of a raven's cry broke his contemplation, and Bentley looked back to the prison entrance. The door was slightly ajar, as if beckoning him to enter.

He remembered the layout of the foreboding structure, and found himself walking the halls to the warden's office. He found the loathsome man sitting at his desk, as Tianna's vision had shown him, hunkered over a pile of papers, pen clasped tightly in his swollen hand. The floor was obscured by the preternatural fog as a single light burned at the desk's corner, and Bentley was compelled to go behind the desk, to verify what it was that would have the warden working so late.

The warden had indeed been signing William Tuttle's execution papers, the final bit of bookkeeping to put the murderer in the ground. For a moment, Bentley thought there might still be time, that maybe with these papers incomplete, William might have been spared.

Roderick called to him from somewhere close by.

Bentley left the office, following the mist-covered corridor to another more secure building that housed the general population of prisoners. He remembered the clamor of his last visit and was taken aback by the eerie quiet and stillness. The mist had found its way up and into all the cells, blanketing the floors in a roiling carpet of white. As before, the ghosts were there, standing in or outside the cells of those they haunted, but tonight their focus appeared to be on Bentley.

And where he was going.

The raven called out, his voice echoing in the distance, and Bentley moved toward the sound. As he traveled the twisting halls, Bentley freely passed through normally locked metal doors meant to keep the wretched population from escaping, now ajar, allowing him to go as he pleased. To his right, he passed the meeting room where he and William Tuttle had first talked, and where he had become doubtful of the large man's guilt.

A fat lot of good that had done him, Bentley chided himself, finding his way to a staircase that descended into the bowels of the prison.

The raven's caw drew him down.

Bentley needed to hold on to the railing as he traveled downward, the roiling gray fog so thick upon the stairs that it obscured his feet. That was all he needed—to trip and fall upon the steps and break his neck.

The lower level was even darker and more depressing than the floor above, if that was even possible. There was a smell in the air, like a hot August night just before a powerful storm. The smell of burnt ozone.

Two guards were in the corridor, and he immediately froze, watching them through the holes of his mask. They were very much like all the others, awake but almost in a kind of trance. One stood very still, staring down at his polished black shoes, his mouth moving ever so slightly as if in prayer, and the other leaned against the stone wall, staring at the caged lightbulb on the ceiling. Bentley passed them, completely unnoticed.

At the end of the corridor was where the action against William Tuttle was taken. He entered the room where the electrocution had taken place. The heavy wooden chair, which often went by the name of Old Sparky, sat there looking satisfied over its latest offering. The burnt ozone smell was incredibly strong, but there was another smell as well. Something sickeningly sweet, and greasy, and strangely—horribly—appetizing.

The smell of cooked meat.

His stomach burbled hungrily, and he suddenly felt the need to vomit, but Roderick again cried out for his attention, distracting him from the urge.

He left Old Sparky's room and went around the corner, where he found another heavy door standing ajar. This led to a stone corridor with a rounded ceiling.

The sound of the raven came from somewhere at the end, and he knew deep down in his soul that this was where he would find William Tuttle.

Bentley walked the corridor to the end, the burnt ozone smell slowly starting to fade, to be replaced by something heavier, an antiseptic smell of bleach and isopropyl alcohol. He was in the infirmary. An old, grizzled, bespectacled doctor stood outside his examining room, a cigarette burning in his mouth, an incredibly long piece of ash dangling precariously at the end, ready to fall. There was a stethoscope around his long, scrawny neck. Bentley looked inside the room for any sign of William, but he was nowhere to be found.

And then Roderick cried out from somewhere in the room.

Bentley passed through the doctor's office, then through the infirmary itself with its four beds. Two of the beds held prisoners, gripped in the hold of unusual sleep. The mist swirled around their beds, and they moaned ever so slightly, caught in the grip of nightmare, their sins haunting them as they slept.

Beyond the infirmary was another, smaller passage, which led to an area of the lower section of the prison reserved for those who had escaped in a far more finite way.

The morgue was nothing fancy: a square room with a heavy metal door, compressors humming and rattling nearby as the contents of the room were kept at a temperature much colder than the rooms outside it.

The door was closed, but it opened with an ominous click and an inner sanctum–type creak, beckoning him to enter. The mist roiled at his feet as he walked through the doorway into the frigid confines of the chamber. A stretcher sat in the room's center, the large form upon it covered with a sheet.

Bentley's heart sank at the sight of the figure lying perfectly still upon the stretcher.

His failure.

The ghost of Tianna Hoops materialized from the fog upon the floor, standing over the sheet-covered corpse of her lover.

"I'm so sorry," Bentley told her. "I tried to get here in time, but . . ."

She looked at him, but he did not feel the sadness leaking from her that he'd experienced before. *There's something different in her face*, Bentley thought. *A look of . . .*

Tianna raised her delicate hand, pointing to the figure upon the stretcher.

. . . expectation.

Chapter Thirty-six

BEFORE:

Phillip lay in a crumpled heap at the bottom of the marble staircase, still alive but unable to rise.

The man twitched and moaned pitifully where he lay. There was an enormous gash on the side of his head, which bled freely onto the marble floor at the foot of the stairs.

Grim Death slowly descended the stairs, the ghost of the man's mother floating by his side.

Phillip was positioned in such a way, at the steps' end, that he could see Grim Death's approach.

"Puh . . . please," he begged, blood bubbling up from somewhere broken inside.

"It's useless to beg," Grim Death said, standing on the steps above where Phillip sprawled. "For the act you carried out, a price must be paid."

The man squirmed and moaned, a pathetic attempt to escape Grim Death, who now loomed over him.

"Yes, your mother was dying . . . her time in this world was limited, but it was still her time."

Grim Death paused to let his words sink in.

"You took that time from her. You stole the life she had left."

Phillip was trying to move, to rise, but he was unable to, his injuries crippling him.

"The penance for the crime you committed?" Grim Death asked him.

Phillip's mouth was bloody, and he tried to speak, to beg for mercy, but his pleas went ignored.

"The death you deserve," Grim Death said, reaching down with both hands. One pinched Phillip's nostrils closed, while the other clamped over his mouth.

"A grim death."

Philip moaned briefly, his body struggling to hold on to the life it still contained, but he did not last for long.

The ghost of his mother looked down upon the corpse of her son, wearing an expression both satisfied and sad.

She then looked to Grim Death.

"Good?" he asked.

And she smiled, nodded, and faded away like so much smoke.

Yet strangely fulfilled.

Chapter Thirty-seven

Bentley did as the ghost wanted.

Reaching out with a tentative hand, he grabbed the sheet, preparing himself for what he would see lying beneath.

His failure personified.

"Are you sure?" he asked the ghost of Tianna Hoops.

The ghost did not answer, continuing to stare at the shape upon the stretcher.

Bentley pulled back the sheet and looked upon the body of William Tuttle. He was still wearing his prison uniform, and his head of curly brown hair had been shaved at the top, where the metal cap would have been placed to allow the current to course through his body and fry his brain. A severe burn had charred the bare skin there, making it look as though he were wearing a black beanie. Though he was very dead, Tuttle's skin was still a bright red from the electrical current that had passed through him. The man's handsome face was locked in a painful grimace, as if he had steeled himself against the onslaught of death.

Bentley stared, not really knowing what he was supposed to do. He could have used Roderick to guide him further.

"I'm sorry I didn't get here sooner, William," Bentley said, his voice echoing strangely in the freezer. "I tried . . . I really did."

Tianna's spirit had drifted closer, and gazed down at the man she loved.

"I doubt I would have been able to save you, even if I had gotten here in time," Bentley said. "But at least I would have been able to tell you that you didn't do this."

He looked at the ghost.

"You didn't kill her," he said. "Yes, it was you physically, but you weren't in control. Somebody . . . something else did that. But I took care of that, and they'll never do it to anybody ever again."

Bentley felt a bit foolish talking to the corpse, but it seemed like the best idea in the moment.

He was finished now, unsure if there was anything more that he should do.

"I think I'm done here," he told Tianna's ghost, feeling the weight of the evening's activities starting to weigh upon him, his eyelids growing heavier by the second behind his mask. He would need to sleep, to heal, if he were to function again as an agent of Death.

The ghost did not move, continuing to float there, gazing down at her lover's body.

As he started to pull the sheet back up and over the man's grimacing face, she reached out and laid a spectral hand upon the body. Bentley thought it a nice gesture, just as he was about to cover William's face.

A jagged bolt of what looked to be static electricity crackled to life, momentarily connecting him to the dead man. Bentley yelped, yanking back his hand and frantically moving his fingers. There was a numbness there now, and he wanted to get the feeling back. He had no idea where the spark had originated—if it had come from him and entered the corpse of William Tuttle, or if somehow the body of the man had held on to some of the electrical charge that had ended his life.

Still wriggling the feeling back into his fingers, Bentley looked over to see that Tianna was almost gone, her spectral form fading away. Soon, all that remained was the most beautiful of smiles, like Alice's Cheshire cat, and then that, too, was gone, leaving behind only a memory of what had been there.

Bentley wondered if Tianna was somehow satisfied with what had happened, if she had received enough closure to move on to her next adventure. Whatever had occurred, she'd seemed happy at the last of it.

William Tuttle sat up on the stretcher, the name of his lover on his lips. "Tianna."

Bentley stepped back in surprise as the dead man turned his head to look at him.

From somewhere close by came the caw of a raven and the fluttering of ebony wings.

Chapter Thirty-eight

Pym helped him from the car, into their home.

The sun had just begun to rise as they maneuvered themselves inside.

"Are you sure you don't require a doctor?" the manservant asked him, as they moved through the front of the house to the back.

"I'm fine, Pym," Bentley said, his words slurring. "Just tired . . . so very tired."

Pym managed to pull out a kitchen chair and helped him to sit. Bentley, still wearing the face of Grim Death, swayed upon the seat.

"I'm surprised," Bentley said, struggling to keep from sliding from the chair to the kitchen floor.

Pym watched him with stern eyes, finally coming forward and pulling the skull mask from his face.

"I can't talk to you that way," he said, throwing the mask down upon the kitchen table. The way he looked at it, Bentley expected it to scuttle off into the darkness to escape, like some loathsome insect.

"What surprises you?" Pym continued. He'd grabbed a dishtowel from somewhere and was wiping the hand that had touched the mask.

"How exhausting it all is," Bentley said.

He could see that Pym wanted to say so much, but the butler kept it to himself, which was probably for the better. The less Pym knew about this strange new facet of the world that he'd been indoctrinated into, the safer he would be.

"Maybe some coffee," the butler said, moving toward the stove.

Bentley watched the man through bleary eyes as he prepared to make them coffee. For a moment he put himself in Pym's place, and felt a nearly overwhelming guilt, mixed with sadness. *How strange this must be for him*, Bentley thought, looking to the mask lying upon the table. *But he continues to unswervingly serve me.*

Even though he thinks me mad.

It was then and there that he decided Pym could not be involved. No matter how much he trusted the man, he couldn't drag him in any further. And besides, it wasn't Pym who owed a debt to Death—it was Bentley.

Slouching in the chair, barely having the strength to sit upright, Bentley wondered, *Do I even have what it takes to perform this function? To serve the needs of this powerful, demanding cosmic force?*

Pym placed a steaming cup of coffee down in front of him.

"Drink up, sir," the butler said. "And while you're doing that, I'll draw you a nice hot bath."

And can I do it alone?

Chapter Thirty-nine

A m I . . . am I dead?" William Tuttle asked from his place atop the stretcher.

"I believe you were," Bentley answered, still attempting to understand what was happening. "But you don't appear to be now."

"But aren't you . . . Death?"

"Me?" Bentley asked, remembering then that he was still wearing the mask. He pulled it from his face, sticking it inside the pocket of his trench coat. "No, I just work for him."

William looked at him closely.

"Don't I know you?" William asked.

"Yes, we've met."

"You're the priest."

Bentley shook his head. "Not really. I was just pretending to be."

William continued to stare, brow furrowed—confused.

"I came to see you, to determine whether or not you murdered—"

"Tianna," William finished, lowering his gaze sadly.

"You didn't, William," Bentley told him. "You didn't harm her."

The big man threw his legs over the side of the stretcher.

"Yeah, the bird explained it all to me."

"The bird?" Bentley asked him.

William nodded. "Yeah, a big black raven. He explained it all to me in that place."

Bentley didn't understand. "That place?"

"The place where I was after . . ." He brought one of his large hands up to the burn mark on top of his head. "Ow, that still smarts."

"I'm sure it does." Bentley moved closer to where the big man sat. "So the bird told you—everything?"

William nodded. "Yeah, pretty much. Also said that since they brought me back, I owe them."

Bentley felt a chill of familiarity run up and down his spine.

"You owe them," Bentley repeated as the big man slowly nodded.

"And to pay back the debt, I've got to help you out," William said as he hopped off the table and almost collapsed to the floor.

Bentley rushed forward, attempting to catch the man, but he weighed nearly a ton.

"Maybe you should rest a little more before—" Bentley began.

"No," the big man said. "No, I think I'd like to leave this place now."

Bentley could hear the desperation in the man's voice and completely understood. "Okay, I'll help you."

He got beneath one of the big man's arms, and the two of them left the cold room, passing through the infirmary where the physician still stood, though the ash from his cigarette had finally fallen to the floor.

They slowly climbed the stairs up from the prison's lower depths and into the prison itself.

The mist still rolled about the floor, and all within the prison confines were still held in the grip of some strange, dreamlike state.

"Did you do this?" William asked Bentley, who still supported him as they walked.

"No," Bentley said.

"Was it the bird?" William asked.

"Most likely," Bentley answered as they made their way from the prison to the administration area. "Him, and his boss."

"His boss?" William questioned.

Bentley pulled the skull mask from his pocket and held it up. "The boss."

"Oh," William said.

They were passing the warden's office, and they peered in as they went. William pulled away from Bentley to stand in the doorway.

"William?"

The big man went inside.

Not knowing what he was going to do, Bentley followed and found him standing in front of the man's desk, staring.

"We should go," Bentley said.

"This was a very bad man," William said, and Bentley could not argue, having spent some time with the loathsome example of a human being.

"He was," Bentley agreed. "But you'll never have to see him again."

Bentley felt a sliver of fear as the large man walked around the desk to stand alongside the warden. He had no idea what William was going to do, and began to wonder if somehow this place had transformed him into something other than the good man he'd been when he arrived.

"William," Bentley said to him again. "We should go."

William ignored him, bending down to see what it was the warden had been working on.

"These papers are about me," William said. "They're my execution forms. And he signed them."

Bentley stood in the doorway, waiting.

"According to them, I'm officially dead," he said, bringing the fingertips of one large hand down upon the paperwork.

"So it must be true," Bentley said.

William thought about this a little more before coming around the desk again.

"Must be," he said, joining Bentley, as the two of them continued on through the administration building, and then out into the dark, early morning.

Bentley watched the writhing fog, and believed that it had started to recede.

"We should hurry," he told the large man, walking down the path, past the guardhouse and outside the high, barbed-wire fence. "We don't want to be seen."

"Where are we going?" William asked.

"The car is parked out here," Bentley said, leading the man to their means of escape. He opened the back passenger door, allowing the big man to crawl inside. Bentley went around to the other side to get in.

"Bentley?" Pym said from the driver's seat.

"This is William, Pym," Bentley said. "I believe he is going to be assisting me in my mission." He looked over to the large man sitting there, waiting for a comment.

"Bill," he said.

"Excuse me?" Bentley asked.

"It's Bill," he said. "I've always hated being called William."

"Ah," Bentley said. "I completely understand. Pym, this is Bill, and he will be helping me on my mission."

"Hello, Bill," Pym said.

"Hello," Bill grunted, his hand slowly going up to touch the burnt and blackened area upon his head.

"We should go, Pym," Bentley said. "Before anybody notices us."

"Very good, sir," Pym said, pulling out onto the road and pointing them away from the prison.

———

The sound of the car's tires passing over the road filled the silence within the vehicle.

"Where are we going?" Bill finally asked.

"We're going home," Bentley said, roused from near sleep. "Back to Hawthorne House, where you will stay with me . . . with us, and—"

"No," Bill said forcefully. "I think I'll get out here." He pointed to an exit sign for a town off the highway.

"You can't do that," Bentley informed him.

"Yeah, I can," Bill said. "And I will. I need some time alone. I need some time to think about the way things are now."

"But where will you go?" Bentley asked.

"Used to live around here before the circus," Bill answered. "I've got some friends close by."

Pym did as he was told, taking the next exit and driving into the dingy town.

"Here is good," Bill told them as they drove through the center of the town in the predawn hour.

Bentley took his wallet from his pocket and emptied it of money. "Here, take this," he told the man, shoving the cash into his large hand. "Pym, give him what money you have."

Pym brought the car to a stop and searched his pockets.

"Take this also," Bentley said, removing his trench coat. "It's got some blood on it, and it'll be a little small on you, but it should tide you over until you can get another."

"Thanks," Bill said, taking the coat. "I'll get it back to you soon."

The large man climbed from the car, slipping into the trench coat to hide his prisonwear.

Bentley leaned over the seat, tossing him his slouch hat.

"You might want to wear this as well," he said to the man. "To cover up . . ." Bentley touched the top of his head.

"Good point," Bill said, placing the hat over the burnt circle on his scalp.

Bill stood there, looking around.

"Will you be all right?" Bentley asked, still leaning over to address the large man through the open car door.

A cold wind started to blow, and Bill pulled up the collar on his borrowed trench coat. "I'll be fine," he said, slowly starting to turn away from them. "And thanks."

"Until we meet again, William Tuttle," Bentley called out.

Bill stopped, and turned for a moment.

"Yeah, until then."

He started to walk again, losing himself in the dwindling shadows of the quickly approaching dawn.

—

Bentley's eyes had begun to slowly close as the tug of sleep drew him into her lovely embrace.

"I thought he was to be executed?" Pym asked, his voice like a shot of gunfire.

Bentley's eyes flicked open.

"What was that?"

"That man . . . William—Bill," Pym said as he drove the car.

"What about him?"

"I thought he was going to be executed."

"He was."

"But he wasn't?" Pym questioned, looking at Bentley in the rearview mirror.

"But he was."

"I don't understand."

"And it's probably best that it stays that way," Bentley said. He glanced out the side window, guessing that there was at least another hour of driving before they returned home.

"Let's get home, Pym," he said, nestling into the corner of the backseat. "I'm going to need to rest before I'm needed again."

He closed his eyes, but knew that he was being watched. He opened his eyes to see the reflection of Pym's gaze in the rearview mirror, staring into the backseat.

"Until Grim Death is needed again," he corrected himself, closing his eyes and quickly falling deeply asleep.

Escorted into the arms of sweet unconsciousness by the beating of ebony wings.

Epilogue

t was not long until he was needed again.

Grim Death.

Bentley had been sleeping when the visitation occurred: two little boys—twins—their sad, cherubic faces stained with streaks of gore. Someone had taken their eyes.

They sat upon his bed, watching him awaken, and though he feared what it was they would show him, Bentley beckoned for them to come.

The twins eagerly did what was asked of them, crawling down the bed-clothes toward where he lay.

Bentley watched them with an unwavering stare, his gaze focused upon their empty sockets and the blackness they contained.

Becoming lost in the stygian darkness, which once held the windows to their souls.

———

Bill Tuttle sat in the far darkness of Snookey's Tavern, nursing his second beer of the night.

Nobody bothered him there, almost as if they knew there was something not quite right about the man, even though there wouldn't be any way to tell by looking at the large figure, sitting alone at the back table with his drink. He'd taken to wearing a watch cap pulled down tight around his head, to hide the circular burn mark the electric chair head piece had made on his scalp.

He'd been lying low, calling in a few favors from the early days before the circus. No questions were asked. Clothes, spending money, and a roof over his head were given freely, and he appreciated it.

Bill had enough questions of his own, without the questions of others to muddy up the works. Sitting, staring into his drink, he remembered the day—

The day he died.

He'd spent the last day of his life thinking, as he usually did. Thinking about the circus, and of her—Tianna—and how he hoped he'd see her again so that he might apologize for what he'd done.

For what he could not remember.

They'd let him have whatever he wanted to eat, and he'd decided on a nice steak, a rib-eye—medium-rare—with a baked potato. It had been one of Tianna's favorites.

Bill drank some more of his beer; it had gone warm as he sat.

As he waited.

A priest had come to read him last rites, and to hear his confession. He'd decided to just keep his mouth closed to hurry things along. The quicker they got things done, the quicker he'd get to see her again.

They'd walked him down from the special cell they'd had him in, the priest reading from his old bible as they walked to the room where the chair was kept.

Once they reached the room, they'd begun the preparations for what was to follow, shaving the top of his head and his chest, and strapping him into the heavy wooden chair.

Bill squeezed his mug in a powerful grip, remembering the terror he had felt, as well as the anticipation. It would be over soon, he'd told himself. The only fear he carried was that he wouldn't see her after he was gone, that there would be some punishment in the afterlife that would deny him his only wish.

He'd prayed he was wrong as they wet a sponge in salt water and placed it upon the spot they'd shaved, then lowered the metal cap onto his head.

Despite its warmth, Bill finished his beer, slamming the empty mug down onto the tabletop loud enough for Mickey, working the bar, to hear. He'd known the barkeep since they were kids, when he'd helped Mickey deal with some bullies who had been taking away the money he'd earned selling papers on the corner.

Mickey asked with a gesture if he wanted another. Bill nodded yes.

Dying had only hurt for a little bit. There was this sudden, intense jolt of pure agony that shot through his body, and then a comforting, floating warmth as his body shut down. They'd shocked him at least one more time for good measure, but by then he was already gone.

His spirit had flown the coop to someplace else. And that was where it got a little bit strange.

Bill felt his mouth go dry, and he wondered where his new beer was. Mickey was serving some customers, so he would have to wait. And remember.

After he'd died, he'd gone to someplace special. He was suddenly back at the circus commissary, having a late-night snack with the woman who had stolen his heart. It was exactly as he remembered it, down to the last detail of Tianna getting a little bit of mustard on the corner of her beautiful mouth as she'd bitten into the wiener that they'd shared.

He did as he remembered doing, reaching out to gently wipe away the smear of yellow.

And that was when everything had stopped—frozen—except for him.

"*She's a looker, I'll give you that,*" a strange voice had said from somewhere in the commissary tent.

Bill remembered turning around, but all he could see was a bird.

A crow . . . or was it a raven?

"Was that you?" he'd asked the bird.

With the question the bird had spread its wings, flying over to perch upon Tianna's shoulder, so that they could talk.

So that they could have a discussion about what had happened, and what was going to happen.

That was when he'd learned that it was the mermaid that had been responsible for Tianna's murder, that he'd been taken over and controlled by her strange song, his body manipulated like some kind of puppet.

Mickey came over with Bill's new drink and set it down, grabbing the empty mug.

"Everything all right, Bill?" he asked.

Bill nodded, even though he was lying. He wasn't sure if things would be all right ever again, now that he'd been brought back from the dead.

For a purpose.

The raven had told him he was being sent back to help with a mission. The guy who had helped avenge him, and avenge the woman he loved, needed some help with the job he'd been given.

Bill remembered how he'd looked at the bird, and then at the form of his beloved Tianna, frozen in the moment, and had asked:

"What if I don't want to go back?"

The bird had looked at him then, tilting his head oddly to fix him in one of his dark beady eyes. And the bird had said:

"If you ever wanna see this cute little thing again, you'll do what we're asking you to do."

What choice did he have? He went back to the pain of living, of remembering a woman gone from this world but waiting for him in the next.

So he would just have to wait and do what was asked of him. Do his job until they didn't need him anymore, and then he could finally rest.

He could finally be with her again.

Bill drank deeply from his mug. The bird had come to him when he slept, telling him to be ready. That he would be called on to do what was expected of him.

Bill was ready. He had been ready for the last three nights, coming to the bar and waiting.

Waiting to be called.

He was drinking more of his beer when he noticed how quiet the bar had become, nervous murmurings passing through the crowd of desperate drinkers. He lowered his mug to see that he was being watched.

The tall, fedora-wearing figure stepped from the shadow and briefly into the light as he approached. It was the skull-faced man. The one he had been ordered to help.

The one he had been waiting for.

"Come, William," the deathly visage called to him in a compelling tenor.

"Bill," he said as he stood, finishing his beer and setting the mug down on the table.

"Excuse me?"

"Bill," he corrected. "Remember? Not William."

"Right," the skull-faced man said, snapping his fingers, his voice no longer sounding quite so menacing. "Sorry, I forgot."

Bill shrugged, waiting.

"Come, Bill," the man said, the creepy edge having returned to his voice. "Grim Death has need of your services tonight." He turned, heading for the door.

And Bill followed, answering Death's call as he had been asked to do.

There was work to be done.